HAMLYN
CAKE DESIGN AND
DECORATING COURSE

HAMLYN
CAKE DESIGN AND
DECORATING COURSE

Edited by
Suzy Powling

FACTS AND FIGURES

Oven temperatures

The cooking times in the recipes in this book may vary slightly depending on the individual oven. Tins should be placed in the centre of an oven unless stated otherwise. Preheat the oven to the specified temperature in all cases. The table below gives recommended equivalents.

Conversion Chart

	°C	°F	Gas Mark		°C	°F	Gas Mark
Very cool	110	225	¼	Moderately hot	190	375	5
	120	250	½		200	400	6
Cool	140	275	1	Hot	220	425	7
	150	300	2		230	450	8
Moderate	160	325	3	Very hot	240	475	9
	180	350	4				

Metrication

In this book quantities are given in metric and Imperial measures. Exact conversion from Imperial to metric does not usually give very convenient working quantities and so the metric measures have been rounded into units of 25 grams. In baking particularly quantities can be crucial. Because of this in some cases the same Imperial quantity will appear to have a different metric equivalent: 4 ounces can be converted as 100 g or 125 g in different recipes, for example. When following a recipe, use only one set of measurements – do not mix them. The table shows generally recommended equivalents.

Ounces	Approx. g to nearest whole figure	Recommended conversion to nearest unit of 25	Ounces	Approx. g to nearest whole figure	Recommended conversion to nearest unit of 25
1	28	25	11	312	300
2	57	50	12	340	350
3	85	75	13	368	375
4 (¼ lb)	113	100	14	396	400
5	142	150	15	425	425
6	170	175	16 (1 lb)	454	450
7	198	200	17	482	475
8 (½ lb)	227	225	18	510	500
9	255	250	19	539	550
10	283	275	20 (1¼ lb)	567	575

Sizes

All spoon measures given in this book are level. Eggs are size 2 unless otherwise stated.

CONTENTS

INTRODUCTION

For many of the important occasions in life, a beautifully decorated cake forms the centrepiece of the event, whether it be a wedding, christening or birthday party or a celebration like Christmas. The creation of a suitably elegant cake can be achieved successfully at home with impressively professional results.

The Hamlyn Cake Design and Decorating Course aims to cover the range of techniques – from the simple to the specialized – involved in producing wonderful cakes for every possible occasion, and to point the way towards creative cake design after mastering these techniques. As well as giving basic recipes for all the mixtures for cakes suitable for decorating, the first section describes how to make the icings and fillings most commonly used, how to apply them with skill and how to master the decorative techniques appropriate to each. Of these, piped designs are most important, and the varied effects that can be achieved are clearly illustrated, together with run-outs. Decorations made from marzipan and moulding paste, whether cut out or moulded, are another feature which can be used to ornament cakes for all sorts of occasions, from a grand

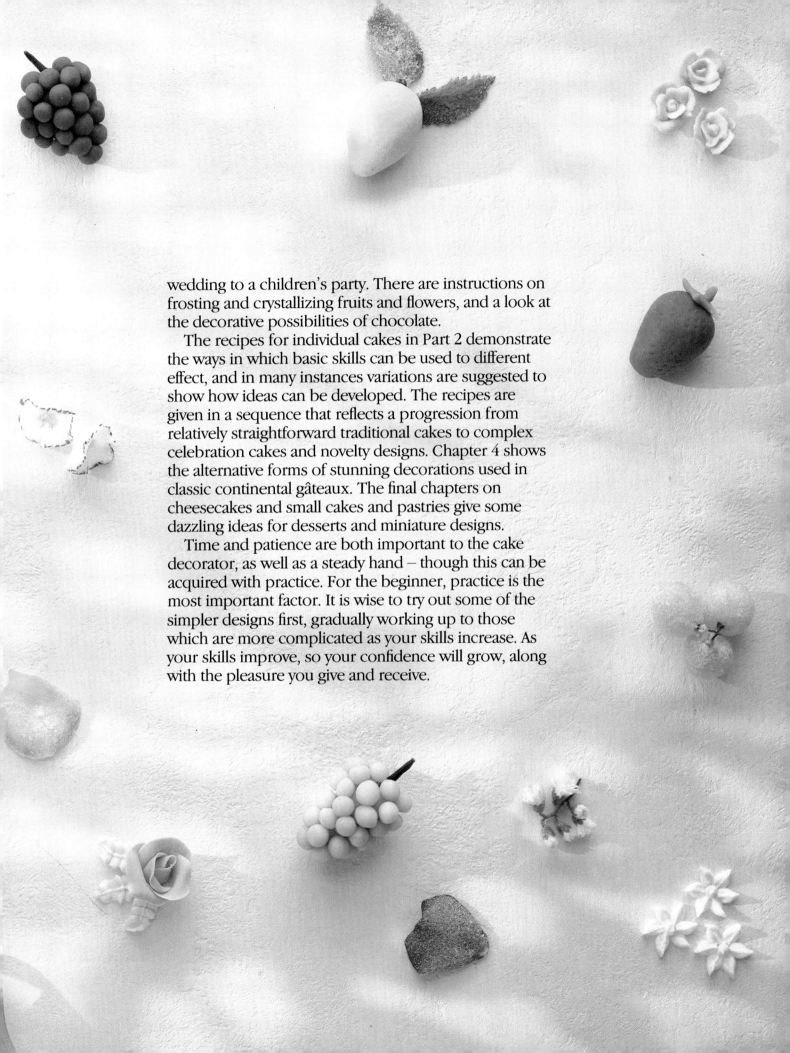

wedding to a children's party. There are instructions on frosting and crystallizing fruits and flowers, and a look at the decorative possibilities of chocolate.

The recipes for individual cakes in Part 2 demonstrate the ways in which basic skills can be used to different effect, and in many instances variations are suggested to show how ideas can be developed. The recipes are given in a sequence that reflects a progression from relatively straightforward traditional cakes to complex celebration cakes and novelty designs. Chapter 4 shows the alternative forms of stunning decorations used in classic continental gâteaux. The final chapters on cheesecakes and small cakes and pastries give some dazzling ideas for desserts and miniature designs.

Time and patience are both important to the cake decorator, as well as a steady hand – though this can be acquired with practice. For the beginner, practice is the most important factor. It is wise to try out some of the simpler designs first, gradually working up to those which are more complicated as your skills increase. As your skills improve, so your confidence will grow, along with the pleasure you give and receive.

INTRODUCTION
PART 1

This first section lays the foundations of the course, beginning with a survey of the equipment needed for cake-making (icing and piping equipment is discussed on page 54) and the ingredients you will need to have in your store-cupboard. The ability to make a good basic cake is of key importance in cake decorating. The recipes given here include mixtures for the different types of cake suitable for decorating; in part 2 individual recipes also include other ideas to extend your repertoire.

For continental gâteaux and cheesecakes, a special pastry is often used. These pastries are described here, as well as the different kinds of meringue, a very useful item in the decorator's repertoire. Many cakes need a layer of marzipan to separate the cake from the icing. The base icing is carefully applied on top of the marzipan to give a background for the piped icing designs and other decorative features. With any icing, and especially with the more complicated designs, it is very important to read through the whole recipe first. Most decorated cakes will take several days to complete and many of the extra decorations need to be made well in advance to give them time to dry completely.

An important factor in cake decorating is planning a design that fits the occasion. Some complex designs have a template to work from, most of these are given on pages 52 and 62, others are with the individual recipe. Cakes made from unusual shapes are discussed on page 53.

No cake decorating course would be complete without a section on chocolate, invaluable in decorating and delicious in the mixture. Frosted fruits and flowers, included here, can add a really special touch. And Part 1 ends with with some suggestions of how you can use simple bought decorations to create easy and effective designs and decoration.

BASICS

A good cake should be made from the best ingredients and should turn out cleanly from the tin when baked, without sticking to the sides. This section describes the basic store-cupboard ingredients and equipment you will need, and shows how to prepare and line different shapes of tin for baking.

If you enjoy cooking, your kitchen will already be equipped with certain basic items, but for cake-making an additional range of specialized equipment is necessary. On pages 12–13 is a list of the spoons, bowls, tins and so on that you will find essential. As you become more adventurous and as your range extends to cakes of different shapes, gâteaux, small cakes and pastries you will want to acquire more aids to creative cake-making. These are available from a number of specialist shops and suppliers and make (tell your friends) welcome birthday presents! Invest in good equipment which, if well cared for, will last for years. Over time a good cook gets to know his or her equipment and gets increasingly better results with it.

Preparing tins correctly for baking is very important if the cake is to be turned out cleanly without sticking to the sides. Instructions for different mixtures and different-shaped tins are given on page 14.

Like everything else you cook, a cake should be made from the best ingredients for a good result, especially if it is a formal cake for a special occasion. Absolute freshness is vital for eggs and cream; butter too must be fresh but can be kept in the freezer. Listed opposite are the basic store-cupboard ingredients which you will require. They do not all have an indefinite shelf life, but if you make cakes frequently there is little risk of the ingredients deteriorating in quality because they have been stored too long. Be ruthless with flavourings that have lost their potency. Throw them away and buy fresh. Spices, like dried herbs, lose strength very quickly if exposed to light. Add some simple decorative extras such as glacé cherries, angelica, silver dragees and crystallized fruits to your store and you will always have to hand the makings of a splendid cake.

INGREDIENTS

Almond essence is an extract of bitter almonds, and is so powerful that only 2–3 drops are needed to flavour a cake. It is an essential ingredient of marzipan. Use a pure essence without synthetic additives.

Black treacle is a byproduct of sugar production, the residue after the crystallization of commercial sugar from sugar cane. It is an excellent sweetener as it is high in iron and calcium, with some Vitamin B. The flavour is stronger than sugar, and using treacle in a recipe will deepen the colour, for example in a Rich Fruit Cake (pages 24–5).

Butter is used in cakes and icings. Unsalted butter is to be preferred for cake mixtures, though this is not essential. It is certainly the best choice for buttercream and enriched butter icings. Store, covered or wrapped, in the refrigerator, away from strong-smelling foods, but allow to soften at room temperature for 1–2 hours before use.

Chocolate has many useful qualities, not only in cake mixtures (and desserts) where it gives added texture, but in fillings and frostings. *Couverture*, the professional confectioner's chocolate, has a fine flavour and a glossy appearance but is difficult to work with because of its sensitivity to temperature; it is also rather expensive. The most suitable chocolate for cooking is a plain or bitter chocolate with a minimum of 50 per cent cocoa solids. Some chocolate bars are specifically made for baking. Good quality milk cooking chocolate is available. Sweeter than plain chocolate, it is more suitable for children's party cakes.

Adding cocoa powder is the most economical way to achieve a good chocolate flavour in cakes. It must be blended evenly into the mixture, either by sifting it with the other dry ingredients or by blending it with a little boiling water to make a paste which can be combined with the mixture.

Cocoa powder will keep for up to 1 year in a cool dry place. Chocolate bars should be stored in a cool dry place and used by the 'best before' date given on the packet. If you keep chocolate in the refrigerator in hot weather, it will lose some of its gloss. Wrap it well as it easily absorbs odours. The so-called bloom that sometimes appears on chocolate happens when cocoa butter and sugar crystals rise to the surface after exposure to variations in temperature. It has no effect on flavour and disappears on melting.

Cream must be kept cool, clean and covered. For covering and filling cakes and for piped decorations double or whipping cream may be used. Everything must be really cold before whipping – the bowl, the whisk and the cream itself. Whip quickly until a matt surface appears then slowly to avoid overwhipping and making it buttery (a tablespoon of cold milk added to the bowl helps to prevent this). Once fresh cream has been added to a cake it must be used the same day.

Eggs must be stored cool, in a refrigerator or cold larder, away from strong-smelling foods and with the rounded ends uppermost. Before use, allow eggs to reach room temperature. When beating egg whites, make sure the bowl and whisk are scrupulously clean and grease-free for the best results. Separate the yolks from the whites very carefully – a suspicion of egg yolk and the whites will not bulk out. Powdered albumen (egg white) can be used in icing and solves the difficulty of using up leftover egg yolks. It is sold at health food shops. To make up, mix 1 teaspoon with 4 tablespoons of cold water per 450 g (1 lb) icing sugar, or follow the packet instructions. Strain before use.

Flour of many kinds is available, but for making cakes you will need plain flour (fruit cakes, whisked and Genoese sponges) and self-raising flour (Victoria sandwich and Quick-mix). A Madeira cake uses both. Wholemeal flours are heavier, but, if you wish, a small quantity of white flour can be replaced by wholemeal flour for a healthier family cake. Cornflour is used to lighten some mixtures, and to dust the rolling pin and your hands when working with fondant moulding paste. Potato flour, the continental equivalent of cornflour, is used in some cheesecake recipes.

Flour does not have an indefinite shelf life. Once the packet is opened, store the remainder in an airtight tin in a cool dry place. Use within 2 months of purchase.

Fruit and peel for fruit cakes includes raisins, currants and sultanas, dried peel (from the citron, a relative of the orange) and glacé cherries. Dried fruit bought loose will need washing (see page 12), but packaged fruit from a reputable supplier should already be well cleaned. It is still worth checking to ensure that no stalks have slipped through. Peel can be bought ready-chopped, but often it needs to be cut more finely. Before use, glacé cherries should be rinsed to remove the syrup and halved or chopped according to the recipe. Use all dried fruits within 3 months of purchase.

Glycerine is a harmless, sweet, colourless viscous liquid which may be added to royal icing to prevent it from setting too hard. It is available from chemists and specialist cake decorating shops.

Liquid glucose is a sticky, colourless substance which is mixed with icing sugar and egg white to make fondant moulding paste (page 44). It is available from chemists and cake decorating shops.

Raising agents, to make cakes lighter, work by expanding the air bubbles in the flour as it is heated. Baking powder is most commonly used, a mixture of cream of tartar and soda, but bicarbonate of soda may be used alone in certain recipes. Always follow precisely the instructions about the quantity of a raising agent to be used – too much can result in a cake that rises well at first and then collapses, giving a heavy texture.

Spices are indispensable in the storecupboard. The most commonly used are cinnamon, in the form of quills or powder; ginger, either ground or preserved (Jamaican ginger is the best) and nutmeg (ground, or bought whole and ground in a special grater whenever required). Mixed spice is a useful item, but must be used soon after purchase – as with all spices bought in ground form, the flavour quickly fades.

Vanilla essence is used as a flavouring agent for cake mixtures, creams and icings. Choose one made from pure vanilla, with no synthetic ingredients. Vanilla beans are the dried pods of the vanilla plant. To make vanilla sugar, cut a bean in half and store it in a jar of caster sugar. After 2–3 days the sugar will be deliciously scented (but leave the bean in the jar).

Washing Dried Fruit

Most packaged dried fruit is pre-washed.

Dried fruit bought loose may require rinsing in cold water and thoroughly drying before use. Excess moisture can be removed with absorbent kitchen paper or clean tea cloths and the fruit should then be spread out on baking sheets covered with absorbent kitchen paper or clean cloths and left in a fairly warm (not hot) place to dry. This will take up to 24 hours and fruit should be moved round once or twice during this time. Never use wet fruit in cakes, as it will sink immediately.

EQUIPMENT

Basic equipment is listed below, while icing equipment is discussed on pages 54–5.

a selection of bowls and basins (china or glass)
large and small measuring jugs
a set of measuring spoons
tablespoons and teaspoons
nylon sieves
large metal spoon
wooden spoons
spatulas
pastry brush
kitchen scissors
large and small palette knife/spreader or a round-bladed knife
skewers
string
rolling pin
greaseproof paper, non-stick silicone or waxed paper and foil

A selection of cake tins is necessary and these should be made of a good firm metal. If you can, try to collect a set of tins that graduate in size at 2.5 cm (1 inch) intervals – always measuring across the base of the tin. Tins that are round, square, hexagonal, horseshoe-shaped or heart-shaped or in other unusual shapes are all available in graduated sizes. If you need an unusual shape, write to one of the specialist suppliers. If they cannot help, bake the cake in a large tin and cut to the required shape using a template (see page 53 for details of shapes). Tins can sometimes be hired.

Loose-based or springform tins are useful for removing cakes such as whisked sponges and Victoria sandwich cakes or cheesecakes which are easily damaged. Cake tins can be non-stick or otherwise but do ensure that the corners of square tins really are square. If not it is difficult to get a true square edge to the cake unless you build it up with marzipan

before adding the icing.

Some of the newer cake tins, particularly the larger deep ones used for rich cakes, measure a little larger than those which have been available for many years. This is a result of metrication. While the old style of 7 inch tin measured nearer 6½–6¾ inches, for example, the new tins measure around 7¼ inches. This means that some recipes will produce a slightly shallower cake when baked in new tins and may need a slightly shorter cooking time.

Always keep your cake tins in a special cupboard when not in use to prevent them

getting knocked and misshapen. It is also a good idea to keep a few wooden spoons aside just for cake-making and icing. They are better than metal spoons but in general use can become tainted with strong-smelling food and have stains which could be transmitted to the icing with horrific results! Always use nylon rather than metal sieves in cake-making, to avoid any danger of flour or icing sugar becoming tainted when sieved. A rubber rather than a wooden spatula is best for scraping cake mixture from the side of a mixing bowl.

A selection of cake tins and boards

Cake Boards

Round and square cake boards ranging from 17.5 cm (7 inches) to 40 cm (16 inches) are readily available from department stores. Other shapes available from specialist suppliers and some stores include the heart and the hexagon. Cake boards are usually finished in silver, but gold boards are also available. These cake boards are ideal for special occasions, but a wooden bread or meat board covered with ordinary kitchen foil is quite adequate for a child's party cake or an informal tea-party.

Electrical Items

While most cakes can be mixed successfully with nothing more sophisticated than a wooden spoon, and simply iced with the aid of a spatula, there are occasions when electrical equipment is a boon. A food mixer or processor is very useful for making certain pastries, for instance and is particularly useful for the Quick Mix Cake on page 16. At the very least, a well equipped kitchen should include a hand-held electric whisk. In the absence of a food processor, a blender will make short work of crushing praline or nuts.

We have not given microwave instructions in this course as we feel that conventional cooking gives the best results for the cake recipes here. However, a microwave can be very useful for melting butter or chocolate, softening marzipan, plumping dried fruit and even making glazes. Consult your manufacturer's handbook for more information.

LINING CAKE TINS

If using special non-stick tins, follow the manufacturer's instructions. With all other tins it is necessary either to grease and flour, or grease and line with greaseproof paper and grease again. Use oil, melted lard or melted margarine for greasing. If you wish to use non-stick silicone or waxed paper, there is no need to grease the paper. The cake tin, whether plain or with a non-stick coating, must be scrupulously cleaned before it is lined.

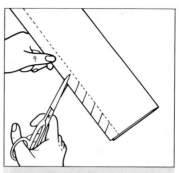

Round tin, base
Making slanting cuts along the unfolded bottom edge of the greaseproof strip.

Round tin, side
Placing the strip into the greased tin to fit the sides. Cut edges spread over base.

Base-Lining a Round or Square Tin

This method prevents the bottom of the cake from falling out or sticking and is used for sponge and sandwich mixtures and lightly fruited cakes, but not for the rich cakes.

1. Cut a single piece of greaseproof paper to fit the bottom of the tin.

2. First grease the inside of the tin completely, then position the paper in the base and grease.

To Double-Line a Deep Round Tin

For rich mixtures which require long cooking you should use a double thickness of greaseproof paper and line both the sides and base of the tin. With the richer fruit cakes tie two or three thicknesses of brown paper or newspaper round the outside of the tin as an added protection against overcooking the outside of the cake.

For less rich mixtures follow the instructions below, using only single thickness greaseproof paper.

1. Cut one or two strips of double greaseproof paper long enough to reach round the outside of the tin with enough to overlap, and wide enough to come 2.5 cm (1 inch) above the rim of the tin. Fold the bottom edge up about 2 cm (¾ inch) and crease it firmly. Open out and make slanting cuts into the folded strip at 2 cm (¾ inch) intervals.

2. Place the tin on a double thickness of greaseproof paper and draw round the base, then cut it out a little inside the line.

3. Grease the inside of the tin, place one paper circle in the base and grease just round the edge of the paper.

4. Place the long strips in the tin, pressing them against the sides with the cut edges spread over the base. Grease all over the side paper.

5. Finally position the second circle in the base and grease again.

To Double-Line a Deep Square or Rectangular Tin

Follow the instructions for the deep round tin but make folds into the corners of the long strips.

Rectangular tin, base
Cutting from the corners of the greaseproof paper to the corners of the tin.

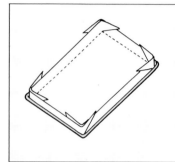

Rectangular tin, sides
Fitting the paper into the greased tin so corners overlap to make angles.

To Line a Shallow Rectangular Tin

It is always wise to line and grease tins for easy removal of Swiss rolls and similar cakes.

1. Cut a piece of greaseproof about 7.5 cm (3 inches) larger than the tin (and larger still if the sides of the tin are deeper than 2.5 cm/1 inch).

2. Place the tin on the paper and make a cut from the corners of the paper to the corners of the tin.

3. Grease inside the tin, put in the paper so that it fits neatly, overlapping the paper at the corners to give sharp angles, and grease again.

To Line a Loaf Tin

Use the same method as for lining a shallow rectangular tin but cut the paper at least 15 cm (6 inches) larger than the top of the tin. Grease the tin, position the paper, fitting the corners neatly, and grease again.

CAKE MIXTURES & MERINGUES

These classic recipes cover the basic sponge and fruit cakes you will need. The art of making meringues, used as a basis for some Gâteaux recipes, is also described here.

Most of the cakes in the book are based upon the classic recipes which follow, and for the majority of these quantities are given in chart form, making it easy to see how much mixture is required for a particular size of tin.

None of these cakes is made by the simple 'rubbing-in' method used for coarser textured cakes. Achieving a really light cake is the hallmark of an experienced cake maker and the lightest of all is the Victoria sandwich, the texture of which is achieved by thoroughly creaming butter with sugar in the first stage, as is also done for Rich fruit cake. This preliminary creaming process, after which the butter and sugar mixture is very pale and fluffy, is extremely important. If it is incomplete, the mixture will not accept the rest of the ingredients as it should. The Whisked sponge does not require the same amount of effort, but it is still important to incorporate as much air as possible into the eggs-and-sugar mixture at the initial stage. Thorough blending is required for the Quick mix cake, but by combining all the ingredients simultaneously the preparation time is considerably reduced, leaving you with time in hand for elaborate decorations (this mixture is the basis of a number of novelty cakes in chapter 4).

The keeping qualities of the basic plain cakes vary. The whisked sponge is best eaten on the day it is cooked, or frozen for up to 2 months; the Genoese sponge should be eaten within 3 days or frozen for up to 1 month; the quick mix cake keeps well for 1 week; and the Madeira and Victoria sandwich cakes will keep for 7–10 days. These last three can also be frozen, the Quick mix and Victoria sandwich for 1–2 months, the Madeira for 6 months. If you do not intend freezing them, store the cakes in an airtight container in a cool, dry atmosphere.

Quick Mix Cake

This is a very quick and easy cake to prepare and bake to use for many occasions. However, as it is made without proper creaming, it does not keep as well as a Victoria sandwich or Madeira, so it should be baked, iced and used within a week for the best results. Consequently it is not advisable to use this mixture for an elaborately iced and decorated cake using royal icing for a special occasion. In this instance, for non-fruit cake eaters, a Madeira cake should be used, as it will stay fresh for much longer.

The Quick mix cake can be baked in a variety of shapes and sizes. If you want to bake in something a different shape from those in the chart, simply fill your chosen baking container with water and see which size of tin on the chart holds the same amount of liquid – this will tell you the amount of mixture you will require. The baking may have to be watched a little carefully; if the container is shallower allow a little less time and if it is deeper allow a

little longer before testing. Remember always to use a good quality soft tub margarine for this cake and don't forget to add baking powder.

Preparation time: about 5 minutes
Cooking time: see chart
Oven: 160°C, 325°F, Gas Mark 3

1. Put the margarine, sugar, eggs, sifted flour and baking powder and vanilla essence into a bowl.

2. Mix together with a wooden spoon or hand-held electric whisk, then beat hard for 1–2 minutes until smooth and glossy.

3. Turn into a greased and floured (or single-lined and greased) tin and level the top. Bake in a preheated oven for the time suggested in the chart or until well risen, just firm to the touch and the sides of the cake are just beginning to shrink from the sides of the tin.

Step 1
Put all the ingredients together into a bowl.

Step 2
Mix together well, then beat hard until smooth and glossy.

4. Cool for about 30 seconds in the tin, then loosen the sides of the cake from the tin and turn on to a wire rack. Invert the cake on to another wire rack, unless baked in a ring mould or basin. This prevents ugly marks from the wire rack which can show through a thin icing. Leave to cool.

5. The cake is now ready to fill and/or ice.

Step 4
Turn cake on to a wire rack. Invert on to another wire rack so top does not mark.

QUICK MIX CAKE INGREDIENTS

CAKE SIZES	2 × 18 cm (7 inch) sandwich tins	18 paper cake cases or patty tins	20 cm (8 inch) sandwich tin 20 cm (8 inch) ring mould 18 cm (7 inch) deep square tin	900 ml (1½ pint) pudding basin*	about 26 paper cake cases or patty tins	2 × 20 cm (8 inch) sandwich tins
soft (tub) margarine, chilled	100 g (4 oz)	100 g (4 oz)	100 g (4 oz)	100 g (4 oz)	175 g (6 oz)	175 g (6 oz)
caster sugar	100 g (4 oz)	100 g (4 oz)	100 g (4 oz)	100 g (4 oz)	175 g (6 oz)	175 g (6 oz)
eggs (size 1 or 2)	2	2	2	2	3	3
self-raising flour	100 g (4 oz)	100 g (4 oz)	100 g (4 oz)	100 g (4 oz)	175 g (6 oz)	175 g (6 oz)
baking powder	1 teaspoon	1 teaspoon	1 teaspoon	1 teaspoon	1½ teaspoons	1½ teaspoons
vanilla essence	4 drops	4 drops	4 drops	4 drops	6 drops	6 drops
approx. cooking time	25–30 minutes	15–20 minutes	35–40 minutes	about 50 minutes	15–20 minutes	30–35 minutes

*add 25 g (1 oz) cornflour sifted with the flour

Fatless Sponge

Variations

Chocolate Omit the vanilla essence and add 1 tablespoon sifted cocoa powder for the 2-egg mixture; 1½ tablespoons for the 3-egg mixture; 2 tablespoons for the 4-egg mixture; and 2½ tablespoons for the 5-egg mixture.

Coffee Omit the vanilla essence and add 2 teaspoons instant coffee powder (not granules) or 1 tablespoon coffee essence for the 2-egg mixture; 1 tablespoon coffee powder or 1½ tablespoons coffee essence for the 3-egg mixture; 4 teaspoons coffee powder or 2 tablespoons coffee essence for the 4-egg mixture; and 5 teaspoons coffee powder or 2½ tablespoons coffee essence for the 5-egg mixture.

Orange or Lemon Omit the vanilla essence and add 2 teaspoons finely grated orange or lemon rind for the 2-egg mixture; 3 teaspoons for the 3-egg mixture; 4 teaspoons for the 4-egg mixture; and 5 teaspoons for the 5-egg mixture.

Spiced Add 1 teaspoon mixed spice, ground cinnamon or ground ginger for the 2-egg mixture; 1½ teaspoons for the 3-egg mixture; 2 teaspoons for the 4-egg mixture; and 2½ teaspoons for the 5-egg mixture.

Nut Add 40 g (1½ oz) finely chopped or grated walnuts, hazelnuts, pecans, unsalted peanuts or toasted almonds to the 2-egg mixture; 50 g (2 oz) to the 3-egg mixture; 65 g (2½ oz) to the 4-egg mixture; and 75 g (3 oz) to the 5-egg mixture.

Fudgy Replace from half to all the caster sugar with sifted soft light brown sugar for all the sizes of cake.

This very light sponge makes the ideal base for a rich topping such as cheesecake or whipped cream and fruit. It can be made 1–2 days in advance if kept in an airtight tin, or may be frozen for 2–3 months.

1 tablespoon flour mixed with 1 tablespoon sugar, for dusting
120 g (4½ oz) caster sugar
5 eggs, separated
1 tablespoon grated lemon zest
120 g (4½ oz) plain flour, well sifted

Preparation time: 20 minutes
Cooking time: 30 minutes
Oven: 180°C, 350°F, Gas Mark 4

1. Grease a 24 or 26 cm (9½ or 10½ inch) round cake tin and line the base with non-stick silicone paper. Grease again and dust with the flour and sugar mixture. Shake off any excess.

2. Set aside 2 tablespoons of the sugar. Whisk the egg yolks with the remaining sugar until they are thick, pale and creamy. Mix in the lemon zest.

3. Whisk the egg whites until they hold firm snowy peaks, then whisk in the reserved sugar.

4. With a large metal spoon mix 2 tablespoons of the beaten egg white into the egg and sugar mixture. Fold in the remaining egg white in batches, alternating with dredgings of sifted flour. Do not beat the mixture, but let it retain as much air as possible.

5. Turn the batter into the prepared tin. Lightly smooth the surface. Rap the tin once on the worktop to disperse any air bubbles, and bake immediately in a preheated oven for 30 minutes.

6. When the cake is well risen and browned remove from the oven and leave to stand on a wire rack for 10 minutes. Turn out of the tin and leave to cool completely.

QUICK MIX CAKE INGREDIENTS							
23 cm (9 inch) deep sandwich tin	2 oval oven-proof 600–700 ml (1–1¼ pint) glass dishes	28 × 18 × 4 cm (11 × 7 × 1½ inch) slab cake 20 cm (8 inch) round or petal-shaped tin 20 cm (8 inch) square tin	1 litre (2 pint) pudding basin*	29 × 21 × 4 cm (11½ × 8½ × 1½ inch) slab cake	23 cm (9 inch) round or petal-shaped tin 23 cm (9 inch) square tin	30 × 25 × 5 cm (12 × 10 × 2 inch) slab cake
175 g (6 oz)	175 g (6 oz)	175 g (6 oz)	175 g (6 oz)	225 g (8 oz)	225 g (8 oz)	275 g (10 oz)
175 g (6 oz)	175 g (6 oz)	175 g (6 oz)	175 g (6 oz)	225 g (8 oz)	225 g (8 oz)	275 g (10 oz)
	3	3	3	4	4	5
175 g (6 oz)	175 g (6 oz)	175 g (6 oz)	175 g (6 oz)	225 g (8 oz)	225 g (8 oz)	275 g (10 oz)
1½ teaspoons	1½ teaspoons	1½ teaspoons	1½ teaspoons	2 teaspoons	2 teaspoons	2½ teaspoons
drops	6 drops	6 drops	6 drops	8 drops	8 drops	10 drops
about 45 minutes	40–45 minutes	35–40 minutes	about 1 hour	about 40 minutes	about 1 hour	50–60 minutes

The cakes in this book which are based on the **Quick Mix** mixture are: Easter Egg Cake, page 120; Easter Basket, page 122; Numeral Birthday Cakes (alternative, Madeira), pages 138–9; Pirate's Treasure Chest, page 140; Basket of Chocolates (alternative, Madeira) page 140; Hickory Dickory Dock Cake, page 144; Executive Case, page 145; Humpty Dumpty, page 148; Rocket Cake, page 156; Peppermint Racer, page 157; Willie Wasp, page 158; Gâteau Japonaise, page 165 and Sponge Dice, page 210.

Victoria Sandwich Cake

This mixture produces one of the lightest textured cakes, perfect simply sandwiched with good jam and dusted with icing sugar. The quantities in this light mixture are fairly critical, so cannot be given for different sized tins as in the other recipes. However, to make a larger cake, use 200 g (8 oz) of caster sugar, butter or margarine and flour, with 4 eggs and just over 1 tablespoon of water. Bake in a 20 cm (8 inch) deep round cake tin, allowing about 1 hour to cook (a square tin of the same size will take a little less time). The same quantity can be baked in a 23 cm (9 inch) deep round tin and will need 45–50 minutes' cooking time.

150 g (6 oz) caster sugar
150 g (6 oz) butter or soft
*   margarine*
3 eggs (size 1 or 2)
150 g (6 oz) self-raising flour
1 tablespoon cold water
a few drops of vanilla essence.

Preparation time: about 30 minutes
Cooking time: 20–25 minutes
Oven: 190°C, 375°F, Gas Mark 5

1. Grease two 20 cm (8 inch) round sandwich tins and either dust with flour or base-line with greaseproof paper and grease again. Alternatively grease and flour or base-line a rectangular tin measuring 28 × 18 × 4 cm (11 × 7 × 1½ inches).

2. Cream the sugar and butter or margarine together until light, fluffy and very pale in colour.

3. Beat in the eggs, one at a time, following each with a spoonful of the flour.

4. Sift the remaining flour and fold it into the mixture alternately with the water. Finally add the vanilla essence.

5. Divide the mixture between the cake tins, or fill the larger tin, and level the tops. Bake in a preheated oven for 20–25 minutes or until well risen and firm to the touch. The larger cake may take a few minutes longer. Turn out on to a wire rack and leave to cool.

Variations

Chocolate Replace 25 g (1 oz) of the flour with sifted cocoa powder and add ½ teaspoon baking powder with the flour.

Coffee Replace the water with coffee essence or dissolve 2 teaspoons instant coffee powder or granules in 1 tablespoon boiling water, cool and use in place of the water.

Lemon or Orange Omit the vanilla essence and add the very finely grated rind of 1 lemon or 1 orange. The water may be replaced with fruit juice.

Fudge Replace the caster sugar with sifted soft light brown sugar.

Cakes in this book which are based on the Victoria Sandwich cake mixture are: the Mother's Day cakes, pages 104–5; Lion Cake, pages 150–1 and Orange Coffee Gâteau, page 180.

From the top: Madeira cake, Victoria sandwich cake.

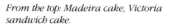

CAKE SIZES	15 cm (6 inch) round or square tin	18 cm (7 inch) round tin	18 cm (7 inch) round tin* 900 g (2 lb) loaf tin	18 cm (7 inch) square tin	20 cm (8 inch) round or petal-shaped tin	20 cm (8 inch) round or petal-shaped tin*
butter	100 g (4 oz)	100 g (4 oz)	150 g (6 oz)	150 g (6 oz)	150 g (6 oz)	200 g (8 oz)
caster sugar	100 g (4 oz)	100 g (4 oz)	150 g (6 oz)	150 g (6 oz)	150 g (6 oz)	200 g (8 oz)
self-raising flour	100 g (4 oz)	100 g (4 oz)	150 g (6 oz)	150 g (6 oz)	150 g (6 oz)	200 g (8 oz)
plain flour	50 g (2 oz)	50 g (2 oz)	75 g (3 oz)	75 g (3 oz)	75 g (3 oz)	100 g (4 oz)
eggs	2	2	3	3	3	4
grated lemon rind	½–1 lemon	½–1 lemon	1 lemon	1 lemon	1 lemon	1½ lemons
approx. cooking time	1 hour	50 minutes	1¼ hours	1 hour and 5–10 minutes	1 hour	1 hour and 15–20 minutes

MADEIRA CAKE INGREDIENTS

*These quantities make a deeper cake

Madeira Cake

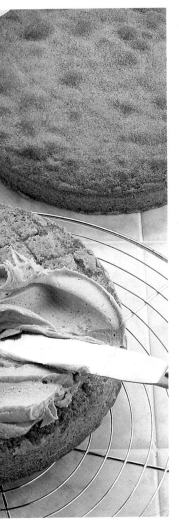

Madeira cake can be covered with marzipan and royal icing or fondant moulding paste or other icing. It may also be brushed with apricot glaze and simply covered in fondant moulding paste. The traditional flavouring of lemon rind and juice may be replaced with orange for an Orange Madeira or altered as in the variations below.

Preparation time: about 15–20 minutes.
Cooking time: see chart
Oven: 160°C, 325°F, Gas Mark 3

1. Grease and single-line the chosen tin (page 14).

2. Cream the butter and sugar together until light, fluffy and very pale.

3. Sift the flours together. Beat in the eggs, one at a time, following each with a spoonful of the flours.

4. Fold the rest of the flours into the creamed mixture followed by the grated lemon rind and juice.

5. Turn into the prepared tin and level the top.

6. Bake in a preheated oven for the time suggested or until well risen, firm to the touch and golden brown.

7. Cool in the tin for 5–10 minutes, then turn out on to a wire rack and leave until cold. Do not peel off the lining paper but wrap as it is in foil or store in an airtight container until required. If you plan to ice the cake, leave it for at least 24 hours to allow it to settle. Madeira cakes may be frozen for up to 6 months. Thaw still in the wrappings at room temperature.

Variations

Ginger Omit the lemon rind and add 1 teaspoon ground ginger to the 2-egg mixture plus 2 pieces finely chopped stem ginger, if liked. Add 1½ teaspoons ground ginger to the 3-egg mixture; and 2 teaspoons to the 4-egg mixture with more chopped stem ginger as desired.

Coffee Walnut Omit the lemon rind and replace the lemon juice with coffee essence. Add 40 g (1½ oz) finely chopped walnuts to the 2-egg mixture; 50 g (2 oz) walnuts to the 3-egg mixture; and 65 g (2½ oz) walnuts to the 4-egg mixture.

MADEIRA CAKE INGREDIENTS

0 cm (8 inch) square tin	23 cm (9 inch) round tin	28 × 18 × 4 cm (11 × 7 × 1½ inch) slab cake	23 cm (9 inch) round or petal-shaped tin*	23 cm (9 inch) square tin	25 cm (10 inch) round or petal-shaped tin	30 × 25 × 5 cm (12 × 10 × 2 inch) slab cake
00 g (8 oz)	200 g (8 oz)	200 g (8 oz)	250 g (10 oz)	250 g (10 oz)	250 g (10 oz)	250 g (10 oz)
00 g (8 oz)	200 g (8 oz)	200 g (8 oz)	250 g (10 oz)	250 g (10 oz)	250 g (10 oz)	250 g (10 oz)
00 g (8 oz)	200 g (8 oz)	200 g (8 oz)	250 g (10 oz)	250 g (10 oz)	250 g (10 oz)	250 g (10 oz)
00 g (4 oz)	100 g (4 oz)	100 g (4 oz)	125 g (5 oz)	125 g (5 oz)	125 g (5 oz)	125 g (5 oz)
	4	4	5	5	5	5
½ lemons	1½ lemons	1½ lemons	2 lemons	2 lemons	2 lemons	2 lemons
hour and 5–20 minutes	1 hour and 10 minutes	1–1¼ hours	1 hour and 30–40 minutes	1 hour and 25–30 minutes	1 hour and 20 minutes	1 hour and 15–20 minutes

akes in this book which are based on the Madeira mixture are: Santa's Stocking, page 112; Numeral Birthday Cakes (alternative, Quick Mix), pages 138–9; Basket of Chocolates (alternative, Quick Mix), page 142 and Flower Cake, page 152.

Whisked Sponge Cake

The butter in this recipe is added for extra keeping quality but it can be omitted if preferred. Without the added fat the cake should be eaten within 48 hours, with fat it should keep for 48 hours longer, but it does not keep indefinitely in prime condition.

This cake will freeze for up to 2 months if wrapped securely in foil or put into a rigid container; take care as it can easily be damaged without good protection.

Preparation time: 10–15 minutes
Cooking time: see chart
Oven: see chart

1. Line the chosen tin with non-stick silicone paper or greased, greaseproof paper.

2. Put the eggs and sugar into a heatproof bowl set over a saucepan of hot but not boiling water. Whisk until the mixture becomes very thick and pale in colour and the whisk leaves a heavy trail when lifted. Remove the bowl from the saucepan and continue whisking until the mixture is cool. Alternatively the whisking may be done in a food processor. It is not possible to add heat in this case but the result is satisfactory.

3. Sift the flour and baking powder together, then sift again over the whisked mixture. Using a metal spoon, fold in the flour quickly and evenly, followed by the cooled but still runny butter (if used).

4. Turn into the prepared tin(s) and shake gently or spread out lightly with a palette knife until even, making sure there is plenty of mixture in the corners. Bake for the time suggested in the chart or until the cake springs back when gently pressed with the finger-tips and has begun to shrink a little from the sides of the tin.

5. Turn on to a wire rack and remove the lining paper. Leave to cool.

6. If making a Swiss roll, invert the cake on to a sheet of greaseproof paper sprinkled liberally with caster sugar or on to a sheet of non-stick silicone paper without the sugar, unless specified. Quickly peel off the lining paper and trim the edges of the cake with a sharp knife. Fold the top short edge of the cake in about 2.5 cm (1 inch), then roll up the cake loosely with the paper inside. (This process must be done immediately the cake is taken out of the oven for it will not roll up without cracking if it is allowed to cool any more than necessary.) Fold back the top of the paper, so that it does not stick to the cake as it cools and spoil the top surface.

7. Leave to cool for a few minutes to allow the cake to set, then carefully unroll and remove the paper.

8. Fill with jam, buttercream or fruit and whipped cream, and roll up again.

Whisked sponge cake with (top left) Swiss roll variation.

WHISKED SPONGE CAKE INGREDIENTS

CAKE SIZES	2 × 18 cm (7 inch) sandwich tins	20 cm (8 in) sandwich tin 18 cm (7 inch) square tin	28 × 18 cm (11 × 7 inch) Swiss roll tin	18 sponge drops	20 cm (8 inch) round cake tin	2 × 20 cm (8 inch) sandwich tins
eggs (size 1 or 2)	2	2	2	2	3	3
caster sugar	50 g (2 oz)	50 g (2 oz)	50 g (2 oz)	50 g (2 oz)	75 g (3 oz)	75 g (3 oz)
plain flour	50 g (2 oz)	50 g (2 oz)	50 g (2 oz)	50 g (2 oz)	75 g (3 oz)	75 g (3 oz)
baking powder	½ teaspoon	½ teaspoon	½ teaspoon	½ teaspoon	½ teaspoon	½ teaspoon
melted butter (optional)	15 g (½ oz)	15 g (½ oz)	15 g (½ oz)	15 g (½ oz)	25 g (1 oz)	25 g (1 oz)
approx. cooking time	20–25 minutes	25–30 minutes	10–12 minutes	5–10 minutes	35–40 minutes	20–25 minutes
oven	180°C, 350°F, Gas Mark 4	180°C, 350°F, Gas Mark 4	190°C, 375°F, Gas Mark 5	190°C, 375°F, Gas Mark 5	180°C, 350°F, Gas Mark 4	180°C, 350°F, Gas Mark 4

The cakes in this book based on a Whisked Sponge mixture are: Sugar Plum Fairy Castle, page 141 and Ballet Shoes, page 146.

Step 2
Whisk the eggs and sugar over hot water until mixture is thick and creamy.

Step 4
The cake will shrink a bit from the sides of the tin and feel 'springy' to the touch.

Step 6, Swiss roll
Rolling the Swiss roll up with the greaseproof paper inside. A teatowel is used to help.

Step 8, Swiss roll
Spreading a buttercream filling over the unrolled sponge before re-rolling.

28 × 18 × 4 cm (11 × 7 × 1½ inch) slab cake	30 × 23 cm (12 × 9 inch) Swiss roll tin	33 × 23 cm (13 × 9 inch) Swiss roll tin
3	3	4
75 g (3 oz)	75 g (3 oz)	100 g (4 oz)
75 g (3 oz)	75 g (3 oz)	100 g (4 oz)
½ teaspoon	½ teaspoon	½ teaspoon
25 g (1 oz)	25 g (1 oz)	25 g (1 oz)
30–35 minutes	12–15 minutes	15–20 minutes
180°C, 350°F, Gas Mark 4	200°C, 400°F, Gas Mark 6	190°C, 375°F, Gas Mark 5

Variations

Lemon or Orange Add the grated rind of ½ lemon or orange with the flour.

Chocolate Replace 15 g (½ oz) flour with sifted cocoa powder.

Coffee Add 2 teaspoons instant coffee powder (not granules) to the mixture with the flour.

Spiced Add ½ teaspoon ground cinnamon, mixed spice or ground ginger sifted with the flour.

Walnut Add 25–40 g (1–1½ oz) very finely chopped or ground walnuts, folded into the cake mixture with the butter.

Genoese Sponge

A Genoese (also known as a Torten) sponge is a type of whisked sponge to which butter is always added. This improves its keeping qualities, but the texture remains light and moist. This is a good cake for cutting into fingers or into different shapes for icing and decorating (Genoese pastries).

40 g (1½ oz) butter
2 eggs
65 g (2½ oz) caster sugar
50 g (2 oz) plain flour, sifted

Preparation time: 20 minutes
Cooking time: 35–40 minutes
Oven: 180°C, 350°F, Gas Mark 4

1. Brush an 18 cm (7 inch) square tin with melted butter. Line with greased greaseproof paper and dust lightly with sifted flour.

2. Place the butter in a bowl set over a saucepan of hand-hot water and let it melt without becoming hot.

3. Place the eggs in a mixing bowl and whisk for 1 minute. Add the sugar, set the bowl over a pan of hot, not boiling water and whisk until the mixture is light and creamy and has doubled in volume. The whisk should leave a trail when pulled across the surface. Remove the bowl from the heat and continue to whisk until the mixture is cold.

4. Pour in half the melted butter, leaving the sediment behind. Add half the flour and fold in carefully with a metal spoon. Fold in the remaining melted butter and flour in the same way.

5. Pour the mixture into the prepared tin and place in a preheated oven. Bake for 35–40 minutes or until the sponge is golden brown, firm to the touch and begins to shrink from the side of the tin.

6. Leave in the tin for 1 minute and then turn the sponge out on to a folded tea-towel to cool. (This light cake is easily marked by the lines on a wire rack.)

Step 4
Add the flour after the melted butter and fold into the whisked egg and sugar.

Step 6
To avoid marks, the sponge should be turned out onto a folded teatowel to cool.

Cakes in this book that are based on a Genoese sponge mixture are: Gâteau de Pâques, page 104; Praline Gâteau, page 160; Coffee Chestnut Gâteau, page 164; Italiens, page 194 and Printaniers, page 194.

Healthy Sponge Cake

The carrots and apples in this version of a Quick-mix sponge give sweetness as well as a moist texture to the cake. With the addition of nuts and honey it is delicious, and not over-sweet. The mixture is very quick and easy to combine because vegetable oil is used rather than butter or margarine.

The cake will keep for up to 7 days in an airtight tin. While it can be substituted for any recipe based on the Quick-mix Sponge, it is versatile enough to take any of the classic icings or frostings.

Preparation time: about 10 minutes
Cooking time: see chart
Oven: 180°C, 330°F, Gas Mark 4

1. Put the apple, carrot, nuts, oil, sugar, honey and eggs in a bowl and mix well.

2. Sift together the flours, bicarbonate of soda, salt and cinnamon. Stir into the carrot mixture until well blended.

3. Turn into a greased and base-lined tin and level the top. Bake in a preheated oven for the time given in the chart or until well risen, just firm to the touch and the sides of the cake are just beginning to shrink from the sides of the tin.

4. Cool for about 2 minutes in the tin then loosen the sides of the cake from the tin and turn out on to a wire rack. Leave to cool.

Healthy sponge cake

CAKE SIZES	2 × 18 cm (7 inch) sandwich tins	18 paper cake cases or patty tins
apple, chopped	100 g (4 oz)	100 g (4 oz)
carrot, grated	100 g (4 oz)	100 g (4 oz)
nuts, chopped	50 g (2 oz)	50 g (2 oz)
vegetable oil	100 ml (3½ fl oz)	100 ml (3½ fl oz)
soft brown sugar	75 g (3 oz)	75 g (3 oz)
clear honey	1½ tablespoons	1½ tablespoons
eggs	1	1
egg yolk	1	1
plain flour	75 g (3 oz)	75 g (3 oz)
wholemeal flour	75 g (3 oz)	75 g (3 oz)
bicarbonate of soda	¾ teaspoon	¾ teaspoon
salt	pinch	pinch
ground cinnamon	1½ teaspoons	1½ teaspoons
approx. cooking time	25–30 minutes	15–20 minutes

HEALTHY SPONGE CAKE INGREDIENTS

20 cm (8 inch) sandwich tin or ring mould 18 cm (7 inch) deep square tin	900 ml (1½ pint) pudding basin	2 × 20 cm (8 inch) sandwich tins	23 cm (9 inch) deep sandwich tin	2 oval ovenproof 600–700 ml (1–1¼ pint) glass dishes	28 × 18 × 4 cm (11 × 7 × 1½ inch) slab cake 20 cm (8 inch) round or square tin	30 × 25 × 5 cm (12 × 10 × 2 inch) slab cake
100 g (4 oz)		175 g (6 oz)	175 g (6 oz)	175 g (6 oz)	175 g (6 oz)	225 g (8 oz)
100 g (4 oz)	100 g (4 oz)	175 g (6 oz)	175 g (6 oz)	175 g (6 oz)	175 g (6 oz)	275 g (10 oz)
50 g (2 oz)	50 g (2 oz)	75 g (3 oz)	75 g (3 oz)	75 g (3 oz)	75 g (3 oz)	150 g (5 oz)
100 ml (3½ fl oz)	100 ml (3½ fl oz)	125 ml (4 fl oz)	125 ml (4 fl oz)	125 ml (4 fl oz)	125 ml (4 fl oz)	250 ml (9 fl oz)
75 g (3 oz)	75 g (3 oz)	100 g (4 oz)	100 g (4 oz)	100 g (4 oz)	100 g (4 oz)	225 g (8 oz)
1½ tablespoons	1½ tablespoons	2 tablespoons	2 tablespoons	2 tablespoons	2 tablespoons	4 tablespoons
1	1	2	2	2	2	4
1	1	—	—	—	—	—
75 g (3 oz)	75 g (3 oz)	100 g (4 oz)	100 g (4 oz)	100 g (4 oz)	100 g (4 oz)	225 g (8 oz)
75 g (3 oz)	75 g (3 oz)	100 g (4 oz)	100 g (4 oz)	100 g (4 oz)	100 g (4 oz)	200 g (7 oz)
¾ teaspoon	1 teaspoon	1 teaspoon	1 teaspoon	1 teaspoon	1 teaspoon	2½ teaspoons
pinch	pinch	pinch	pinch	pinch	pinch	pinch
1½ teaspoons	1½ teaspoons	2 teaspoons	2 teaspoons	2 teaspoons	2 teaspoons	4 teaspoons
35–40 minutes	50 minutes	30–35 minutes	45 minutes	40–45 minutes	40 minutes	55 minutes

Rich Fruit Cake

This fruit cake improves with keeping and makes a delicious Christmas cake. When making the smaller cakes, especially the top tiers of a wedding cake, it is often a good idea to add a little gravy browning (about 1 teaspoon) to the mixture, so that it will be the same colour as the larger cakes, which tend to go darker during the longer cooking time.

Preparation time: about 30 minutes
Cooking time: see chart
Oven: 150°C, 300°F, Gas Mark 2

1. Grease and double-line the chosen cake tin (page 14).

2. Mix together the currants, sultanas and raisins in a large bowl.

3. Cut the glacé cherries into quarters. Rinse them under warm water and dry thoroughly on absorbent kitchen paper or a clean cloth.

4. Add the cherries to the dried fruit mixture with the mixed peel, almonds and grated lemon rind. Mix well.

5. Sift the flour, ground cinnamon and mixed spice together.

6. Cream the butter until soft, then add the sugar and continue creaming until light, fluffy and much paler in colour. Do not overbeat or the cake will become coarse in texture and heavy.

7. Add the eggs to the creamed mixture one at a time, beating in thoroughly and following each with a spoonful of flour.

8. Fold in the remaining flour, followed by the dried fruit mixture.

9. Add the black treacle, if liked.

10. Turn the mixture into the prepared tin and level the top. Using the back of a spoon, make a slight hollow in the centre of the mixture, so that the top of the cake comes out flat when baked.

11. Fold sheets of brown paper into long narrow strips of about six thicknesses and tie around the outside of the tin for protection during cooking. Place in a preheated oven and bake for the time suggested in the chart. If the cake seems to be overbrowning, lay a sheet of greaseproof paper lightly over the top. With very large cakes it is sometimes better to turn the oven down to 140°C, 275°F, Gas Mark 1 after about three-quarters of the cooking time has been completed.

12. To test if the cake is done, insert a skewer in the centre: it should come out clean. Remove from the oven and leave to cool in the tin. Turn on to a wire rack and remove the lining paper.

13. Prick the top of the cake all over with a skewer, then spoon several tablespoons of brandy or other spirit over the top. Wrap in greaseproof paper and foil and store. If possible repeat this process at intervals of 2 weeks while the cake is maturing. This cake should be allowed to mature for 2–3 months but can be used after 2 weeks or so. It will keep for 6–8 months.

Step 6
After creaming the butter, add the sugar. Cream until just light and fluffy.

Step 8
Fold in the remaining flour after all the egg has been incorporated.

Step 10
Level the top of the mixture and make a slight hollow in the centre.

Step 11
Tying strips of brown paper around the outside of tin to protect during cooking.

RICH FRUIT CAKE INGREDIENTS

SQUARE	13 cm (5 inch)	15 cm (6 inch)	18 cm (7 inch)	20 cm (8 inch)	23 cm (9 inch)	25 cm (10 inch)	28 cm (11 inch)	30 cm (12 inch)
ROUND or PETAL-SHAPED	15 cm (6 inch)	18 cm (7 inch)	20 cm (8 inch)	23 cm (9 inch)	25 cm (10 inch)	28 cm (11 inch)	30 cm (12 inch)	
SLAB CAKE				29 × 21 × 4 cm (11½ × 8½ × 1½ inch)	30 × 25 × 5 cm (12 × 10 × 2 inch)			
currants	150 g (5 oz)	225 g (8 oz)	350 g (12 oz)	450 g (1 lb)	625 g (1 lb 6 oz)	775 g (1 lb 12 oz)	1.2 kg (2 lb 8 oz)	1.4 kg (3 lb)
sultanas	50 g (2 oz)	90 g (3½ oz)	125 g (4½ oz)	200 g (7 oz)	225 g (8 oz)	375 g (13 oz)	400 g (14 oz)	500 g (1 lb 2 oz)
raisins	50 g (2 oz)	90 g (3½ oz)	125 g (4½ oz)	200 g (7 oz)	225 g (8 oz)	375 g (13 oz)	400 g (14 oz)	500 g (1 lb 2 oz)
glacé cherries	40 g (1½ oz)	65 g (2½ oz)	75 g (3 oz)	100 g (4 oz)	150 g (5 oz)	225 g (8 oz)	300 g (10 oz)	350 g (12 oz)
mixed peel, chopped	25 g (1 oz)	50 g (2 oz)	50 g (2 oz)	75 g (3 oz)	100 g (4 oz)	150 g (5 oz)	200 g (7 oz)	250 g (9 oz)
blanched almonds, chopped	25 g (1 oz)	50 g (2 oz)	50 g (2 oz)	75 g (3 oz)	100 g (4 oz)	150 g (5 oz)	200 g (7 oz)	250 g (9 oz)
lemon rind, grated	¼ lemon	½ lemon	¾ lemon	1 lemon	1 lemon	1 lemon	1½ lemons	2 lemons
plain flour	100 g (3½ oz)	175 g (6 oz)	200 g (7½ oz)	350 g (12 oz)	400 g (14 oz)	600 g (1 lb 5 oz)	700 g (1 lb 8 oz)	825 g (1 lb 13 oz)
ground cinnamon	½ teaspoon	½ teaspoon	¾ teaspoon	1 teaspoon	1½ teaspoons	2 teaspoons	2½ teaspoons	2¾ teaspoons
ground mixed spice	¼ teaspoon	¼ teaspoon	½ teaspoon	¾ teaspoon	1 teaspoon	1¼ teaspoons	1½ teaspoons	1¾ teaspoons
butter	75 g (3 oz)	150 g (5 oz)	175 g (6 oz)	275 g (10 oz)	350 g (12 oz)	500 g (1 lb 2 oz)	600 g (1 lb 5 oz)	800 g (1 lb 12 oz)
soft brown sugar	75 g (3 oz)	150 g (5 oz)	175 g (6 oz)	275 g (10 oz)	350 g (12 oz)	500 g (1 lb 2 oz)	600 g (1 lb 5 oz)	800 g (1 lb 12 oz)
eggs (size 2)	1½	2½	3	5	6	9	11	14
black treacle (optional)	1 teaspoon	1 teaspoon	1 tablespoon	1 tablespoon	1 tablespoon	2 tablespoons	2 tablespoons	2 tablespoons
approximate cooking time	2 hours	2½ hours	2¾ hours	3¼ hours	3¾ hours	4¼–4½ hours	5¼–5½ hours	6–6½ hours
approximate cooked weight	750 g (1½ lb)	1.25 kg (2½ lb)	1.5 kg (3¼ lb)	2 kg (4½ lb)	2.75 kg (6 lb)	4 kg (9 lb)	5 kg (11 lb)	6.5 kg (14 lb)
brandy, added after cooking	2 tablespoons	3 tablespoons	3 tablespoons	4 tablespoons	5 tablespoons	6 tablespoons	7 tablespoons	8 tablespoons

Cakes in this book based on a Rich Fruit Cake mixture are: Hexagonal Wedding Cake, page 92; American Wedding Cake, page 94; Three-tier Wedding Cake, page 98; Christening Cakes, pages 100–1; Round Christmas Cake, page 108; Square Christmas Cake, page 109; Christmas Cake with Angels, page 114; Golden Wedding Cake, page 128; Good Luck Horseshoe, page 126; Confirmation Cake and Good Luck Cake, pages 124–5; Eighteenth Birthday Cake, page 132; Sporting Birthday Cake, page 134 and Square Birthday Cake, page 130.

Light Fruit Cake

This is a well-flavoured cake made more moist by the inclusion of grated apple, but it does not keep for longer than about 2 weeks. It is therefore better to use it only for a simply decorated cake. Like all fruit cakes, it can be covered with marzipan and with any of the icings.

The currants suggested in the recipe may be replaced with finely chopped, stoned dates or with a mixture of finely chopped, no-need-to-soak dried apricots and chopped, stoned prunes.

This fruit cake will keep well in the freezer for up to 3 months. Do not remove the lining paper from around the cake once it has cooled, but overwrap it securely in foil.

Preparation time: about 20 minutes
Cooking time: see chart
Oven: 180°C, 350°F, Gas Mark 4

1. Grease and double-line the chosen tin (page 14).

2. Sift the flour, bicarbonate of soda, spice and ginger into a bowl.

3. In another bowl cream the butter or margarine with the sifted brown sugar until very light, fluffy and pale in colour.

4. Beat in the eggs one at a time, following each with a spoonful of the flour mixture, then fold in the remaining flour.

5. Mix the raisins, currants, sultanas, peel and fruit rind together and add to the mixture.

6. Peel, core and coarsely grate the apples, add to the mixture and stir through evenly.

7. Turn the mixture into the prepared tin, level the top and bake for the time suggested on the chart, in the centre of the oven. The largest size of cake cooks better if the oven is turned down to 160°C, 325°F, Gas Mark 3 after 1½ hours to prevent overbrowning.

8. To test if the cake is done, insert a skewer into the centre. It should come out clean. Cool the cake in the tin for 5 minutes. Turn out on to a wire rack and leave until cold. When cold, wrap in foil or put into an airtight container for 24–48 hours before use.

Variations

An even more sumptuous fruit cake can be made by modifying the Rich Fruit Cake mixture.

Reduce the quantity of currants slightly, increasing the quantity of glacé cherries accordingly; add the grated rind of half an orange and a good pinch of nutmeg to the mixture. Add sherry with the flour, using 2 teaspoons for the smallest size, graduating up to 5–6 tablespoons for a 30 cm (12 inch) cake.

Before wrapping the cooked, cooled cake in foil (it must be kept for 2 weeks before use) prick the top all over with a skewer and spoon 2–8 tablespoons sherry or brandy over the surface (depending on the size of the cake).

Both fruit cake recipes can be finished in Dundee-cake style with blanched whole almonds arranged on top of the unbaked cake to cover it completely.

Another luxurious way of finishing a fruit cake which is not to be formally iced is to add glacé fruits and nuts to the top with a coating of warmed and sieved apricot jam.

Use this decoration of colourful fruits on a light fruit cake, arranging them on a topping of glacé icing which is just beginning to pour over the sides of the cake. The contrast of dark cake, white icing and red, green and yellow fruits is very effective. If you increase the amount of grated orange or lemon peel in the mixture, use an orange or lemon-flavoured and coloured glacé icing and the appropriate crystallized fruits.

See Gâteau de Pâques (page 119) and Cassata alla Siciliana (page 194) for examples of decorating with crystallized fruits.

Opposite page: Light fruit cake

LIGHT FRUIT CAKE INGREDIENTS

CAKE SIZES	18 cm (7 in) round 15 cm (6 in) square	20 cm (8 in) round 18 cm (7 in) square	23 cm (9 in) round 20 cm (8 in) square	25 cm (10 in) round 23 cm (9 in) square
plain flour	175 g (6 oz)	225 g (8 oz)	350 g (12 oz)	450 g (1 lb)
bicarbonate of soda	⅓ teaspoon	½ teaspoon	¾ teaspoon	1 teaspoon
mixed spice	⅓ teaspoon	½ teaspoon	¾ teaspoon	1 teaspoon
ground ginger	good pinch	¼ teaspoon	⅓ teaspoon	½ teaspoon
butter or margarine	100 g (4 oz)	175 g (6 oz)	250 g (9 oz)	350 g (12 oz)
light soft brown sugar	100 g (4 oz)	175 g (6 oz)	250 g (9 oz)	350 g (12 oz)
eggs	2 (size 3 or 4)	2 (size 1 or 2)	3 (size 1 or 2)	4 (size 1 or 2)
raisins	175 g (6 oz)	225 g (8 oz)	350 g (12 oz)	450 g (1 lb)
currants	75 g (3 oz)	100 g (4 oz)	175 g (6 oz)	225 g (8 oz)
sultanas	75 g (3 oz)	100 g (4 oz)	175 g (6 oz)	225 g (8 oz)
cut mixed peel	40 g (1½ oz)	50 g (2 oz)	75 g (3 oz)	100 g (4 oz)
grated orange or lemon rind	1	1	1½–2	2
cooking apple	100 g (4 oz)	175 g (6 oz)	250 g (9 oz)	350 g (12 oz)
approx. cooking time	1–1¼ hours	1¼–1½ hours	about 1¾ hours	2–2¼ hours

MERINGUES

The ability to make good meringue is invaluable to the cake maker and decorator. Many continental gâteaux are based on meringue – in layers or shells sandwiched with whipped cream and fruit, or as a decoration, perhaps dusted with cocoa. This section takes the mystery out of making meringues and gives recipes for all applications.

There are several types of meringue but the most commonly used is called Meringue Suisse. This is made by whisking egg whites until they are very stiff, then whisking in half the sugar gradually and folding in the rest. This is piped or spread for discs and other shapes as well as the usual teatime meringues. Meringue Cuite is easier to handle and holds its shape better. It is made by heating the egg whites and sugar over a pan of gently simmering water while the mixture is being whisked. The meringue is used mainly for basket and shell shapes. It will also 'hold' chopped nuts or other tiny pieces of flavouring baked into it.

With all meringue making the bowl and whisk must be scrupulously clean and free from all traces of grease to obtain the best results and most bulk. Weigh the sugar accurately. If you use too much the result will be sticky, soggy meringues. The type of whisk you use will affect the result. A balloon whisk gives greater volume but takes longer than a rotary whisk. An electric mixer saves time but gives the least volume. If you use a balloon whisk, put the egg whites in a wide bowl; a rotary whisk works best in a narrow deep bowl.

The best sugar to use is caster sugar, or a mixture of half caster sugar and half icing sugar, which gives very white, crisp meringues. For delicious pale brown meringues make Meringue Suisse and replace 50–75 g (2–3 oz) white sugar with light soft brown sugar, and sift it with the caster sugar before adding it to the egg whites. Bake in the same way.

Meringue Suisse

4 egg whites (size 1 or 2)
225 g (8 oz) caster sugar

Preparation time: about 10 minutes
Cooking time: 2 hours (shells, stars, bars); 2½–3 hours (discs)
Oven: 110°C, 225°F, Gas Mark ¼

1. Place the egg whites in a large grease-free bowl. Whisk the whites using a rotary whisk, balloon whisk or electric whisk, until the mixture is thick, white and stands in stiff peaks.

2. Whisk in half to two-thirds of the sugar about a tablespoon at a time, making sure it is completely incorporated and the mixture is stiff again after each addition.

3. Using a metal spoon, fold in the remainder of the sugar, again a little at a time. The meringue is now ready to pipe or spread and should be used immediately; it will deflate if left before cooking.

Step 1
Whisk the egg whites until they are thick, white and stand in stiff peaks.

Step 2
Stiffly whisk in half to two-thirds of the sugar, a tablespoon at a time.

Step 3
Use a metal spoon to fold in the remaining sugar a little at a time.

Meringue Discs

Makes 2 circles + 6–8 individual meringues for decoration

1. Cover 2 baking sheets with non-stick silicone paper, waxed paper, or greased greaseproof paper and draw a circle of the required size on each: 20–23 cm (8–9 inches) are the usual sizes but discs may be made larger if you are baking for a party. Alternatively draw three circles each 2.5–4 cm (1–1½ inches) smaller than the last to give graduated sizes, beginning with the largest at 18–20 cm (7–8 inches).

2. Fill a piping bag fitted with a large plain nozzle 1–2 cm (½–¾ inch) in diameter or a large star vegetable nozzle, and beginning in the middle of the circle, pipe a continuous spiral to fill the drawn circle. Repeat with the second circle.

3. Bake in a preheated oven, reversing the sheets in the oven after each hour. Cool on the paper, then peel off and store in an airtight container.

Meringue Shells, Stars and Bars

Makes 24–36, depending on size and shape

1. Line 2 baking sheets with non-stick silicone paper, waxed paper or greased greaseproof paper.

2. Fit a piping bag with a large star vegetable nozzle and fill with meringue.

3. On the paper pipe out shell shapes, stars or whirls or any other shapes to use to decorate the top of meringue discs or to form the sides for a meringue basket. For bars, use the same nozzle and pipe out straight lines of mixture about 10–12.5 cm (4–5 inches) long or squiggle the nozzle back and forth to give zigzag bars. Piping a continuous twisted line will give a meringue bar with a professional appearance.

4. Bake in a preheated oven, reversing the baking sheets in the oven after an hour to give even cooking on both sheets. When ready the meringues should be crisp and dry and should peel easily away from the paper. Leave on the paper to cool, then store between sheets of greaseproof paper in an airtight container.

Meringue Cuite

Makes about 8 nests or 1 large basket

250 g (9 oz) icing sugar
4 egg whites
few drops vanilla essence

Preparation time: about 20 minutes
Cooking time: about 2 hours
Oven: 110°C, 225°F, Gas Mark ¼

1. Sift the icing sugar at least twice to ensure it is completely free of lumps.

2. Put the egg whites into a heatproof bowl and whisk until frothy.

3. Add the icing sugar and whisk until blended. Stand the bowl over a saucepan of very gently simmering water and whisk the mixture until it becomes thick, white and stands in peaks. Whisk in the essence. The meringue cuite is now ready for piping into the shape you want.

4. For meringue nests, put the meringue into a piping bag fitted with a 1 cm (½ inch) plain nozzle or a large star nozzle. Line 2 baking sheets with non-stick silicone paper and draw circles of 10–12.5 cm (4–5 inches) over them.

5. Use the meringue to fill these circles beginning in the centre of each; then pipe a ring on top of the outside of the meringue circle to form the raised sides of the nest. Alternatively, instead of the outside ring, a series of dots or rosettes may be piped around the edge of the circle.

6. Bake in the oven for about 2 hours, reversing the sheets in the oven after 1 hour. Cool on the paper before peeling off. A large basket may be made in the same way beginning with a circle of about 23–25 cm (9–10 inches) and piping at least 2 rings on top of each other to form the sides.

Step 3
Whisking the mixture over a pan of simmering water to stiff white peak stage.

Meringue Based Cakes

Meringue discs can be sandwiched together with whipped cream and fruit or a combination of whipped cream and crème patissière. Any of the light, fruity cheesecake mixtures could also be used as an unusual filling: use half to sandwich the meringue layers and spread the remainder on top. Decorate with frosted or crystallized fruits.

To use meringue as the base for a cheesecake, make meringue cuite with 50 g (2 oz) chopped nuts for a firmer result. Layers can be made in a rectangular shape if you prefer. The recipe opposite for meringue suisse will make 3 layers. Draw rectangles of 30 × 10 cm (12 × 4 inches) on lined baking sheets. Pipe in the meringue in a backwards and forwards pattern. Bake in a preheated oven for 2½–3 hours.

Recipes in this book based on meringue are Austrian Meringue Basket (page 166), Petits Vacherins (page 215), Yellow Chicks (page 210) and Marrons Meringues (page 218).

Note: Baked meringues of all shapes and sizes will store satisfactorily for 7–10 days before use if kept in an airtight container.

PASTRY

Good pastry making is an important skill in the cake maker's repertoire. Many of the continental-style gâteaux so popular today are based on different types of pastry – such as rich puff pastry or pâte sucré. Pastry is also frequently used as a base for cheesecakes.

In the area of cakes and cake decorating, boundaries are becoming blurred. Tradition has it that a special occasion calls for a fruit or sponge cake with a suitable, often elaborate icing. Different countries, however, have different traditions. In France, many wedding feasts include a huge *galette de pommes*, a flat apple tart in which thin apple slices are carefully arranged in circles over a filling of apple purée and glazed. *Croquembouche* appears at weddings in France and Italy – a pyramid of tiny choux buns filled with liqueur-flavoured cream and swathed in spun sugar.

The continental influence has spread, introducing pastry-based confections as the centrepiece of a celebration, with layers of custard or cream and a message or name scripted in piped chocolate. Luxurious gâteaux such as these and cheesecakes are also frequently presented as dinner-party desserts. For this category of cakes the ability to make good pastry of various kinds is an invaluable skill, and extends your range to include fruit flans and exquisite little cakes for tea.

The great quality of pastry-based cakes, flans and cheesecakes is the contrast between the light, crisp, delicately flavoured pastry and the filling it contains. A shell of pâte sucrée may hold an array of jewel-like raspberries and redcurrants arranged on a layer of crème patissière or little choux buns may be filled with whipped cream and covered in melted chocolate. To make the famous *mille feuille*, sheets of puff pastry are layered with cream and crème patissière, covered in glacé icing and sliced into fingers.

Shortcrust pastry and its enriched variations, puff pastry and choux pastry are described in this chapter. Strudel pastry is included in the recipe for Cranberry Apple Strudels on page 204.

like cake-decorating, pastry-making is an art, and to be successful it is essential to master the basic techniques. Plain flour must be used for all the dessert pastries described here – self-raising flour results in a spongy texture. The fats used should be butter or hard margarine (hard fats are easier to rub in) with a proportion of lard in some cases to give a crisp texture when baked.

Keep everything cool. Make the pastry at a time when the kitchen is cool; chill any water that may be needed; the fats too should be cold when used. When rubbing the fat into the flour, always use only the fingertips as this is the coldest part of the hand. If you have warm hands, hold them under cold running water for a few moments to cool down before you start.

Rubbing or cutting in the fat can be done with two round-bladed knives used to cut the fat into small pieces in opposite directions, shaking the bowl from time to time to bring the larger lumps to the surface. Finish the rubbing in using the fingertips. A food processor or food mixer will give similar results in seconds.

The amount of water added to the fat and flour to bind them together will vary each time, as some flours will absorb more water than others. Make sure that enough water is added, as too dry a mixture will make the pastry crumbly and impossible to handle, and too wet a mixture will result in a crust that is too tough to eat. Add the water a little at a time, stirring it quickly into the flour with a round-bladed knife. Ensure that at least two-thirds of the given liquid is added.

The pastry is moist enough when it will gather together to form a soft ball without much kneading. If the pastry is dry and crumbly, add a drop more water to bind it together. Turn the dough out of the bowl on to a lightly floured work surface

and knead quickly until it is smooth, handling the pastry as little as possible. Wrap in cling film and chill for 10–15 minutes before using – this allows the pastry to firm up and relax before being used, and makes rolling out easier.

Rolling Out

Roll out carefully using light even pressure with both hands on the rolling pin – light flowing movements are better than heavy abrupt actions. Always roll away from yourself. Keep the pastry in a round shape and lift and turn it often to make sure that it does not stick to the work surface and that it keeps its shape. Sprinkle with a little flour to prevent it sticking to the table or rolling pin, but do not turn the pastry over, as this will incorporate too much flour into the pastry. Before baking the pastry should be lightly chilled in its finished shape to prevent excessive shrinkage.

To Bake

It is essential to bake the pastry in a preheated oven at a fairly high temperature to ensure quick rising and 'set' before it has a chance to shrink and collapse.

Proportions If a recipe calls for 225 g (8 oz) pastry, this means 225 g (8 oz) flour and does not refer to the sum total of all the ingredients. Any pastry recipe can be doubled or halved, but always keep the proportions the same in each case. It is a good idea to master shortcrust pastry before attempting any others.

Lining a flan tin

1. Choose a flan tin with a loose bottom, or a flan ring used on a baking sheet. China flan dishes do not conduct the heat quickly enough.

2. Roll the pastry out thinly, about 3 mm (⅛ inch) thick, to a circle 4 cm (1½ inches) larger than the diameter of the flan tin.

3. Lift the pastry on the rolling pin and lower it into the flan. Press it carefully into the base and sides, taking care not to stretch it at any time.

4. Trim the edges, using a rolling pin to roll the pastry level with the rim.

5. Prick the base with a fork to allow any steam to escape while cooking.

6. Chill the lined flan tin for at least 10 minutes.

Decorations for flans

Pastry trimmings can be used to make decorations. Roll them out thinly and cut into small shapes with pastry cutters, or make leaf shapes or tassels.
To make leaves, cut the pastry into 2.5 cm (1 inch) strips and then diagonally across into diamond shapes. Mark the shapes with the back of a knife to represent veins on the leaves.
To make a tassel, cut a 2.5 cm (1 inch) strip, then cut three-quarters of the way through at intervals of 5 mm (¼ inch) and roll up neatly. Open up like a flower and place on the pastry topping.

Baking Blind

A flan case is baked blind when the filling is to be cooked for only a short time or not at all.

Oven: 200°C, 400°F, Gas Mark 6

1. Line the pastry case with greaseproof paper, foil, or a double layer of absorbent kitchen paper.

2. Weight it down with dried beans (kept specially for this purpose, they can be used indefinitely). You can also buy special ceramic beans. Take care to put in enough beans to compensate for the filling. Push them well to the edges to support and hold up the sides.

3. Bake the pastry case in the centre of a preheated oven for about 15 minutes.

4. Remove the beans and paper and bake for a further 10 minutes or until the pastry is dry and golden brown.

5. Allow to cool on a wire rack before carefully removing from the flan tin (or follow the recipe instructions).

Glazing Brush the decorated flan with glaze before baking to give it a really professional look. For savoury pastry, a whole egg, beaten with a large pinch of salt, gives a rich golden colour. For sweet pastry, brush with a little milk or beaten egg white and dust with caster sugar before baking to give a frosted look.
To make a lattice pattern for open flans see the instructions given with Franzipan Tart on page 184. For a more decorative effect the strips of pastry can be twisted before being laid in position, sealed and trimmed in the usual way.

SHORTCRUST PASTRY

Shortcrust is the standard pastry for tarts, pies and shells. It is very easy to make and provided you follow the golden rules of handling it no more than is necessary and avoiding adding too much water, it will reward you with excellent texture and taste. For a special occasion, decorate the crust with appropriate pastry shapes or letters, or add warm glacé icing, pouring it over the cooked crust while the pastry is warm. If you wish to increase the quantity, remember that there should be half the weight of fat to flour, a pinch of salt and a measured amount of water: for 175 g (6 oz) flour, use 1½ tablespoons, for 225 g (8 oz) flour, no more than 2½ tablespoons.

The combination of half butter or hard margarine and half lard gives the colour and flavour of butter with the crisp texture characteristic of white fat. Shortcrust pastry should be light and crisp with a delicately tinted colour.

Basic Shortcrust Pastry

Makes 100 g (4 oz): 1 × 20 cm (8 inch) pastry shell or 12 tartlet shells

100 g (4 oz) plain flour
pinch of salt
25 g (1 oz) butter
25 g (1 oz) lard
1 tablespoon water

Preparation time: 10 minutes
Cooking time: 25 minutes for pastry case; 15 minutes for tartlet shells
Oven: 200°C, 400°F, Gas Mark 6

1. Sift the flour and salt into a bowl. Add the fats and, using a round-ended knife or palette knife, chop finely. Rub the fat into the flour with the fingertips.

2. When the mixture looks fine – like breadcrumbs – shake the bowl to bring any remaining lumps of fat to the surface and rub them in.

3. Add a little cold water and mix, first using a round-ended knife and then the fingertips, to bind the pastry together to a ball of dough. Add a little more water if necessary, but a wet dough makes a tough pastry.

4. Knead the dough lightly on a floured board. The pastry can be used immediately or wrapped in cling film and kept in a cool place for 15–30 minutes.

For perfect Pâte Brisée

Use iced water or the coldest possible. A touch of lemon juice will give a good flavour.

Use as little water as possible. Although damper pastry is easier to handle, because it is not so crumbly, it will be tough when cooked.

Handle the pastry as little as possible.

Always roll the pastry in one direction only – straight ahead of you. Turn the pastry round as you roll, do not change the direction of rolling.

Never overstretch the pastry – it will only shrink back as it cooks.

Pâte Brisée (Rich Shortcrust Pastry)

Use this pastry for flans and tarts with a moist filling. It has a firmer texture than shortcrust pastry and is very elastic, making it easy to roll out without breaking. Allow it to rest for a few minutes after rolling to let it spring back before lining the tins. The traditional French way to make this pastry is directly on a board avoiding the use of a bowl.

Makes 100 g (4 oz): 1 × 20 cm (8 inch) pastry case or 10 tartlet shells

100 g (4 oz) plain flour
15 g (½ oz) caster sugar
pinch of salt
50 g (2 oz) butter, chilled and diced
1 egg yolk
2 teaspoons chilled water or egg white

Preparation time: 15 minutes
Cooking time: 25 minutes for a pastry case; 15 minutes for tartlet shells
Oven: 200°C, 400°F, Gas Mark 6; then 180°C, 350°F, Gas Mark 4 (for pastry case)

1. Sift the flour, sugar and salt on to a board or into a bowl. Make a well in the centre and add the butter, egg and water or egg white.

2. With the fingertips of one hand only work the butter, egg and water mixture until the butter is smooth and pliable.

3. With a palette knife bring the flour in over the wet ingredients and cut it in very lightly.

4. As soon as the mixture is we coated use the heel of the han to bring the pastry together, squeezing it firmly, letting go straight away and turning it ove as it falls. Continue to work in this way until the pastry comes together, adding a little more water if it seems very dry. Knea very lightly until smooth.

5. Wrap in foil or cling film and chill for at least 20 minutes. Th pastry is then ready to use. Bak a pastry case in a preheated moderately hot oven for 10 minutes and then reduce the temperature for 15 minutes. Bake tartlet shells in a preheated oven for 15 minutes only.

âte Sucrée (Sweet Shortcrust Pastry)

is famous French pastry is
sp and thin when baked. It is
ed for the most delicate sweet
ts and flans. Like Pâte Brisée,
ly the fingertips – of one
nd – should be used in
xing, and it is made on a
ard. Because it is very soft
en made, it must be wrapped
d thoroughly chilled for at
ast an hour after preparation
it will be difficult to roll out.
must be rolled thinly; if this
oves tricky, roll it between
o sheets of non-stick silicone
per or cling film. Alternatively,
nay be pressed into the tins
hand, patching any little cracks
th small pieces of pastry.

akes 100 g (4 oz): 1 × 20 cm
inch) pastry case or 10
rtlet shells

0 g (4 oz) plain flour
nch of salt
g (2 oz) caster sugar
g (2 oz) butter (at cool room
temperature)
egg yolks
drops vanilla essence or ½
teaspoon grated lemon zest
(optional)

eparation time: 15 minutes
us chilling
ooking time: 25 minutes for a
stry case; 15 minutes for
rtlet shells
ven: 200°C, 400°F, Gas Mark 6;
en 180°C, 350°F, Gas Mark 4
or pastry case)

Sift the flour and salt into a
le on a working surface or
ard and make a well in the
ntre. Add the sugar, diced
tter, egg yolks and vanilla
sence or grated lemon zest, if
ing.

Using the fingertips of one
nd 'pinch and peck' the
tter, sugar and yolks together
til the mixture is smooth and
le. Try not to work in too
uch flour at this stage as it will
ughen the finished pastry.

3. Clean your fingertips with a
palette knife and use the knife
to draw the flour over the yolks.
Use your fingertips and then the
heel of the hand to bring the
pastry together in a ball. Knead
lightly until smooth.

4. Shape the ball of dough into
a flattened round. Wrap in cling
film and chill for 1–2 hours
before use. To use, roll out very
thinly on a lightly floured
surface.

5. Line a flan tin or tartlet tins.
Bake a pastry case in a preheated moderately hot oven for
10 minutes, then reduce the
temperature for 15 minutes.
Bake tartlet tins in a preheated
moderately hot oven for 15
minutes only.

Step 1
Make a well in the centre of
the flour and salt and add the
remaining ingredients.

Step 2
Work the butter, sugar and
yolks together until the
mixture is smooth and pale.

Step 3
When you have worked in
the flour, form the pastry
into a ball and knead lightly.

Step 4
Roll the chilled pastry out
very thinly on a lightly
floured surface.

PUFF PASTRY

Puff pastry (pâte feuilletée) is
the lightest and richest of all the
pastries and rises in the most
dramatic way. It is also the most
difficult to make. Homemade
puff pastry is unrivalled for taste
and texture; however, ready-
made puff pastry can be
purchased which rises well too.

The secret of successful puff
pastry lies in making the dough
soft enough to be elastic, but
not so wet that it becomes
soggy and sticky. Care must be
taken when rolling out the
pastry to keep it even in shape,
as poor layering gives an
uneven rise. The pastry needs to
be kept cool all the time, so use

iced water to mix if the kitchen
is warm and handle it as little as
possible. Butter, rather than
margarine, should be used, as
the flavour is important to the
taste of the pastry. Always keep
the butter chilled in the refrigerator until it is needed.

It is best to make the pastry
the day before it is required,
which gives it time to relax and
chill thoroughly before rolling
out. If you wish, make the
pastry as far as the fourth rolling
on one day, and complete the
rolling and folding and shaping
on the next day. When chilling
the pastry make fingermarks on
the pastry to indicate the

number of rollings given – it is
easy to forget where you are
when doing other things at the
same time.

For a well-risen pastry, the
oven must be correctly preheated and really hot when the
cold pastry is put in so that the
sudden heat makes it rise into
light, flaky layers. The baking
sheet need not be greased as
the pastry contains so much fat;
instead, dampen it with a little
cold water. This turns to steam
and helps the pastry to rise well.
A breadmaking flour gives
elasticity to the dough and also
helps make the pastry rise well.

Basic Puff Pastry

Makes 225 g (8 oz): 8 vol-au-vent cases

225 g (8 oz) plain flour
½ teaspoon salt
225 g (8 oz) butter
about 150 ml (¼ pint) iced
   water with a squeeze of
   lemon juice added

Preparation time: about 50 minutes, plus chilling
Cooking time: See individual recipes
Oven: 220–230°C, 425–450°F, Gas Mark 7–8

1. Sift the flour and salt into a bowl. Take about 40 g (1½ oz) of the butter and rub into the flour until the mixture is like fine breadcrumbs.

2. Use the iced water to bind to a fairly soft dough, working it in with a knife. You may not need all the liquid. Knead lightly in the bowl until smooth. Wrap in cling film and chill for 15 minutes.

3. Place the butter between 2 sheets of cling film or grease-proof paper. Soften it by beating it with a rolling pin, and form it into an oblong measuring 20 × 10 cm (8 × 4 inches).

4. On a lightly floured surface roll out the pastry to a square of about 23 cm (9 inches) and about 1 cm (½ inch) thick. Take the butter and place it on the pastry.

5. Fold the pastry over the butter, corner by corner, to form an enclosing envelope. Seal the edges of the pastry with the rolling pin.

6. Turn the pastry envelope if necessary so that the fold is on the right. 'Rib' the pastry by pressing the rolling pin across the pastry at regular intervals. This helps to distribute the air evenly through the pastry and makes the butter easier to roll out.

7. Roll the pastry into a long thin strip straight in front of you so that it is three times as long as it is wide, to measure approximately 10 × 30 cm (4 × 12 inches).

8. Fold the bottom third of the strip upwards and the top third downwards over the rest of th[e] pastry so it is quite even.

9. Seal the edges with the rolli[ng] pin and 'rib' it as before. Put [the] pastry into a polythene bag an[d] chill for 15–20 minutes.

10. Repeat the rollings and foldings (steps 7 and 8) four times more, giving the pastry [a] quarter turn each time so that the fold is always on the right. Mark the dough each time wit[h] fingerprints to show how ofte[n] it has been rolled. Wrap and c[hill] for 30 minutes after every two rollings. If the pastry is still str[eak]ed with fat, roll and fold it aga[in].

11. Wrap the dough in cling fi[lm] and chill for 30 minutes befor[e] using.

CHOUX PASTRY

Often known as a paste, choux pastry differs from all other types of pastry: it is much softer in texture, and is piped or spooned on to dampened baking sheets rather than being rolled out. It has many uses, both sweet and savoury. Success in making it begins with accurate weight and measuring. Make certain that the butter has melted before the water starts to boil, and the water must be boiling when the flour is added. Do not open the oven door until at least three-quarters of the cooking time has elapsed.

Step 1
Place the butter into a saucepan with the measured water.

Step 3
Add the sifted flour and salt to the pan and mix in with a wooden spoon.

Step 4
Beat the mixture until it is smooth. When it forms a ball, remove pan from heat.

Choux Buns

Makes 6–8

65 g (2½ oz) plain flour
pinch of salt
50 g (2 oz) butter
150 ml (¼ pint) water
2 eggs, beaten

Preparation time: about 15 minutes, plus cooling
Cooking time: see inividual recipes
Oven: 220°C, 425°F, Gas Mark 7; then 190°C, 375°F, Gas Mark 5

1. Sift the flour and salt on to a piece of greaseproof paper. Put the butter into the saucepan with the water.

2. Heat gently until the butter melts then bring quickly to the boil.

3. Add the flour to the pan all [at] once and mix in with a woode[n] spoon or spatula.

4. Beat until the mixture is smooth and forms a ball, leaving the sides of the pan clean. Do not over-beat.

FAULT FINDING GUIDE FOR PASTRY

FAULT	Causes & Solutions	FAULT	Causes & Solutions
RUBBED IN PASTRIES – Shortcrust, pâte brisée (rich shortcrust), pâte sucrée (sweet shortcrust)		**PUFF PASTRY (continued)**	
Crumbly dough	Insufficient mixing. Knead lightly to form a ball. Not enough liquid. Add more, a few drops at a time.	Uneven rising	Poor folding – corners must be eased out and pastry folded neatly into 3 layers. Uneven rolling.
Sticky dough	Too much liquid. Add a little more flour. Flour not weighed accurately. Pâte sucrée and pâte brisée not chilled before rolling.	Fat breaking through the dough	Fat too hard so that it breaks through when rolling. Insufficient chilling. Over-handling. Over-heavy rolling.
Cooked pastry hard and tough	Too much water worked in. Over-handled. Rolled out in too much flour. Flour sprinkled over pastry during rolling.	Fat running out during cooking	Fat broke through the dough while making (see above). Oven temperature too low.
Cooked pastry soft and crumbly	Too much fat used. Too little liquid added. Self-raising flour used for pâte brisée and pâte sucrée.	Pastry hard and tough	Too much water or too little water added to dough – it should be soft but not sticky.
Pastry shrunk	Stretched during lifting or shaping. Pâte brisée and pâte sucrée not allowed to relax before using. Pastry cooked in too cool oven.	Pastry shrinking	Insufficient resting. Pastry stretched during cutting, shaping or lifting.
Flan sides collapsed	Oven temperature too low. Insufficient baking beans used, or they were not piled up against sides of flan.	Damp and soggy inside	Insufficiently cooked. Vol-au-vents not put back into the oven to dry after the insides have been removed.
Soft under-cooked pastry	Oven temperature too low. Oven not properly preheated. Baking sheet not used under a flan tin. Too much liquid used in a pie. Top of pie or turnover not slit to allow the steam to escape.	**CHOUX PASTRY**	
PUFF PASTRY		Mixture too soft	Wrong proportions of ingredients used – weigh and measure accurately. Water not boiling when flour added. Mixture not cooked until it leaves sides of pan. Too much egg added at once. Insufficient beating when each amount of egg is added.
Sticky dough	Flour incorrectly weighed. Too much water added. Add a little more flour before rolling out. Dough not chilled enough.	Mixture not risen	Wrong proportions of ingredients used. Mixture too soft. Mixture not beaten enough. Oven too cool. Temperature lowered too soon. Oven doors opened during cooking. Not cooked long enough.
Pastry not risen	Fat not cool enough. Dough too tight; insufficient water added. Insufficient resting and chilling. Over-heavy rolling.	Sinking when removed from oven	Not cooked long enough – return to the oven quickly.
		Soft and soggy inside	Bases not pricked to allow the steam to escape. Not returned to oven after pricking to dry.

Remove quickly from the heat and spread the paste out evenly over the base of the pan. Leave to cool for about 10 minutes.

5. Beat the egg vigorously into the paste, a little at a time, to give a smooth glossy paste. A hand-held electric whisk is best for this as it helps to incorporate the maximum amount of air required for a good rise. The paste may not take the last spoonful of beaten egg.

6. The pastry must have a dropping consistency but remain stiff enough to pipe or spoon and hold its shape. The pastry is now ready for use.

CINGS, FROSTINGS & FILLINGS

Perfect icing is the key to successful decorating. Here are icings ranging from rich buttercreams, crème pâtissière and frostings to royal icing and fondant moulding paste.

Decorating cakes is an art which requires a good deal of practice as well as endless patience. Part of the art is knowing how to make the basic icings and fillings for cakes and which are the uses most appropriate to each. Icings can be divided into those that are simple to make and easy to apply, such as glacé icing and buttercream and its variations, and the more advanced types such as fondant moulding paste and royal icing. Glacé icing is suitable for light sponges, small cakes and pastries. Buttercream can be used for all these as well as gâteaux, flans and tarts. Crème pâtissière is used for filling flans, tarts and choux buns. Fondant moulding paste is suitable for covering fruit cakes, Madeira cakes and sponges, while royal icing is only used on rich fruit cakes or sometimes a Madeira as it is too heavy for sponges. Frostings give an informal 'roughed-up' finish to gâteaux. Frosted cakes should be decorated – with nuts, crushed caramel or frosted fruits – before the frosting sets. All frostings involve making a syrup first. Syrup-making is included in this section as it has many uses in baking and sweet-making.

Apricot glaze is brushed over the surface of a cake to prevent crumbs being drawn into a covering of fondant moulding paste or marzipan. It is also good for joining together different shaped pieces of cake before covering them with icing, as when assembling a sponge shape for a novelty cake, for example.

Good almond paste or marzipan is a vital element in cake decorating. Home-made almond paste is superior in flavour to commercially prepared marzipan, which is made from the same ingredients but includes food additives and preservatives. Almond paste is paler in colour and can be soft to use, while marzipan has the advantage of being smoother and easier to handle for a beginner.

Glacé icing is the simplest to make but must be used rapidly as it dries quickly. It can only be used for covering cakes, and feather icing. Once it has been poured over the cake it must be left to set completely, as a sudden movement may crack the surface. It can be flavoured and coloured.

Buttercream consists basically of creamed butter and sugar with a little flavouring. It can be used as a filling, covering and for piping, although the results are not as refined as with royal icing. It can be smoothed with a palette knife or whirled into patterns.

Continental buttercream is made from a sugar syrup base. It differs from simple buttercream in that, while the proportion of sugar is lower, more butter may be used and the mixture is enriched with egg yolks. The thicker texture makes it unsuitable for piping, but the flavour is more luxurious and it is good for filling and covering gâteaux. Crème au beurre mousseline is a slightly lighter variation.

Crème au beurre is a butter icing made lighter with the addition of a meringue mixture. This makes it perfect for filling light sponge cakes or for meringue baskets or layers. It can be flavoured. Not suitable for piping.

Crème pâtissière is a rich, delicious custard which has a velvety smooth texture and combines well with fresh fruit.

Frostings are icings and fillings that give an attractive finish to gâteaux and cakes. All are based on a syrup. The best known is American frosting, which sets quickly into stiff peaks but remains soft underneath.

Fondant moulding paste is available ready made but is easily made at home. Soft and pliable, it can be used to cover cakes and to mould decorations. As a cake covering it gives a beautifully smooth, slightly polished finish and gently rounded edges. Once on a cake or moulded into shape, it should be left for 2–3 days to dry. It can be coloured and flavoured, which makes it ideal for 'novelty' cakes. If used on tiered cakes it is advisable to apply a coat of royal icing to the tops to take the weight of the other tiers without sinking.

Fondant icing is softer than fondant moulding paste and is used for covering cakes only, not for moulded decorations, as the consistency when ready to use is that of thick cream. It keeps for up to 2 months and can be coloured and flavoured.

Satin icing can be used like fondant moulding paste to cover cakes, but the icing sugar is bound with butter melted with lemon juice, giving a slight flavour to the finished product.

Royal icing gives an exceptionally smooth finish and can be sculpted into exact corners. The range of piped work possible with royal icing is limitless – it is an extremely versatile medium. Too heavy for light-textured sponges, it is the most appropriate icing for rich fruit cakes, and can also be used on a Madeira, if you wish to make a formal cake but prefer a lighter texture.

MARZIPAN OR ALMOND PASTE

Almond paste is generally homemade and marzipan shop-bought. Both are used for covering all cakes to be coated with royal icing and for most cakes to be covered in fondant moulding paste, especially if a fruit cake; for decorative tops to cakes; or for moulding all sorts of shapes, such as flowers, leaves and animals.

Make up in quantities of not more than 900 g (2 lb) at a time, otherwise it becomes unmanageable. You can make up small quantities using 50 g (2 oz) ground almonds, etc. However, if you need small amounts for colouring, it is often best to use a commercial marzipan. The remainder, if it is securely wrapped in polythene, will keep for up to a month or so.

To make a creamy-white marzipan, the natural colour of almonds, use 2 lightly beaten egg whites instead of the egg or egg yolks for mixing.

Marzipan does not freeze.

Adding Colour To colour marzipan, simply add several drops of the chosen food colouring or colourings, then knead and squeeze the marzipan until the colour is evenly distributed throughout with no streaking. Powder or paste colourings can be used in the same way, adding sufficient until the required colour is obtained. If the marzipan becomes a bit soft, knead in a little sifted icing sugar as well.

Makes 450 g (1 lb)

100 g (4 oz) caster sugar
100 g (4 oz) icing sugar, sifted
225 g (8 oz) ground almonds
1 teaspoon lemon juice
few drops almond essence
1 egg or 2 egg yolks, beaten

Preparation time: about 10 minutes

1. Combine the sugars and ground almonds and make a well in the centre.

2. Add the lemon juice, almond essence and sufficient egg or egg yolks to mix to a firm but manageable dough.

3. Turn on to a lightly sugared surface and knead until smooth. Take care not to overknead or the marzipan may begin to turn oily. (There is no remedy for this and it then becomes difficult to use.) It can be wrapped securely in polythene or kitchen foil and stored for up to 2 days before use.

Commercial marzipan is available ready to roll in the traditional yellow or 'white' which is in fact the natural colour. They are both good and easy to use and the natural one is ideal for adding colours to for moulding as it gives truer colours than the yellow version.

Make sure you buy fresh marzipan, either by checking the date on the packet or by pressing it with your finger. If it is so hard that you cannot make a slight indentation, you should not buy it.

MARZIPAN (approximate quantities)								
Square Cake size		15 cm (6 inch)	18 cm (7 inch)	20 cm (8 inch)	23 cm (9 inch)	25 cm (10 inch)	28 cm (11 inch)	30 cm (12 inch)
Round Cake size	15 cm (6 inch)	18 cm (7 inch)	20 cm (8 inch)	23 cm (9 inch)	25 cm (10 inch)	28 cm (11 inch)	30 cm (12 inch)	
Marzipan	350 g (¾ lb)	450 g (1 lb)	575 g (1¼ lb)	800 g (1¾ lb)	900 g (2 lb)	1 kg (2¼ lb)	1.25 kg (2½ lb)	1.4 kg (3 lb)

Apricot Glaze

As well as forming a layer between the surface of a cake and its covering of fondant moulding paste or marzipan, apricot and other jam glazes can also be brushed over fruits in tarts.

The cooled, sieved glaze can be stored in an airtight container in the refrigerator for up to a week, but it must be boiled and cooled again before applying it to the cake. The smallest quantity you can make up is 2 tablespoons of jam and 1 teaspoon of water.

Makes about 5 tablespoons

175 g (6 oz) apricot jam or
preserve
2 tablespoons water

Preparation time: about 5 minutes
Cooking time: about 5 minutes

1. Put the jam into a small saucepan with the water and heat gently, stirring until the jam has completely melted.

2. Rub through a sieve and return the purée to a clean saucepan.

3. Bring back to the boil and simmer for 1 minute or until it is the required consistency. Allow to cool before use.

Applying apricot glaze to the top of a fruit cake. Marzipan has been used to level the top of the cake.

Covering a Cake in Marzipan

The same method is used for both round and square cakes and any other shape you wish to cover. For fancy shapes, such as petal or oval, simply use the cake tin as a pattern for cutting out the top section of marzipan.

To calculate quantities for different shapes, calculate roughly what the finished size of the baked cake will be and allow about 100 g (4 oz) more than the amount given in the chart for a similar-sized round or square cake.

1. Place almost half of the marzipan on a working surface dredged with icing sugar, or between two sheets of polythene. Roll out evenly until 2.5 cm (1 inch) larger than the top of the cake.

2. Brush the top of the cake with apricot glaze (see picture, left) and if the surface is uneven or very curved, build up the edges or fill in any holes with scraps of marzipan. If the cake is very uneven, roll it out as smoothly as possible, or cut off the bumps and turn the cake upside down and cover the base with marzipan instead.

3. Invert the cake on to the marzipan and carefully turn the cake the right way up. Alternatively lift the marzipan shape on to the top of the cake, keeping it even. Trim off any excess and smooth the edges with a small palette knife.

4. Stand the cake marzipan side up on a cake board and brush the sides with apricot glaze.

5. Cut two pieces of string, one the exact height of the cake and the other the complete circumference. Roll out the remaining marzipan and using the string as a guide, cut a strip to the height and circumference of the cake. Two shorter lengths can be cut if this is easier.

Step 3
Invert the cake on to the rolled-out marzipan.

Step 3 continued
With the cake right way up, trim off any excess marzipan and smooth the edges.

Step 6
Unroll the measured marzipan strip around the side of the cake.

Step 7
Smooth the joins at the end of the strip and where it meets the marzipan on top.

6. Loosely roll the marzipan strip(s) into a coil. Place one end on the side of the cake and unroll carefully, moulding the marzipan as you go and making sure the base of the marzipan touches the board.

7. Using a small palette knife, smooth the join at the ends of the strip and where the strip meets the marzipan on top of the cake. If the marzipan seems unduly moist, rub it all over with sifted icing sugar, and brush off the surplus.

8. Store the cake, uncovered, in a warm and dry, but not too hot, place for at least 24 hours before applying any icing. For tiered wedding cakes and those which you want to keep for a while after icing, allow up to a week; otherwise the oils from the marzipan will seep through into the royal icing and leave unsightly marks.

Note

Some people prefer to add the sides of marzipan to the cake before the top; it doesn't really matter which way you do it as long as it is kept neat and even and you fill in any holes or dents before you start.

For notes on making decorative items from marzipan, see pages 66 (holly and mistletoe leaves and berries), 64–5 (fruits) and 63 (rose buds, flowers and leaves).

ROYAL ICING

Royal icing can be made in any quantity as long as you allow 1 egg white to each 225 g (8 oz) icing sugar. However, it is better to make up not more than a 900 g (2 lb) quantity of icing at a time because the icing keeps better if made in small quantities. It is difficult to make up very small quantities, although it is possible to use ½ egg white and 100 g (4 oz) icing sugar.

The icing can be stored in an airtight container in a cool place for about 2 days. However, it must be stirred very thoroughly before use, and if necessary a little extra sifted icing sugar added to correct the consistency. The icing often seems to soften if left to stand for more than a few hours.

While using the icing, cover the bowl with a damp cloth to prevent a skin forming. Egg albumen powder, available from specialist cake decorating shops, can be made up according to the instructions on the packet and used in place of fresh egg whites.

Glycerine can be added to help soften the icing and make cutting easier. It should be omitted from the icing for the first 2 coats on the top surface of the bottom tier of a wedding cake and the first coat on the top surface of the middle tier, as a hard surface is needed to take the weight of other tiers. It should be used carefully as too much glycerine will make a very soft icing.

CONSISTENCY CHART FOR ROYAL ICING

Royal icing can be made to varying consistencies suitable for different purposes. In each case, beat for 1 minute before adding the required water or icing sugar.

Consistency	Method	Appearance
1 For coating; flooding for run-outs	Add 4 tablespoons water to the rest of the ingredients.	A soft consistency which should form a blob thick enough to cover the back of a spoon. It should not be runny.
2 For lines, trellis, scroll, lacework, writing, outlines for run-outs, scallops, beading, bells, doves.	Add 3 tablespoons water to the rest of the ingredients.	To test for correct consistency, use the back of a spoon to pull up some of the mixture; it should form a small peak. Add more sugar if the mixture is not stiff enough.
3 For borderwork, shells, rosettes, leaves, edging, frills and basketwork.	Add 3 tablespoons water to the rest of the ingredients. Add more icing sugar to achieve the required stiffness.	The mixture should form a peak which stands erect, slightly curling over at the top.
4 For flowers and snow; also for securing decorations to the cake.	Add 2 tablespoons water to the rest of the ingredients.	The mixture should form a stiff erect peak. If the mixture is too soft the petals of the flowers will spread out and blend into one another.

Makes 675 g (1½ lb)

3 egg whites
approx. 675 g (1½ lb) icing sugar, sifted
3 teaspoons strained lemon juice
1–1½ teaspoons glycerine (optional)

Preparation time: about 15 minutes, plus standing

1. Put the egg whites into a clean, grease-free bowl and beat until frothy. Using a wooden spoon, gradually beat in half the sifted icing sugar. (A hand-held electric whisk can be used but it will incorporate a lot of air and the resulting bubbles will be difficult to disperse.)

2. Add the lemon juice, glycerine and half the remaining sugar. Beat well until smooth and very white.

3. Gradually beat in enough of the remaining icing sugar to give a consistency which will just stand in soft peaks.

4. Put the icing into an airtight container or cover the bowl with a damp cloth and leave to stand for an hour or so, if possible, to allow most of the air bubbles to come to the surface and burst.

5. The icing is now ready for coating a cake; or it can be thickened a little with extra sifted icing sugar for piping stars, flowers, etc.; or thinned down for flooding run-outs, etc., by adding a little lightly beaten egg white or lemon juice. See above for guide to consistency. Several cakes in chapters 2 and 3 include decorative elements, such as flowers, fans, birds and butterflies, made from the basic white or tinted royal icing.

ROYAL ICING

Approximate quantities of icing sugar for two thin coats of royal icing on round and square cakes. Calculate for other shapes from these amounts allowing a little extra.

Square		15 cm (6 inch)	18 cm (7 inch)	20 cm (8 inch)	23 cm (9 inch)	25 cm (10 inch)	28 cm (11 inch)	30 cm (12 inch)
Round	15 cm (6 inch)	18 cm (7 inch)	20 cm (8 inch)	23 cm (9 inch)	25 cm (10 inch)	28 cm (11 inch)	30 cm (12 inch)	
Icing sugar	450 g (1 lb)	575 g (1¼ lb)	675 g (1½ lb)	900 g (2 lb)	1 kg (2¼ lb)	1.25 kg (2½ lb)	1.4 kg (3 lb)	1.6 kg (3½ lb)

Covering a Cake in Royal Icing

Some people prefer to ice the top of the cake first, then the sides; others do it the other way round. It doesn't really matter, so long as you add several thin coats rather than one thick coat, since this gives the smoothest surface for flat-icing. It is wise to apply the icing to one surface at a time rather than all in one go, allowing each application time to dry before continuing, or you may spoil the surface already put on the cake.

After each coat to the top or sides, it is important to pare or cut off any lumps or bumps in the icing, using a finely serrated-edge knife.

An ordinary royal iced cake requires two coats on the top and sides. Sometimes an extra coat on the top is necessary, if it is not as smooth as you would like. A wedding cake, however, requires three coats all over, with an extra coat on the top for the lower tiers, to help them hold the weight of the other cakes.

To Flat Ice the Top

1. With a dab of icing, attach the cake to a cake board, which is 2.5–5 cm (1–2 inches) larger than the cake. Put a quantity of icing in the centre of the cake and smooth out with a palette knife, using a paddling movement. This helps to remove air bubbles and distribute the icing evenly. Remove the surplus icing from the edges.

2. Take an icing ruler or long palette knife and draw across the cake towards you, carefully and evenly, keeping the ruler or knife at an angle of about 30° Take care not to press too heavily or unevenly.

3. Remove surplus icing by running a palette knife around the top edge of the cake, holding it at right angles to the cake.

4. If not sufficiently smooth, cover with a little more icing and draw the ruler or knife across the cake again, repeating until smooth. Leave to dry.

Step 2
Draw an icing ruler across the top of the cake towards you at an angle of about 30°

Step 3
Straighten the edges with a palette knife held at right angles to the cake.

To Flat Ice the Sides

Place the cake on an icing turntable if possible, or use an upturned plate.

For a Square Cake

The best way of achieving good even corners is to ice two opposite sides first, leave to dry, then ice the other two.

1. Spread some icing on one side, then draw the comb or palette knife towards you, keeping the cake still to give an even finish.

2. Cut off the icing down the corner in a straight line; cut the surplus off the top and base of the cake. Repeat with the opposite side and leave to dry.

Step 1
Icing the second side. Smooth the icing, drawing the comb towards you.

Step 2
Using a palette knife, cut surplus icing off the top.

3. Repeat the process with the two remaining sides, keeping the corners neat and tidy. Leave to dry.

For a Round Cake

1. Spread a thin but covering layer of icing all round the sides of the cake. Again use a paddling action to push out as much air as possible, keeping the icing fairly smooth.

2. Hold an icing comb or scraper or a palette knife at an angle of about 45° to the cake. Starting at the back of the cake, with your free hand slowly rotate the cake, and at the same time move the comb slowly and evenly round the sides of the

cake. Remove the comb at an angle and fairly quickly, so the join is hardly noticeable.

3. Lift any excess icing from the top of the cake using a palette knife, again rotating the cake. If not sufficiently smooth, wipe the comb and repeat. Leave to dry.

To Flat-Ice Irregular Shapes

Ice a cake according to the basic shape it most closely resembles. Those similar to a round cake, e.g. heart, oval, and petal are smoothed off all in one go after adding a smooth and even coating of icing all round the sides. An oval is very similar to a round; with a petal cake care to dip evenly into the 'dents'.

Other shapes tend to be multi-sided such as octagonal or hexagonal. These are iced in the same way as a square cake, adding the icing to every other side and, when dry, filling in those not already iced.

FAULT FINDING GUIDE FOR ROYAL ICING		
Fault	Causes	Solutions
While mixing Lumpy consistency; icing is not very white, possibly with a yellowish tint; mixture is too soft and misshapen	Icing sugar stored in damp place or container; icing sugar not sifted sufficiently; not enough egg white; not enough beating; too much heat in the atmosphere; too much fluid.	Buy good quality icing sugar; store in a plastic bag in a dry place; always sift well; use the largest grade egg or 2 egg whites from small eggs; beat a little longer; add a drop of water; add more sugar to stiffen.
While coating a cake Air bubbles	These always appear whether beating by hand or with a mixer. There are more when you use a mixer but since it is the easiest, quickest method of beating be prepared for them.	Leave the icing to stand overnight. Before using, stir slowly with a spoon to help disperse the bubbles. Use a pin to disperse any bubbles on the surface of the cake, pricking the bubble at its side.
When first coat has set Rough edges, lines or streaks on the icing	An accumulation of loose particles of icing sugar. Insufficient beating in the early stages.	Cover with a thin layer of flooding icing.
Uneven surface	The icing has set before all air bubbles were dispersed. Insufficient beating, or final stir was not given.	Using a wide clean paintbrush, dab over the icing with a little water. This wets the crust and seeps into the air pockets. When this is dry, apply another coat of icing.
Drip markings down the sides of the cake	Not removing excess icing from the cake.	If the icing is still wet, remove the excess with a spatula. If it has partly set, use a palette knife, dipped in warm water and immediately pressed straight on to the drip mark. The heat and moisture should melt the icing slightly so the drip mark disappears.
When the icing is on the cake Almond paste is visible so cake has a yellowish tint; icing looks dirty	Not enough layers of icing applied.	Add one or two more layers.
Icing has not set hard	Moist atmosphere caused by too much steam.	Move the cake to a dry place.
Uneven surface to the icing	Not applying the coats of icing evenly.	Apply a final layer and vibrate the turntable to allow it to flow into the uneven areas.

Adding Second and Third Coats of Icing

1. Repeat the method for the top and sides when applying each subsequent coat but make sure each layer is dry before adding the next or you may disturb the previous layers. Drying will usually take from 3 to 6 hours, but can vary according to the room atmosphere.

2. Leave the cake to dry, uncovered, for 24 hours after completing the icing. The cake is now base-iced ready for the decoration.

Rough Icing

As an alternative to a smooth finish, royal icing can be pulled up into peaks with a round-bladed knife to give a snow-peaked effect. The Christmas cakes on pages 110, 113, and 117 demonstrate how attractive this finish can be. Royal icing can also be used on novelty cakes to represent water, if the icing is tinted a pale blue. The contrast between a smooth sided cake and its rough-iced top (or vice versa) can be very decorative.

Icing the Cake Board

Sometimes it is a good idea to ice the cake board too, either before adding a decoration to it, or simply to cover up the expanse of silver board which some people find unsightly. To do this, first completely base ice the cake on its board and leave to dry. Then stand the cake on its board on an icing turntable and coat the board with a thin layer of icing (it may spread more easily if thinned slightly with a little egg white or lemon juice). Either run a palette knife round the edge while revolving the cake or hold an icing comb at an angle to the icing while rotating. Remove surplus icing from the edge of the board with a palette knife. With a square cake use the same method but take care with the corners.

The board may also be decorated in other ways. Flowers or other decorations on the cake may be used to decorate the board, too. Piping to match that on the top edge or round the base can be added to the board. If the cake has any lacework decoration on it, the board can be covered with lacework icing to match.

GLACÉ ICING

This is the quickest of icings to make and is useful for icing all kinds of sponges, Victoria sandwich and other cakes, as well as small cakes and biscuits. It cannot be used for piping stars or anything fancy. The icing will remain liquid for a short time if the bowl is placed in another large bowl containing hot water; otherwise, unless used quickly, it will set in the bowl.

Cakes covered in glacé icing must not be moved until the icing has set completely or it will crack. The cake must be put on to a board which is firm enough not to bend, before the icing is added for it can't be moved after adding the icing.

Glacé icing can be coloured and flavoured in any way you like to blend with any type of coloured decoration and flavour of cake.

Make up a small quantity in the same way as a large one; if it becomes too runny simply add more icing sugar.

Glacé icing must be used at once, as it does not keep. Once on the cake it will keep as long as the cake, i.e. up to 2 weeks. It is not generally used on rich fruit cakes which last much longer.

Makes sufficient to cover the top of a 20 cm (8 inch) round cake. Use double quantities to cover the top and sides.

225 g (8 oz) icing sugar
2–4 tablespoons hot water or fruit juice
food colouring and/or flavouring (optional)

Preparation time: about 5 minutes

1. Sift the icing sugar into a bowl.

2. Gradually beat in sufficient water or juice to give a smooth icing, thick enough to coat the back of a spoon easily. Extra water or sugar can be added to achieve the correct consistency.

3. Add a few drops of food colouring or flavouring, if used. Use at once or place over a bowl or pan of hot water for a short period.

4. Alternatively all the ingredients can be put into a saucepan and heated gently, stirring continuously, until well mixed and smooth; take care not to overheat or the icing will crystallize. Use very quickly.

5. If a crust begins to form on the icing before it is added to the cake, rub it through a sieve before use.

Variations

Lemon or Orange Use strained fruit juice instead of the water. A few drops of food colouring can also be used.

Coffee Use a little coffee essence or very strong black coffee in place of part or all of the water.

Chocolate Sift 1–2 tablespoons cocoa powder with the sugar and continue as recipe. A few drops of vanilla essence may also be added.

Mocha Sift 2 teaspoons cocoa powder and 1 or 2 teaspoons instant coffee powder with the sugar and continue as recipe. Alternatively, you could sift the cocoa with the sugar and add 1–2 teaspoons coffee essence with the water.

To Coat the Top of a Cake with Glacé Icing

1. Make sure the cake is completely ready before you begin.

2. Make the glacé icing, add colour if desired, then, when it is thick enough to coat the back of a wooden spoon, pour it over the middle of the cake. Using a round-bladed knife spread it out quickly and evenly over the top almost to the edge. If the icing drops over the edge, quickly remove it with a knife or palette knife or leave it until it has set, when it can be cut off with a sharp knife. Do not disturb the icing as it sets, or it will crack.

3. Alternatively tie a piece of non-stick silicone paper all round the sides of the cake to come about 2.5 cm (1 inch) above the top of the cake. Pour on the icing, spreading it out almost to the edge. It will then run out by itself and be held in place by the paper. Prick any air bubbles that may appear and leave to set. When set, very carefully ease off the paper.

4. Either add decorations to the glacé icing as it begins to set, or wait until it is quite set.

'o Coat a Whole Cake in Glacé Icing

. It is a good idea to stand the
ake on a thin cake card the
xact size of the cake, as this
eeps the cake rigid when it is
noved and should prevent the
ing from cracking. Stand the
ake on a wire rack over a plate
r tray.

2. Pour almost all of the icing
over the middle of the cake and
spread it out evenly, allowing it
to run down the sides. Use a
palette knife dipped in hot
water to help spread the icing
over the sides; fill in any gaps
with the icing left in the bowl.

3. Leave to set, then trim off
drips. Remove the cake
carefully.

Decorating with Glacé Icing

lacé icing lends itself to an
ttractive design known as
eather icing, used in the
trawberry Feather Bar on page
2. To achieve this design, make
p the amount of glacé icing
equired for the cake plus an
xtra 50 g (2 oz) icing sugar.
emove about 2 tablespoons of
ing and colour it a fairly bright
olour. Put the coloured icing
ito a greaseproof paper piping

bag (see page 56) without
cutting the tip off or adding a
nozzle. Use the white icing to
coat the top of the cake then
immediately cut the tip off the
coloured icing bag and pipe
straight lines across the top of
the cake at 1–2 cm (½–¾ inch)
intervals. Immediately draw a
skewer or the point of a knife
across the lines at right angles
about 2.5 cm (1 inch) apart.

Quickly turn the cake round
and draw the skewer across
again in between the first lines
but in the opposite direction to
complete the feathered effect.
A variation on this idea is the
spider's web design. To make
this, pipe the coloured icing in a
continuous circle, starting in the
centre of the cake and working
towards the outside edge.
Quickly draw a pointed knife

from the centre to the edge,
marking the cake into quarters.
Then draw from edge to centre
between the lines to complete
the pattern. This pattern is
particularly effective if the cake
is iced in coffee-flavoured icing
and the lines are drawn in
chocolate-flavoured icing.

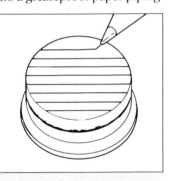

1. Using coloured icing,
pipe evenly spaced straight
lines across the top of the
cake.

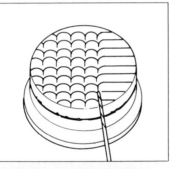

2. Draw a skewer across the
lines at right angles about
2.5 cm (1 inch) apart.

3. Turn the cake around.

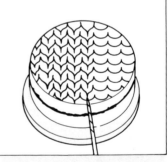

4. Draw the skewer across
again between the first
'feathers' but in the opposite
direction.

FONDANT MOULDING PASTE OR COVERING

This icing is simple to use once you get used to its consistency and you can achieve a professional result more quickly than with royal icing. It is also easy to make, since extra sifted icing sugar can be added until it is sufficiently malleable. Use it for covering cakes either after adding a layer of marzipan to the cake, when it needs to be · brushed lightly with egg white to make the icing adhere, or add it directly to a sponge or Madeira after brushing the cake with apricot glaze.

It should be rolled out on a surface sprinkled with a mixture of sifted icing sugar and cornflour and, for ease of movement, it can be rolled out on a sheet of polythene sprinkled with the sugar mixture. To smooth it, simply rub in a circular movement (take care if you have long nails or are wearing rings) with the fingertips, which have been dipped in icing sugar and cornflour. The paste can be coloured by adding liquid or powder or paste food colourings; and flavourings can be added, too. Apart from cake covering, it is also good for moulding all types of animals, flowers and other shapes. It can be painted with liquid food colouring for extra effect.

Fondant moulding paste can be used almost interchangeably with royal icing but take care when covering tiered wedding cakes for sometimes the paste does not set hard enough to take the weight of heavy top tiers. Make sure it is given extra time for drying out (see step 7 · of recipe) and it may help to add 1–2 coats of royal icing to the tops of the cake before adding the moulding paste.

Liquid glucose or glucose syrup is available from most larger chemists and also from specialist cake decorating shops. A number of these are listed at the end of this book.

It is difficult to make up quantities of more than 900 g (2 lb) because of the kneading required. It blends most easily when made in 450–700 g (1–1½ lb) quantities. Smaller quantities can be used but the egg white and liquid glucose quantities must be weighed very accurately. If only small quantities are required, use a ready-made fondant paste, which will keep for up to a couple of months if wrapped securely in polythene. It is obtainable in supermarkets as well as specialist cake decorating shops.

Makes 450 g (1 lb)

450 g (1 lb) icing sugar
1 egg white
50 g (2 oz) liquid glucose or
  glucose syrup
food colouring and/or
  flavouring (optional)

Preparation time: about 10–15 minutes

1. Sift the icing sugar into a mixing bowl to remove all lumps and make a well in the centre.

2. Add the egg white and liquid glucose. Beat with a wooden spoon or spatula, gradually pulling in the icing sugar from the sides of the bowl, to give a stiff mixture.

3. Knead the icing thoroughly, mixing in any remaining icing sugar in the bowl to give a smooth and manageable paste. To see if it is ready, press your thumb into the icing. If the indentation is perfect, the icing is ready. Add a little more icing sugar if the paste sticks to your thumb.

4. Add colouring and flavouring as desired and extra sifted icing sugar, if necessary, to obtain the correct consistency – i.e. suitable for rolling, which you will soon be able to judge with practice.

5. The icing can be stored in a tightly sealed polythene bag or a plastic container in a cool place for 2–3 days.

Covering a Cake in Fondant Moulding Paste

If the cake is covered with marzipan, first brush the marzipan lightly all over with egg white.

If the cake is without marzipan, brush it first with apricot glaze (page 38).

1. Either roll out the icing on a sheet of polythene dredged with a mixture of icing sugar and cornflour or directly on a working surface dredged with the same mixture. Make sure the rolling pin is also dredged with the icing sugar mixture. Alternatively roll it out between 2 sheets of polythene. Roll it until it is the width of the top of the cake plus the sides, plus about 2.5 cm (1 inch) extra; this usually means about 13–15 cm (5–6 inches) larger than the top of the cake.

2. Support the icing on a rolling pin, pull off the polythene, if using, and place the icing centrally over the top of the cake.

3. Press the icing on to the sides of the cake working it from the centre of the cake out to the edge, then down the sides, using your fingers (dipped in a mixture of icing sugar and cornflour) and using a circular movement to give an even covering.

4. Trim off the excess icing fro around the base of the cake using a sharp knife. Smooth o around the base and trim agai if necessary. Any wrinkles or marks can be removed by rubbing over in a circular movement with the fingers.

5. For square cakes, if you wa straight-edged, rather than rounded-edged corners, you can cut out a piece of icing from each corner, then mould carefully to conceal the join. However, the joy of this icing i the 'soft' edges it gives to corners, which look so good.

6. For any other shaped cake, mould the icing in the same way, but if for a difficult shape such as a horseshoe, it will be necessary to cut the icing in o or two places to achieve a goo even covering.

7. Leave for at least 24 hours t dry and preferably 2–3 days before adding the decoration.

To make moulded decorations from fondant moulding paste see page 63 for roses an other flowers and page 130 fo frills.

lacing the rolled-out paste
n top of the cake.

ressing the paste on to the
ides of the cake.

rimming off excess paste
vith a sharp knife.

FAULT FINDING GUIDE FOR FONDANT MOULDING PASTE

Fault	Cause	Solution
While mixing the paste The ingredients will not mix together.	Missing ingredients; not enough fluid to stick everything together.	Add missing ingredients; add water then knead and squeeze the icing mixture until it forms a soft but firm ball. Use the thumb test (see page 44).
The mixture is a soft sticky mass which will not form a ball.	Too much fluid has been added.	Remove half the quantity of icing and keep it in a separate bowl covered with a lid or cling film so it is not exposed to the air. Add sifted icing sugar to the remaining half, little by little, until you achieve the desired consistency.
After rolling out The fondant cracks or breaks off. It has a scale-like appearance or a dull matt finish.	Not enough fluid has been added.	Add fluid until the mixture is workable. Use the thumb test (see page 44).
The fondant isn't elastic enough; it cracks around the corners and edges as it is placed on the cake.		Work a palette knife gently over the corners until the cracks are sealed. Finish by using your cupped hand to polish and smooth over the corners.
Small air bubbles appear; the fondant is difficult to handle and sticky to the touch.	The consistency is too wet.	Place the fondant back in the mixing bowl and add more sifted icing sugar until the consistency is soft but firm.
The fondant has a wet look.	The atmosphere is causing the icing to sweat.	Leave it and the atmosphere will soon dry it out.
When paste is on the cake The icing is too dry so it is unworkable.		If possible, discard that fondant and use fresh. If this is not possible, take the fondant off the cake in one or two pieces. Remove any yellowish stains (caused by almond paste) and place the icing in a bowl. Dampen your fingers with water and knead the icing until it is workable.
After polishing with cornflour The icing looks dull.	The surface is too dry and has been polished with too much cornflour.	Dampen your hands with a clean cloth. Stroke the top of the cake lightly with a circular movement, polishing it until it is smooth. Dampen your hands again and treat the sides in the same way.

FONDANT MOULDING PASTE (approximate quantities)

Square Cake size		15 cm (6 inch)	18 cm (7 inch)	20 cm (8 inch)	23 cm (9 inch)	25 cm (10 inch)	28 cm (11 inch)	30 cm (12 inch)
Round Cake size	15 cm (6 inch)	18 cm (7 inch)	20 cm (8 inch)	23 cm (9 inch)	25 cm (10 inch)	28 cm (11 inch)	30 cm (12 inch)	
Moulding paste	350 g (¾ lb)	450 g (1 lb)	700 g (1½ lb)	800 g (1¾ lb)	900 g (2 lb)	1 kg (2¼ lb)	1.25 kg (2½ lb)	1.4 kg (3 lb)

OTHER ICINGS AND FILLINGS

Not to be confused with moulding paste, this is a soft icing made from a concentrate and diluted to the consistency of thick cream.

Fondant Icing

To cover a 20 cm (8 inch) round cake

150 ml (¼ pint) water
450 g (1 lb) granulated or cube sugar
1 tablespoon liquid glucose
a few drops of flavouring or colouring (optional)

Preparation time: 15 minutes plus cooling

1. Gently heat the water and sugar in a heavy-bottomed pan until the sugar has dissolved. Bring to the boil slowly and add the glucose. Boil until the sugar registers 115°C (238°F) on a sugar thermometer (the soft ball stage).

2. When the bubbles subside, pour one third of the syrup into one bowl and the remainder into another bowl. Leave to cool until a skin forms.

3. Working with the smaller quantity first, beat with a wooden spoon until it is thick and white. It will change from a liquid to a paste and finally to a solid white mass. Knead with the fingers until smooth. Shape into golf-ball sized pieces.

4. Repeat with the larger quantity of fondant icing. If stored in an airtight jar, this icing will keep for up to 2 months.

5. To use, place 3 or 4 pieces o fondant in a basin over a pan o hot water. Warm gently, stirrin; until the fondant is smooth an the consistency of thick cream Add flavouring or colouring if using. If the icing is too thick, add a little water.

Satin Icing

This is a true moulding icing with a lemony flavour.

To cover a 23 cm (9 inch) round cake

50 g (2 oz) butter
4 tablespoons lemon juice
675 g (1½ lb) icing sugar, sifted
a few drops of food colouring

Preparation time: 20 minutes

1. Place the butter and lemon juice in a small saucepan over a gentle heat and stir with a wooden spoon until the butter has melted.

2. Add 225 g (8 oz) of the icing sugar and heat gently, stirring, until dissolved. When the mixture begins to simmer at the sides of the pan, increase the heat slightly and cook for 2 minutes until it boils gently; do not overboil at this stage or the icing will be too hard.

3. Remove the pan from the heat and add 225 g (8 oz) more icing sugar. Beat thoroughly with a wooden spoon, then turn the icing into a mixing bowl.

4. Gradually mix in enough of the remaining icing sugar to give a soft dough. Turn the dough on to a surface dusted with icing sugar and knead un it is smooth. Add colour at this stage if using.

5. Wrap the ball of icing in cling film and store in the refrigerato for up to 6 weeks. To use, roll out and use as fondant mould-ing paste.

Buttercream

This standard and favourite icing can be coloured and flavoured in a wide variety of ways to complement the type of cake being filled and/or iced; it is also ideal for adding pretty but simple decorations with or without a piping bag and nozzle, on to cakes covered in buttercream or fondant mould-ing paste. It can be applied straight on to a cake or over a layer of marzipan. If the cake to be covered in buttercream appears to be crumbly, it is best to brush it with apricot glaze first to prevent the crumbs from getting mixed into the icing. It is simple to make up half quant-ities of the buttercream. It will also freeze once made.

To cover the top and sides of an 18 cm (7 inch) sandwich cake; or to fill the cake and cover the top.

100 g (4 oz) unsalted butter or soft margarine
175–225 g (6–8 oz) icing sugar, sifted
a few drops of vanilla essence or other flavouring (optional)
food colourings (optional)
1–2 tablespoons milk, top-of-the-milk, evaporated milk or fruit juice

Preparation time: about 10 minutes

1. Cream the butter or margar-ine until very soft.

2. Beat in the sugar a little at a time, adding essence to taste and colouring, if liked, and sufficient milk or other liquid to give a fairly firm but spreading consistency.

3. Store in an airtight container in the refrigerator for up to a week, if wished. Allow to return to room temperature before use.

4. If using for piping lattice or writing the icing may need the addition of a little more milk t make it flow easily without breaking. For piping with a sta nozzle the consistency can be firmer.

Variations

Coffee Omit the vanilla and replace 1 tablespoon of the milk with coffee essence or very strong black coffee; or beat in 2–3 teaspoons coffee powder with the icing sugar.

Chocolate Add 25–40 g (1–1½ oz) melted plain chocolate; or dissolve 1–2 tablespoons sifted cocoa powder in a little hot water to give a thin paste, cool and beat into the icing in place of some of the milk.

Orange or Lemon Omit the vanilla, replace the milk with orange or lemon juice and add the finely grated rind of 1 orange or lemon and a little orange or yellow liquid food colouring.

Mocha Dissolve 1–2 teaspoons cocoa powder in 1 tablespoon coffee essence or very strong black coffee and add in place of some or all the milk.

Almond Replace the vanilla with almond essence and beat about 2 tablespoons very finely chopped toasted almonds if liked. A few drops of green colouring may be added to give a pale almond green coloured icing.

Apricot Omit the vanilla and milk and beat in 3 tablespoons sieved apricot jam, a pinch of grated lemon rind, a squeeze of lemon juice and a touch of orange liquid food colouring.

Minted Replace the vanilla essence with peppermint essence – but in moderation – add a few drops green food colouring and/or 3–4 crushed minted chocolate matchsticks.

Liqueur Omit the vanilla essence and replace the milk with brandy, whisky, rum, sherry or other liqueur. A few drops of an appropriate food colouring can be added.

Continental Buttercream

Rich and creamy, this makes a good covering or filling but is not suitable for piping.

Makes sufficient to fill and cover the top of an 18–20 cm (7–8 inch) sandwich cake

75 g (3 oz) caster sugar
4 tablespoons water
2 egg yolks
100–175 g (4–6 oz) unsalted butter

Preparation time: about 20 minutes

1. Put the sugar into a small heavy-based saucepan with the water and mix gently over a low heat until the sugar has completely dissolved. Put a sugar thermometer into the pan and boil until it reaches the thread stage, 107°C/225°F. If you do not have a thermometer, dip the back of a teaspoon in the syrup and pull the syrup sharply away with the back of another spoon. If no thread forms, boil for a little longer and test again.

2. Put the egg yolks into a bowl and whisk well – a hand-held electric whisk is ideal for this job. Gradually pour the syrup in a thin stream on to the eggs while whisking the mixture continuously.

3. Continue whisking the mixture until it is cold and thick.

4. Put the butter into another bowl and beat until soft and creamy, then beat in the whisked mixture a little at a time, until smooth and of a spreading consistency. Use at once, or add flavourings as for buttercream.

Variations

Crème au beurre mousseline is made in the same way as Continental Buttercream, except that the quantity of water is doubled and the diced butter added bit by bit to the egg and syrup mixture. The result is a little lighter. It can be flavoured with 1–2 tablespoons liqueur or fruit juice or a few drops of vanilla essence. To flavour with chocolate, melt 50 g (2 oz) chocolate in a bowl set over a bowl of hot water. When the chocolate is liquid and smooth, beat it into the crème au beurre mousseline. Leave in a cool place to set.

Crème au Beurre

To cover and fill a 20 cm (8 inch) sandwich cake

2 egg whites
125 g (4 oz) icing sugar, sifted
125 g (4 oz) unsalted butter
a few drops of flavouring or food colouring (optional)

Preparation time: 15–20 minutes

1. Place the egg whites and icing sugar in a mixing bowl set over a pan of simmering water and whisk until the mixture holds its shape. Cool slightly.

2. Place the butter in a mixing bowl and cream until soft. Beat in the meringue mixture a little at a time. Flavour or colour as desired. The crème is ready to use or can be stored in an airtight container in the refrigerator for 2–3 weeks.

Variations

Chocolate Melt 50 g (2 oz) plain chocolate in a bowl set over a pan of hot water. Cool and beat in with the meringue mixture.

Coffee Add 1 tablespoon coffee essence with the meringue mixture.

Praline Add 3 tablespoons crushed praline (see page 49) with the meringue mixture.

Crème Pâtissière

Makes about 450 ml (¾ pint)

300 ml (½ pint) milk
50 g (2 oz) caster sugar
20 g (¾ oz) plain flour
15 g (½ oz) cornflour
1 egg
1 egg yolk
a few drops of vanilla essence
15–25 g (½–1 oz) butter

Preparation time: about 10–15 minutes, plus cooling

1. Heat the milk gently in a saucepan but do not let it boil.

2. Put the sugar, flour, cornflour, egg and egg yolk into a bowl and whisk or beat until very smooth and creamy. Beat in a little of the hot milk.

3. Add the egg mixture to the rest of the milk in the pan and beat until smooth, then cook gently, stirring continuously, until the mixture thickens and comes just to the boil.

4. Add the vanilla essence and butter and cook gently over a low heat for a minute or so, still continuing to stir.

5. Remove from the heat and turn into a bowl. Cover tightly with cling film, or put a piece of wet greaseproof paper on to the surface of the custard to prevent a skin forming. The custard can be stored in the refrigerator for up to 48 hours before use, preferably in an airtight plastic container.

American Frosting

Suitable for most cakes, this frosting has a crisp outer crust with a soft inside. To guarantee success a sugar thermometer must be used, and it is vital to beat until the frosting really does stand in peaks or it may slide off the cake.

To fill and cover a 20–23 cm (8–9 inch) cake

450 g (1 lb) loaf or granulated sugar
150 ml (¼ pint) water
pinch of cream of tartar
2 egg whites
a few drops of food colouring (optional)

Preparation time: 25 minutes

1. Put the sugar and water into a large heavy-based saucepan and heat gently until the sugar has dissolved. Add the cream of tartar.

2. Insert a sugar thermometer. Bring syrup to boil. Boil to a temperature of 115°C (238°F).

3. Meanwhile, beat the egg whites until they are very stiff.

4. Pour the sugar syrup in a thin stream on to the beaten egg whites, beating briskly all the time. Continue to beat until the frosting is thick enough to stand in peaks with the tips just bending over. Add food colouring while beating, if using.

5. Quickly spread the frosting over the cake, pulling it into peaks all over. Leave to set.

Caramel Frosting

To cover and fill a 20 cm (8 inch) round cake

175 g (6 oz) soft brown sugar
1 egg white
2 tablespoons hot water
a pinch of cream of tartar

Preparation time: 5–7 minutes

1. Put all the ingredients in a bowl set over a pan of hot water and whisk for 5 to 7 minutes until the mixture is thick. Use immediately, forming into swirls on the cake with a palette knife.

Variation

Mock Frosting Replace the brown sugar with caster sugar. This can be used as a substitute for American frosting if you do not have a sugar thermometer.

Fudge Frosting

To fill and frost a 20 cm (8 inch) cake

75 g (3 oz) butter
3 tablespoons milk
25 g (1 oz) soft brown sugar
1 tablespoon black treacle
300 g (12 oz) icing sugar, sifted

Preparation time: 15 minutes

1. Put the butter, milk, brown sugar and treacle in a heatproof bowl over a saucepan of hot but not boiling water. Stir occasionally until the butter and sugar have melted, then remove the bowl from the saucepan.

2. Stir in the icing sugar, then beat with a wooden spoon until the icing is smooth.

3. Pour quickly over a cake for a smooth coating, or leave to cool, then spread over the cake and swirl with a small palette knife. Leave the frosting to set, then decorate as desired.

Praline

This delicious ingredient – basically caramelized almonds – is quickly made and can be stored for 6 weeks in a screw-top jar. It is used in desserts and sauces as well as a flavouring for cake icings and fillings. Usually made with almonds, it can be made with any hard nut such as hazelnuts, walnuts or pistachio nuts. Use whole or chopped nuts, skinned or unskinned, toasted or plain, but if making praline powder the nuts should be peeled.

100 g (4 oz) unblanched almonds
100 g (4 oz) sugar
4 tablespoons water

Preparation time: 10 minutes
Cooking time: 20 minutes

1. Wash the almonds in cold water to remove the powder which clings to the skins.

2. Place the sugar and water in a small heavy saucepan over a gentle heat and stir with a wooden spoon until the sugar has dissolved. Remove the spoon and do not stir again (see notes on sugar boiling right).

3. Add the almonds to the syrup, bring to the boil and boil rapidly until it reaches the caramel stage (see right), on the sugar thermometer and turns a rich brown colour.

4. Pour the nuts and caramel on to an oiled baking sheet resting on a pot stand or board to protect the working surface from the heat. Leave to cool.

5. When cold, crush the praline in a pestle and mortar or with a rolling pin. If very fine praline is needed grind it in a blender.

SUGAR SYRUPS

Sugar syrups are used extensively for making some icings and toppings like praline and caramel. In cake-making and decoration it is important to be familiar with the different stages of sugar boiling.

When sugar is boiled, its character changes. First it becomes syrupy, then as the temperature rises, it gets thicker and sets to a soft consistency. The boiled sugar continues to change until it becomes a rich brown caramel which is hard and crisp when set. These changes happen at certain temperatures; because of this it is possible to get good results even without a sugar thermo-meter, although it is a useful piece of equipment. Choose one which is clearly marked. A large handle at the top makes it easy to move and a clip on the side ensures it stands upright in the pan and makes it easier to take an accurate reading.

Utensils

Pan Use a clean pan with a heavy base – thin ones will distort with the extreme heat. Aluminium and stainless steel are excellent, or you may be lucky enough to own a copper sugar boiling pan, which, because it will not be tinned, must only be used for boiling sugar. Enamel pans are not suitable and non-stick pans will be scratched by the sugar grains. To clean the pan after use, let it cool, fill with warm water and cover with a lid. Boil until all the sugar has dissolved.
Spoons Always use wooden spoons or spatulas. Metal spoons will scratch the pans, and if the handle becomes hot, will cause unpleasant burns. Plastic spoons will melt.
Heat diffuser This can be useful on a gas hob when long slow cooking is needed.

Ingredients

Sugar Unless otherwise stated, use granulated sugar.
Butter This will give a good flavour to the finished recipe.
Glucose This is used in some sweet-making recipes to prevent crystals forming in the syrup. Sometimes a very small amount of cream of tartar can be used for the same purpose.

For Successful Sugar Boiling

1. Prepare all utensils before starting to boil the sugar.

2. Keep a small pan of water boiling on the hob and keep the thermometer and spoons in this when not in use.

3. Allow the sugar to dissolve slowly, stirring occasionally.

4. Make certain that all the sugar has dissolved before the syrup comes to the boil.

5. Never stir a boiling syrup unless a recipe states otherwise.

6. Wash any sugar crystals from the side of the pan with a clean pastry brush dipped into water.

7. Remove any scum which forms on the top of the syrup with a metal spoon.

8. Cook over a moderate heat unless told to cook gently.

9. Have patience. Sugar may take a long time to rise from one temperature to another and will then rise very rapidly. When the correct temperature is reached, remove pan from heat.

10. Unless the syrup or caramel is to be used at once, arrest further cooking by plunging the base of the saucepan in a large basin of cold water.

STAGES OF SUGAR BOILING

The temperature at which sugar reaches each stage can be affected by the atmosphere, and even different bags of sugar can react differently. For accuracy the full range of temperatures is stated, but for general use a quick guide is also given.

Thread 107°C (225°F). The sugar looks syrupy. Using a small spoon remove a little of the syrup and allow it to fall from the spoon, on to a dish. The syrup should form a fine thin thread when the correct stage has been reached. Used in crème au beurre mousseline.

Soft Ball 113–118°C (235–245°F). Drop a small amount of the syrup into cold water then mould into a soft ball with the fingers. Used for fudge.

Hard Ball 119–127°C (246–260°F). Drop a little syrup into cold water then mould with the fingers into a ball which is firm but pliable. Used for caramels and marshmallows.

Soft Crack 132–137°C (270–279°F). Drop a little syrup into cold water: it should set hard, but will bend slightly and stick to the teeth when bitten. Used for toffees.

Hard Crack 138–153°C (280–305°F). The syrup dropped into cold water will form brittle threads which snap easily. Used for hard toffee.

Caramel 154–175°C (310–350°F). The syrup becomes a light golden brown. As the temperature rises it gets darker in colour. If it becomes too dark, the flavour is bitter. When it is almost black it can be used as gravy browning. Used for praline.

DECORATIVE TECHNIQUES

Decoration can be modest or elaborate. Whatever style you choose, you can demonstrate your own individual and creative flair. Practise all the different techniques carefully, working through the chapter to learn the decorative skills you require.

One of the most delightful aspects of decorating a cake is that it may be as easy – or as elaborate – as you like. It is literally in your hands whether you sprinkle icing sugar through a doily on to a simple sponge or spend hours creating a masterpiece. It is best to start with simple ideas and work up to the more advanced designs as you gain in confidence and ability.

This chapter takes you through the basics of cake designing and the repertoire of techniques available. The most important of these is piping with royal icing, a delicate and satisfying skill which takes practice to perfect but which has breathtaking results. Making models and novelty shapes with fondant moulding paste is almost equally important for celebration and novelty cakes. The most modest glacé-iced cake can be elevated to elegance with a decoration of frosted fruits, and the versatility of chocolate in cake decoration is unrivalled.

As a beginner, you will find bought decorations a great help, but as your confidence grows, you will probably find yourself buying less and making more, especially when you discover how easy it is to do quite complicated designs after mastering the techniques outlined in this chapter.

It is worth spending some time planning the design of a cake, particularly if it is to be used for a specific purpose. The most important factor in any design (for a cake or anything else) is suitability. Finding the right cake for a particular occasion may not be difficult if that occasion is a little girl's birthday or a family Christmas party, but even then you have the choice of a traditional design or one that is more imaginative. In this book there are ideas for both, and if there is a cake you find attractive, try adapting it and using different decorations for a different purpose.

CAKE TEMPLATES

Very soon after you become interested in decorating cakes, you will want to put patterns or designs on top of the cakes. For this it is necessary to have a guide or template, which is placed on top of the base-iced cake to help achieve an exactly symmetrical design. A template can only be used on a hard icing, such as royal icing or fondant moulding paste, as softer icings are marked by the templates.

It is also possible to buy metal or plastic symmetrical rings and cake markers, which help to make curves and scroll shapes on cakes.

Templates are first drawn on thick paper or thin card with the help of rulers, compasses or anything else which will assist in drawing the design or shape you require. Begin with a square or a circle the same size or about 2.5 cm (1 inch) smaller in width than the cake, depending on the size of the cake. The template must be exact and symmetrical in all ways, because if it is only a little irregular, the whole design of the cake will be spoilt. Once you have made the template it can be kept and used repeatedly. To make it easy to remove the template from the cake it is wise to cut a 'V' in the centre, which can be bent up rather like a handle.

The template should be positioned centrally on the cake. If it is being used for an outline, you then pipe just round the outside using a piping bag and writing nozzle. If it is for some other type of piping, then the design must be pricked out so it remains on top of the cake; simply use a long sharp pin and prick straight through the card or paper to the icing, so that a design is left clearly visible.

A template can also be made for the sides of the cake and is essential if curves or scallops are incorporated into the design.

Don't forget that with tiered cakes you need to make similar templates in graduated sizes to fit each tier.

When piping out the design keep as close as possible to the template, or pipe exactly over the pin-pricked design keeping the curves even. Where sharp corners are required, break the icing at the corner and start again. Trim off with a pin if the icing is not absolutely even. Do not lift off the template until the piped outline is completely dry, otherwise you are likely to disturb the piping.

Other designs can be worked freehand, but if it is to be even in any way, then a template is a necessity.

To Make a Template for a Round Cake

1. Cut a circle of paper the size of the top of the cake or up to 2.5 cm (1 inch) smaller.

2. For an 8-point design, fold the circle in half then into quarters and again into eighths, creasing the folds firmly.

3. For a 6-point design, fold the circle first in half then carefully into three making sure each piece is exactly even (it is most accurate if you use a compass).

4. Check the design and how it needs to be drawn on to the folded paper, then draw it. Cut out carefully and open out the template, to check whether it is correct. If preferred, the template can be drawn on greaseproof paper first to make sure it is right, before transferring to thick paper or card.

Designs suitable for round cakes

Scallop Fold a circle of paper into eight points and draw a scallop.

Hilary Use a circle of paper and fold into eighths (fold into quarters and then once again). Draw a deep curve to come about half way across the paper; then draw a second shallow curve to go right up to the edge.

Curved Both concave and convex curves are suitable. Use a circle of paper, fold into eighths and draw a curve across the end.

Heart Use a circle of paper and fold into eighths. Fold in half again to find the centre of the heart and mark a point 2–4 cm (¾–1½ inches) down the fold. Draw the heart shape from this point round to the other edge.

Petal Use a circle of paper and fold into eighths, then fold again just to mark the centre of each section at the edge. Draw and cut out a deep petal shape coming to the mark.

Laura Use a circle of paper and fold into eighths. Cut out a scroll or scallop, beginning about 2.5 cm (1 inch) down the fold and ending about 2.5 cm (1 inch) along from the corner on the curved edge.

Fleur Use a circle of paper and fold into sixths. Cut out a concave curve. For a **Hexagon** cut a straight edge across the top.

Eighteenth Birthday Cake Use a circle of paper and fold into sixths. See page 132 for full instructions.

Three Tier Wedding Cake Use three circles of paper for the cakes and one for the board. See page 98 for full instructions.

Round Christmas Cake Use a circle of paper and fold into sixths. See page 108 for full instructions.

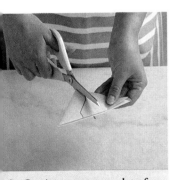

1. Cutting out a template for the Square Birthday Cake on pages 130–1.

2. Lay the template on top of the cake and prick out the design around it.

To Make a Template for a Square Cake

1. Cut a square of greaseproof or other paper the size of the top of the cake or up to 2.5 cm (1 inch) smaller.

2. For a 4-point design, fold the square in half diagonally to give

a triangle, then in half again to give a smaller triangle.

3. For an 8-point design, fold in half a third time to give a still smaller triangle.

Designs Suitable for Square Cakes

The scallop, Hilary and Laura designs can be used on square cakes as well as on round cakes by using a square paper template instead.

Pointed Petal Fold a square of paper into quarters and then

into eighths. Keep the fold to the left and make a mark 5–10 cm (2–4 inches) (depending on size of cake) down the right-hand size. Draw a deep curved arc to the point of the fold.

Eliza Use a square of paper and fold into quarters. Keep the folded edges downwards and

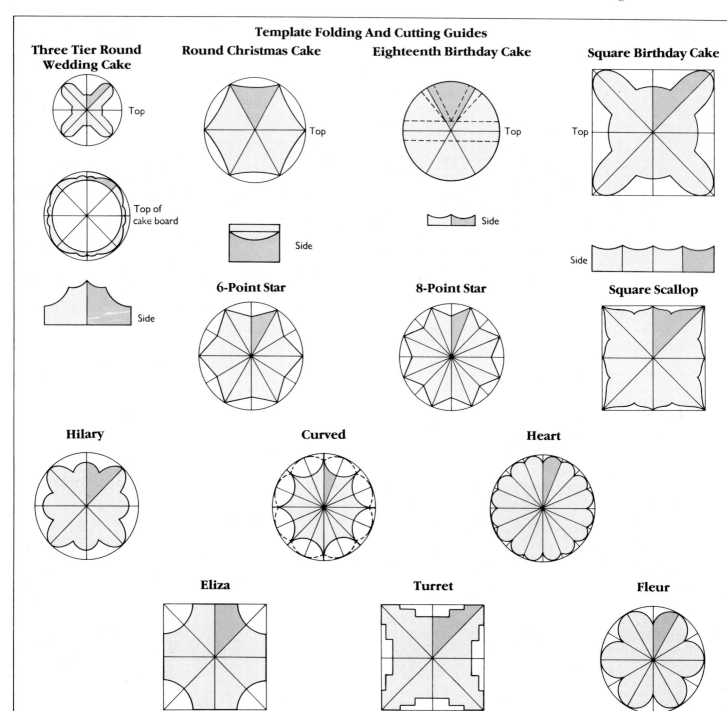

Template Folding And Cutting Guides

Three Tier Round Wedding Cake

Top

Top of cake board

Side

Round Christmas Cake

Top

Side

Eighteenth Birthday Cake

Top

Side

Square Birthday Cake

Top

Side

6-Point Star

8-Point Star

Square Scallop

Hilary

Curved

Heart

Eliza

Turret

Fleur

ut out a semicircle from the
op corner.

urret Fold a square into
eighths. Beginning at the outer
open edge draw two downward
steps towards the opposite
edge. The sizes of the steps can
be varied for different designs,
or make just one step.

Square Birthday Cake Use a
square of paper and fold into a
triangle; fold the triangle in half,
then in half once again. See
page 130 for full instructions.

To Make a Template for the Sides of a Cake

1. For a round cake, measure
the circumference of the cake
with a piece of string, then use
to cut a strip of paper the length
of the sides and the depth of
the cake. If a 4- or 8-point
design, fold the paper into
quarters or eighths, then draw
the design on to the section,
and cut right through the rest to
give a design to reach around
the whole cake. If a 6-point
design, fold into sixths and cut

as before. If preferred, the
shape can be transferred to
thick paper (but not card), so
that it is firm enough to be held
around the sides of the cake
while the design is pricked out
or is outlined in icing. If it is a
difficult pattern to follow, for
instance with lots of curves, it is
simpler if the cake is tilted
slightly while you ice.

2. For a square cake, it is
necessary only to cut a piece of
paper the size of one side of the
cake (provided they are all
symmetrical). Halve this and
draw the design, then cut out,
unfold and use as for a round
cake, holding the template
against each side in turn.

Making Special Shaped Cakes

Cakes made in shapes different
from the traditional round or
square give opportunities for
some different decoration styles
as well. It is not necessary to
have specially designed cake
ins, either; round or square
cakes can be adapted without
difficulty to numerous shapes.

To Make a Horseshoe-Shaped Cake

Begin with a round cake and,
using a paper pattern, first cut
out a central circle 7.5–9 cm
(3–3½ inches) in diameter. Cut
out an even wedge-shaped
piece from the ring to complete
the horseshoe.

A horseshoe-shaped cake in
this book is the Good Luck
Cake on page 110.

To Make a Petal-Shaped Cake

A petal cake can be cut from a
slightly larger 23 cm (9 inch)
round cake. First draw a
template using a pair of
compasses to get it quite even;
then place on the cake and,
using a sharp knife, cut out the
scallops taking it right down to
the base. Trim up until quite
even. It will need a thicker than
usual layer of apricot glaze to
keep the crumbs of cake in
place.

To Make an Oval-Shaped Cake

Select an oval glass dish whose
length matches the diameter of
the round cake you have made.
Using this as a pattern, place on
top of the cake and cut all
around it with a sharp knife,
keeping the sides straight.
Alternatively, draw an oval
shape the size you require on a
piece of card and cut around
this.

To Make a Heart-Shaped Cake

Begin with a round cake. Cut a
heart-shaped paper pattern. The
'V' should be about 4 cm (1½
inches) deep on a 20 cm (8
inch) round cake and gradually
deeper on larger cakes. The
piece taken out should then be
cut in half, reversed and put at
the other end of the cake to
make a point. You will need to
trim off a small triangular piece
to make a good fit. Attach to the
cake with apricot glaze or
buttercream.

Heart-shaped cakes in the
book are the Basket of Chocolates on pages 142–3, and the
Valentine's Day cakes on pages
102–3.

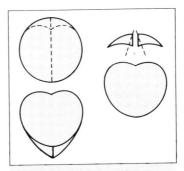

Cutting instructions for
making a heart-shaped cake.

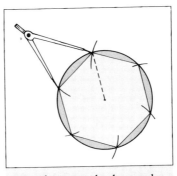

For a hexagonal cake, mark
six points with a compass.

To Make a Hexagonal-Shaped Cake

Begin with a round cake. Take
a compass and measure the
length from the centre of the
cake to the edge. Make a mark
on the edge. Using the same
measurement, position the
compass point at the mark on
the edge and make another
mark with the other end, also
on the edge. Continue in this
way to mark off six equal
sections at the edge. Join the
marks with straight lines and cut
the cake straight downwards
along the lines to make the
hexagonal shape.

A two-tier Hexagonal Wed-
ding Cake is included in this
book on page 92.

To Make an Octagonal-Shaped Cake

An eight-sided cake may be cut
quite simply from a square cake.
Bake a square cake slightly
larger than required, then
carefully cut off each corner as
evenly as possible to give eight
sides all the same length.

All types of shaped cake tins are
usually available to buy or hire
from specialist cake decorating
shops (see page 224) and some
larger kitchen equipment stores.

EQUIPMENT

To decorate cakes with a professional finish it is important to have the correct equipment. The beginner can get started with a few essentials. The more ambitious your projects, the more you will enjoy building up a collection of specialized items that will enable you to achieve a wide range of spectacular effects in your designs.

It is essential to have the items necessary for cake icing and decorating gathered together before you start. Icing does not take kindly to being left while you dash out to buy a forgotten nozzle or icing comb. Some things are everyday kitchen items but others are more specialized and may have to be obtained from cake decorating shops or good hardware stores. Store the equipment carefully so that it does not get damaged. A chip out of an icing ruler will always leave a dent in the icing when used. A bent nozzle will always result in uneven lines.

It is advisable always to buy the best quality equipment available; it will last well and should not rust, bend out of shape or chip in awkward places.

If possible keep some equipment especially for making icing. For instance, wooden spoons and plastic basins pick up flavours from strongly flavoured foods and get stained too. Wooden spoons are better than metal for making and beating royal icing and preferable to using a mixer, because although it makes the task easier, a mixer produces far too many air bubbles. These are difficult to disperse and can ruin the flat surface of a cake if they are not carefully removed.

Stainless steel and plastic icing rulers are available in various lengths. They should be firm enough to keep straight

ut slightly flexible to help keep he icing smooth as the ruler is rawn across the cake. Practice ill soon teach you how much ressure to use when doing his. You can also get serrated lastic rulers which can be used n both royal icing and butter ream to obtain a serrated ffect.

The iced sides of a cake can e smoothed with a palette nife but a plastic icing comb or craper makes the job much asier. They produce perfectly mooth sides and sharp orners, or, in the case of a errated-edged comb, interest g wavy designs. It is easiest to use an icing comb if you have an icing turntable to swivel the cake at a regulated pace as the comb or scraper is pulled round the sides. For the beginner, an upturned plate or a simple turntable will suffice, but as you advance it is wise to invest in a really good one. Whether plastic or metal it should be heavy enough to take any size of cake and should swivel easily and smoothly at the touch of a finger. Choose a high- or low-standing one as you prefer.

CAKE DECORATING EQUIPMENT

The following items are needed to supplement those listed on page 12.

icing ruler
icing comb or scraper
wooden cocktail sticks
small bowls or containers with airtight seals
selection of basic icing nozzles including fine, medium and thick writing, small medium and large, rosette, ribbon, small petal and leaf
piping bags (see below)
tweezers
kitchen scissors
selection of liquid food colourings
As your interest grows and you become more skilful, you may want to add the following to your icing equipment:
icing turntable
icing nail
metal or plastic templates
pair of compasses and/or cake markers
fine paintbrushes

For cutting shapes out of fondant moulding paste, you can use a biscuit cutter, a pastry cutter, a piping nozzle, even lids and tops, as long as they are scrupulously clean. Printing shapes on to fondant paste can be almost as effective as piping on decorations with royal icing.

A selection of icing equipment

PIPING BAGS

Four different types of piping bag are available, either hand-made or bought from department stores. The most useful are greaseproof paper piping bags. They are the simplest to use for all types of icings, and any size nozzle can be used. They are ideal for piping small quantities of icing and it is a good idea to make several at a time. Do not overfill the bag; instead open it carefully and refill it when necessary, taking care not to split it or let it unfold. The filled bag can be kept in a polythene bag for a few hours, while completing another decoration. Because you can make several at a time it is useful if you need to use different coloured icing on the same cake.

Plastic heat-sealed bags are washable and re-usable. Because they prevent moisture seeping through they do not get sticky on contact with your hands. A collar and connector are required for attaching nozzles to the bag. They are difficult for the novice to use, as it is easy to overfill the bags, making them stiff to use and inclined to burst at the seams. Nylon bags also need a collar and connector, and can cause the hands to sweat. They are long-lasting and hygienic. Canvas piping bags are very well made and can be boiled after use. They need a collar and connector to attach the nozzles.

Preparing the Piping Bags

If using a paper piping bag (see page 56), cut about 1 cm (½ inch) off the tip and insert the nozzle. Half to two-thirds fill the bag with icing, using a small palette knife or teaspoon to push it well down into the bag, then fold over the top carefully, continuing to push the icing down to the tip. Do the same with a nylon bag after fitting the special screw collar connector and nozzle, but do not put in too much icing or the bag will be difficult to manipulate. The easiest way to fill a nylon bag is to place the nozzle between the finger and thumb of your left hand and fold the rest of the bag over your hand so it is inside out; in this way as you spoon in the icing with the right hand it can be pressed down to the tip by the left hand and the outside of the bag stays free of icing.

Holding the Piping Bag

You will soon know how you prefer to hold the piping bag to make it work best for you, but here is the easiest way. For paper piping bags, open your hand and place the bag across your palm with tip towards the ends of your fingers. Place the thumb on the folded end of the bag (to keep in the icing), then fold over the other four fingers to hold the bag tightly. Use the other hand to steady it and apply a steady pressure to the bag until the icing begins to come out of the nozzle. With a nylon bag, place the thumb and forefinger round the icing in the bag and twist the bag tightly two or three times to prevent the icing coming out or moving up the bag. Then hold the bag tightly over the twist, again with the thumb and forefinger, with the rest of the fingers folded over the bag. Apply pressure with the other hand.

Alternatively, for fine work and lattice hold the bag in both hands with the thumbs over the end, and the rest of both hands supporting the weight underneath.

Consistency of Icings

It is most important to use icing of the correct consistency for the job in hand. Royal icing varies with the type of icing to be done (see page 39). For dots, shells, rosettes, etc., it should be stiff enough to stand in well formed but not hard peaks, but for writing or trellis it must be slacker or the icing will constantly break. However, it must not be too soft or it will not hold its shape. Glacé icing for piping lines, straightforward, writing, etc., needs to be stiffer than that used to coat a cake: simply add extra sifted icing sugar. Buttercream should be stiff enough to pull into softish peaks, but not too firm or it will not pipe evenly. Buttercream can be used to work designs of shells, stars, rosettes, etc., on a cake.

Trial Run

With all icing, practice makes perfect. Once piped, royal icing becomes hard and cannot be used again, so if you are a complete beginner try practising with a nylon piping bag filled with reconstituted instant mashed potato, using the varying shapes of vegetable nozzles. The potato can be scooped up many times and re-used until you get the 'feel' of handling a piping bag. Even when you are using royal icing, if you are not quite sure or are trying out a new design, practise an edging, border or writing on something other than the cake. An upturned cake tin is ideal and the icing will soak off easily in warm water.

Decorations other than those actually piped on to the cake should be made at least 24 hours in advance. Base-iced cakes are also best left uncovered at room temperature for 24 hours before beginning the decorations.

Making a Greaseproof Paper Icing Bag

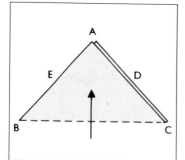

1. Cut a piece of good-quality greaseproof paper to a 25 cm (10 inch) square and fold in half to form a triangle.

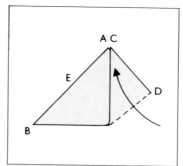

2. Fold point **C** to point **A** on a flat surface and crease firmly.

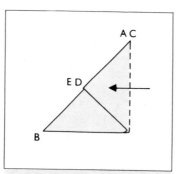

3. Fold point **D** over to point **E** and crease firmly.

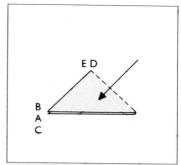

4. Fold point **AC** down to point **B** and crease firmly. Hold the bag at point **ED** and open it up to make a cone.

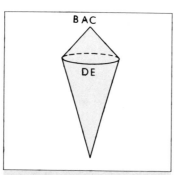

5. Secure the join with tape. Fold the top point down firmly inside the cone.

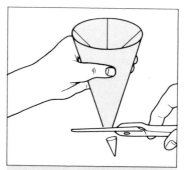

6. Cut off the tip so that the nozzle will fit neatly inside the bag with about one third of the nozzle showing.

COLOURING ICING

It is now possible to buy just about any colour and shade of liquid food colouring, or powder or paste, to tint your icing any colour you may wish. However, if you can only obtain the more basic colours, it is useful to know how to mix them to make other colours.

You get a truer colour when you are adding colourings to a white icing, such as royal or glacé, than you do when colouring buttercreams, because they are cream-coloured to start with.

It is not possible to be precise about the amount of food colouring to add to achieve a specific colour but do remember to add colours very sparingly; it is very easy to add more, but impossible to remove the colour once added. Dip the tip of a skewer into the colouring, then add this to the icing. Continue to add colour in this way, beating the icing after each addition until the correct colour is obtained. It may take longer but is a really safe way of doing it. The colour of royal icing darkens slightly on drying. All these colours can be used with marzipan.

MAKING AND MIXING COLOURS		
Colour required	Mixture	Use for
Pink	Pink colouring or a touch of cochineal.	Christening and birthday cakes.
Peach	Peach food colouring, which may need a touch of pink to prevent it looking too orange; or mix it with pink and yellow and possibly a touch of orange.	Marzipan fruits. Icing and decoration
Flesh tone	Bright red with a little yellow.	For moulded decorations.
Cream	A touch of golden yellow (not primrose) with a touch of pink and/or orange.	Wedding cake piped decorations and flowers.
Red	A paste or powder colouring is needed to produce clear red.	Christmas cake decorations, Ruby Wedding Anniversary Cake.
Mauve/Purple	Use a mauve colour if available, but add a touch of true blue if it is too pink. Make your own with pink and blue but be careful that it does not go too grey.	Piping, and moulded decorations.
Dark green	Add 2 drops of green to 1 of blue.	For marzipan leaves.
Light green	Add 1 drop green to royal icing for a delicate shade.	Run-outs and piping.
Apple green	Bright green shade.	For marzipan fruits.
Golden yellow	1 drop bright orange.	For marzipan fruits.
Orange	Use bright yellow with a little red.	For marzipan fruits.
Brown	Red and green makes a mid-brown; add a touch of blue for a darker tone, a touch of yellow for a sandy tone.	For moulded decorations, e.g. teddy bears.
Black	Black with a touch of blue is very deep. Can be bought as liquorice paste.	For details on novelty cakes.

PIPING NOZZLES

Piping nozzles are also known as tubes and pipes. There is a large range available, in both plain and screw-on types, covering all styles. They are sold by number which can be confusing, because – with the exception of writing nozzles which are uniformly graded from 00 (very fine) to 4 (thick) – not all manufacturers use the same number for the same shaped nozzle. The numbers given here are used by at least two manufacturers, and the name will identify the style in question. Even so, always check on a particular manufacturer's chart before buying. Screw-on nozzles are specially for use with icing pumps or nylon piping bags. Although screw collar nozzles can also be used in paper icing bags, plain nozzles are best because they fit neatly into the bag.

Make sure when you select nozzles that they are perfectly shaped, with no dents or badly fitting seams. For example, misshapen points of rosettes will give unevenly piped stars and writing nozzles which are slightly oval instead of perfectly round will affect the resulting design.

Larger nozzles, often called 'large', 'vegetable' or 'meringue' nozzles are available in metal or plastic. They are used for piping whipped cream, mashed potato, meringues, éclairs and so on. They come in a range of sizes, plain, rope and star-shaped, and are often used on gâteaux or something needing a heavy decoration.

USING THE NOZZLES

Plain Nozzles

Place the nozzle in the piping bag (fine, medium or thick writing) and fill with icing. Before you begin make sure the tip of the nozzle is wiped clean.

Straight lines Place the tip of the nozzle where the line is to begin. Press the icing out slowly and as it emerges lift the nozzle about 2.5 cm (1 inch) above the surface. Move your hand in the direction of the line to be piped using the other hand to guide the bag and keeping the icing flowing evenly. About 1 cm (½ inch) from where the line should finish, stop squeezing and bring the tip of the nozzle gently back to the surface. Break off the icing. By holding the icing above the surface it helps even shaky hands keep straight lines – with a little practice! Some people prefer to pipe lines towards them while others like to work from left to right or vice versa – it doesn't matter which. If you finish with a blob of icing at the end of a line, remove it carefully with a small sharp knife.

Dots Hold the nozzle upright and just touching the surface. Squeeze the bag gently, at the same time lifting the nozzle to allow the icing to flow out. Stop squeezing when you have the size of dot you want and remove the nozzle quickly with a slightly shaking action, to avoid leaving a tail. If a tail does remain, remove it with a hat pin. Dots can be made in all sizes and with any of the writing nozzles. Two-tier dots can be formed by dipping the nozzle downwards into the icing halfway through, giving the dot a large base and small top.

Lattice This attractive way of using straight lines can be worked in many ways. First pipe a series of parallel straight lines

in one direction, keeping them evenly spaced over the area of the cake to be covered. Leave to dry. Turn the cake and pipe a second layer of parallel lines over the first set but at right angles or an angle of 45° to it, to make squares or diamonds. The design can be left at this but is better with a third layer piped over the first lines to give a raised effect. With very fine lattice up to five layers can be worked. Let each layer dry before starting the next so that if a mistake is made, the wet layer can be easily lifted off with a skewer or small sharp knife. Lattice designs can also be worked using curved lines.

Curved lines These can be worked quite easily, once you have mastered control of the icing, to produce loops, plain scrolls, and so on. For curves you really need a template (see pages 51–3), and it is a good idea to practise on thin card or greaseproof paper. Draw a series of curves and pipe over these until you feel confident. Place the tip of the nozzle at the beginning of the curve, lift it up above the surface as for straight lines and allow the icing to follow the curve round, lowering the nozzle to touch the surface between each scallop.

Writing The design should be pricked or traced on to the cake to make sure it is central and will fit in. First write the words on greaseproof paper, then position on the cake and carefully prick out on the surface using a pin. When the paper is removed the guide lines for the writing remain. Pipe the words in white icing first and then, when dry, overpipe with a colour – mistakes in colour on a white cake are difficult to cover up. It is best to begin with capitals. All styles of writing can be used as you progress.

Lacework Using a fine or medium writing nozzle, this is a very effective decoration. It is like scribbling and can be added to set designs on cakes. Lacework is as easy to apply to the top of a cake as it is to sides. Hold the nozzle almost upright and just above the surface so that the icing flows out and move the nozzle around quickly and easily to form the pattern.

Star Nozzles

These vary widely in size and shape of the star they produce. Some have five points, others six or eight and even more points as they become larger. For beginners, concentrate on 5-point (no. 13) or 8-point (no. 8). Many designs can be made using star nozzles.

Stars Place a star nozzle in the bag and fill with icing of the correct consistency. Hold the bag upright and just above the surface. Pipe out sufficient icing to form the star and sharply lift the nozzle away with a down and up movement. Stars should sit fairly flat on the surface, not pulled up into a central point.

Rosettes or whirls These are piped with star nozzles but in a circular movement like making a large dot. Begin just above the surface and move the nozzle in a complete circle to enclose the middle. Finish off quickly to leave a slightly raised point in the centre but not a 'tail'. Varying sizes and slightly differing shapes can be made with different nozzles.

Shells Use either a star nozzle or a special shell nozzle (no. 12); both make good shells and are worked in the same way but the shell nozzle gives a rather fuller and fatter shell. Hold the piping bag at an angle to the surface and a little above it. Start in the centre of the shell and

first move the nozzle away from you, keeping an even pressure of icing, then back towards you with a little more pressure for the 'fat' part of the shell. Release pressure and pull off sharply to form a point. To make a shell edging simply repeat the shells, linking them in a line by beginning the next shell over the tail of the previous one. It is very important to finish off each shell and lift the nozzle between each one or a bulky and uneven border will result.

Scrolls These are useful for tops and sides of cakes but do need a lot of practice, particularly if you want to achieve graduated scrolls. A simple scroll edging can be worked using either a star or shell nozzle, but if they are to be larger or individual scrolls on the top of a cake, a template will ensure evenness (see pages 51–3). Hold the piping bag as for a straight line and with the nozzle almost on the surface. Work a question mark shape beginning with a fairly thick head and gradually releasing the pressure while finishing off in a long pointed tail. A series of scrolls can be worked the same way or several variations can be worked to make attractive designs or double-ended scrolls. Other scrolls can be worked adding twists and graduating the width and size, and using larger and smaller nozzles.

Coils This is a border or edging and is made using a star nozzle. Begin just touching the surface and continue making small circular movements in an anticlockwise direction. Coils can be worked from left to right or vice versa as you prefer, and variations of a coiled border are numerous.

Ribbon or Basket Nozzle

This nozzle (no. 22) is thick, with either one or both sides serrated and is flat to produce a edged ribbon of icing. Some nozzles are evenly ribbed, others are uneven. A ribbon nozzle is used for a flat pleated ribbon edging, is worked continuously by overlapping each pleat, as well as for basket work or 'weaving' on a cake. To do the latter you need one piping bag fitted with a ribbon nozzle and another fitted with a medium or thick writing nozzle. Hold the ribbon nozzle sideways to the cake and at an angle and pipe three short lines the same length as each other, one above each other and with the width of the tip of the nozzle between each one. Pipe a straight vertical line with the writing nozzle along the edge of the three ribbon lines. Next pipe three more straight lines with the ribbon nozzle of the same length as the first ones to fill in the gaps but beginning halfway along those and covering the straight line. Pipe another vertical line at the end of these lines and continue building up first with the ribbon nozzle and then the vertical line.

Three-Point Star Nozzle (Trefoil)

This nozzle (no. 4) is used for borders or small stars on edges or at the base of cakes. It is unusual and very simple and can be worked either upright or upside-down.

Leaf Nozzle

This nozzle (no. 10) has a pointed tip sometimes with an indentation in the centre of the point. You can make three overlapping movements for each leaf or if this sounds a bit difficult, simpler leaves can be made in the same way but without the overlapping movement, and other shaped leaves can easily be devised. Leaves can be piped straight on to cakes, or on to non-stick silicone paper first. Leave to dry before attaching to the cake with a dab of icing.

Petal or Rose Nozzle

This nozzle (no. 18) is used especially for making flowers. Flowers are made separately and when they are dry attached to the cake. Flowers need practice. (To pipe a rose see page 60.)

Top row, from left: fine writing nozzle; medium writing nozzle; thick writing nozzle; 3-point star nozzle; 8-point star nozzle; leaf nozzle.
Bottom row, from left: shell nozzle; fine 5-point star; petal or rose nozzle; ribbon nozzle; fancy star; forget-me-not nozzle; 3-thread nozzle.

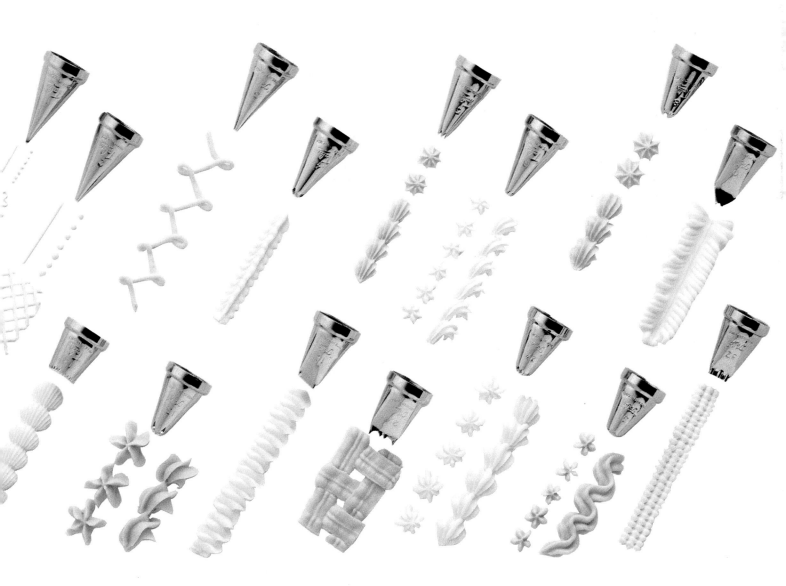

SPECIAL DECORATIONS

A wide range of decorations can be made from royal icing, fondant moulding paste and marzipan, to be attached to an iced cake when it is dry. These include piped flowers and leaves, all types of models, cut-outs and run-outs. All can be made 3–4 weeks in advance, covered in tissue or waxed paper and kept in a dry atmosphere.

PIPED FLOWERS IN ROYAL ICING

All icing takes practice, but making flowers takes a lot of patience too, until you feel confident and can make all sorts of different flowers with ease. Roses are probably the most popular flower to make and are a good start if you are a beginner. There are numerous other flowers you can make by following instructions or by making your own shape.

To make flowers you need an icing nail or a cork impaled on a skewer, a quantity of non-stick silicone or waxed paper cut into 2.5–5 cm (1–2 inch) squares, and a paper or plastic piping bag fitted with a large, medium or fine petal nozzle. For most flowers use a medium nozzle, which is the easiest to obtain and the easiest to use. Half fill the bag with icing and fold down ready to begin. Secure a square of paper to the icing nail with a dab of icing.

Leaves

Use a leaf nozzle and white or green royal icing. Place a sheet of waxed paper on the work surface. Begin with the nozzle touching the paper and the end turned up a fraction. Press gently and as the icing begins to emerge, raise the nozzle slightly. When the leaf is large enough, break off sharply to leave a point. The bag can be gently twisted or moved up and down to give different shapes and the size can be increased by extra pressure.

A piping bag without a nozzle can successfully be used for smaller leaves. Fill the grease-proof paper bag to the half-way point with icing, but don't cut off the tip. Press the tip of the bag flat, then snip off the point in the shape of an arrow. Place the tip of the bag on the paper, holding it at a slight angle. Press out the icing and pull away quickly to make a tapering point. Mark on a vein with a cocktail stick. Serrated fern-like leaves can be made by moving the tube backwards and forwards. When you have had sufficient practice, leaves may be piped straight on to the cake.

Daisy

Probably the simplest of the piped icing flowers, the daisy is also the most effective. Pipe five or six or more slightly rounded but also pointed petals, each separate from the next. Then, using a no. 2 writing nozzle pipe a large dot in the centre of the flower (if preferred several dots can be piped) using a contrasting colour. These flowers can be made in a variety of colours, either with the petals in one colour and the centre white or yellow, or the petals white with a coloured (or yellow) centre.

Primrose

Use yellow icing and work with the thick edge of the petal nozzle to the centre, keeping it flat. Pipe from the centre outwards. Go half way back in, then out again, then back to the centre, to give a heart-shaped petal. Pipe five petals in all. Using a no. 1 writing nozzle and deep yellow or pale orange icing, pipe a dot in the middle.

Rose

Hold the piping bag so that the thin edge of the nozzle is pointing upwards, then, squeezing evenly and twisting the nail at the same time, pipe a tight coil for the centre of the rose. Continue to add five or six petals, piping the icing and twisting at the same time, but taking each petal only about three quarters of the way round the flower. Begin in a different part of the flower each time and make sure the base of the nozzle tips in towards the centre of the flower or the rose will expand at the base and the top instead of just at the top.

For rose buds, keep the petals tight and only add two after the first central coil has been piped.

To make a rose, first pipe a tight coil for the centre.

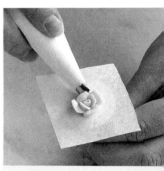

Add five or six petals around the centre to complete.

RUN-OUTS

A run-out is a shaped piece of icing, such as an initial or animal. The outline is piped first, then the centre filled using a technique called flooding. They are also suitable for plaques which can have a further decoration piped or placed on top. They are made from royal icing and can be piped straight on to a cake or on to non-stick silicone paper or waxed paper and attached to the cake when dry. Outlines can be traced from the stencils on page 62 or from designs on greetings cards. Run-outs can be stored in an airtight container for a few months without discolouring.

For simple outline designs, follow the instructions for run-out hearts. If you are making a small number of a complex design proceed as follows. Draw or trace the outlines on to a piece of card. Secure a piece of waxed paper over the card. Using a no. 2 writing nozzle and icing the same colour as that to be used for flooding, trace the outlines of the drawing. Make more than you need – run-outs are very fragile.

To flood the shapes, thin down a little royal icing with lemon juice or egg white (see page 39 for a guide to the correct consistency) so that it flows. Spoon it into the centre of the outline if it is large, or pipe it in using a no. 3 writing nozzle or a piping bag with the end snipped off. Use a cocktail stick to ease the icing into corners and to prick any air bubbles. Leave to dry before completing the details. After 2–3 days, remove the paper; place the run-out on a thick book, slightly overlapping the edge. Pull the paper gently downwards, then turn the run-out round, pulling the paper away until all the edges are loose. Gently pull off the paper.

Butterfly

Use the template on page 62. Outline the wings and body separately. Pipe two antennae with a no. 1 writing nozzle. Decorate the wings with piped lines and dots round the edge using a no. 1 writing nozzle and a contrasting colour. Attach the wings and antennae to the body with a little icing. The wings should tilt upwards slightly; rest them on a little plasticine until they are dry.

Flowers

Outline the edges and the lines of the petals. Flood with icing of the same colour or tinted slightly lighter in tone. Pipe several tiny dots in the centre with yellow icing and a no. 1 writing nozzle. Pansies are extremely pretty, especially when two shades are used in the same flower. Outline the large lower petal in each flower first, flood with icing and leave to dry. When set, outline the remaining petals and fill with a lighter shade. To finish, paint streaks from the centre of the petals with food colouring.

Ivy Leaves

When the flooded leaf is dry, use a no. 1 writing nozzle to pipe a thin line down the centre to make a vein and stalk.

To Make Run-out Hearts

1. Draw a 4 cm (1½ inch) heart shape and trace the number required plus extra for breakages on the underside of waxed or non-stick paper. Turn the paper over and fix it to a board.

2. Tint icing of the correct consistency (see page 39) to the desired colour. Place a little icing in a greaseproof paper piping bag fitted with a no. 2 writing nozzle.

3. Pipe around the outline of the heart design, making sure there are no breaks and that the corners are closed.

4. Thin a little icing with egg white or lemon juice until it is of a flooding consistency (see page 39). Place the icing in a greaseproof paper piping bag without a nozzle. Snip the point off the bag and fill in the design.

5. Use a cocktail stick to ease the icing into the corners and prick any air bubbles. The icing should be level and slightly raised from the outline.

6. Leave to dry for 2–3 days. Peel off the paper very carefully. Store the run-out hearts in an airtight container, layered between sheets of tissue paper.

Step 1
Tracing the outlines of the heart shape on to grease-proof paper.

Step 3
Piping round the outlines.

Step 4
Flooding the outlines, using a piping bag.

Step 6
Removing the dry run-out hearts from the paper.

Original Run-Outs

Once you have become proficient at making run-outs, you can progress from templates of simple shapes to inventing your own designs or using illustrations from greetings cards, magazines or printed papers. This gives you the opportunity to decorate a cake with motifs particularly appropriate for an individual or a special event – two lovebirds for a wedding anniversary, a cradle for a new baby, a teddy bear, kitten or horse. Trace the design on to waxed paper as described on page 61, and when it is dry pipe or paint details and features on as appropriate. If you have a steady hand with a fine paintbrush you can achieve sophisticated results with the range of food colourings now available.

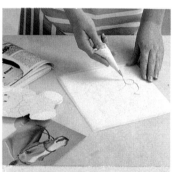

You can make a run-out decoration from any fairly simple design traced on to waxed paper.

Decoration Templates

MOULDED DECORATIONS

Both fondant moulding paste and marzipan can be used for modelling, though moulding paste is best for delicate shapes. It is easier to colour moulding paste to obtain true or bright colours because you start with a white base; but marzipan will turn a good colour if you use a white or natural coloured variety. This is available from some shops or by post from icing specialists, or it can be made at home by substituting 2 egg whites for the egg or egg yolks. Knead food colourings into moulding paste or marzipan until the mixture is evenly coloured and no longer streaky. If the paste or marzipan becomes too soft or sticky, add extra icing sugar. For dark colours use the concentrated colourings, which are available from specialist icing centres. A touch of brown colouring or gravy browning will tone down an overbright colour. Extra colour or features can be painted on with fine paintbrush and liquid food colourings.

For rolling out, use a surface lightly dredged with icing sugar or a mixture of icing sugar and cornflour, or roll out between sheets of polythene or waxed paper. The latter method makes it easier to move the rolled-out paste or marzipan.

Egg boxes are a great help for resting models on as you make them. Wooden cocktail sticks and a fork are other useful implements.

Decorations from Fondant Moulding Paste

This is an extremely pliable icing. It holds its shape even when paper thin, and is excellent for making flowers. Keep the paste to be moulded wrapped in a polythene bag as it dries quickly if exposed to air. Leave the decoration for 24 hours to dry and harden.

Rose

Make a cone with a small piece of paste and press out the base to form a stand. Take a piece of paste the size of a pea, dip it in cornflour and roll it into a ball in the palm of your hand. Take a hard-boiled egg in your other hand and use it to flatten the ball of paste, working with quick gentle strokes. Use more cornflour if it is too sticky. The edge of the petal should be paper thin.

Carefully wrap the petal around the cone, turning the edges outwards. Repeat this process, overlapping each petal, until you have the shape you want. Use a cocktail stick if necessary to help mould the petals. Leave to dry overnight then cut off the base. When using several roses together in a decoration (for example, the American Wedding Cake on pages 94–5), colour some a shade darker for a more elaborate effect.

To mould a rose, attach thin petals to the basic cone.

Continue to add overlapping petals to complete the rose.

To make a daisy, make a base at one end of a ball of paste.

Daisy

Make a small ball of paste and pinch the bottom to form a base. Flatten the ball (as for the petals of a rose) to make a thin round. Using small scissors, cut the edges of the round to form petals, then turn them upwards. Using a cocktail stick, make holes in the centre. Paint the

Painting the tips of the petals to complete the daisy.

centre with yellow food colouring. Using pink food colouring and a fine paintbrush, paint the tips of the petals. Leave to dry. This daisy is very realistic, unlike the stylized version obtained by piping.

Leaves

Colour the paste green and roll out the icing thinly on a surface dusted with cornflour. Cut out leaf shapes with a small knife. Lift the shapes one by one into the palm of your hand and flatten the edges (as for the rose) and pinch each end into a point. Leave to dry overnight.

Mark veins on each leaf, using a fine paintbrush or the point of a knife dipped into colouring.

Christmas Rose

Use the inside of an egg box to mould this flower. Cut a small circle of greaseproof paper for each compartment and cut a line through to the centre to shape a cone. Line each compartment with a circle of paper. Using white paste, shape five petals as for the rose and place them overlapping inside the paper cone. (See illustration overleaf.)

Shape a small piece of yellow moulding paste into a ball and press it lightly into the centre. If liked, use yellow royal icing to pipe stamens in the centre. Leave to dry.

For a Christmas rose, place five white petals overlapping.

To finish, place a ball of yellow paste in the centre.

To shape the chick's beak, use a small pair of scissors.

Attach the mouse's ears to the head with a dab of paste.

Chick

Shape two balls of yellow paste, one half the size of the other. Stick the small ball on top of the large one for the head. Using small scissors, snip the small ball to form a beak shape and paint the mouth with yellow colouring. Position coloured sugar balls for the eyes.

Rabbit

Mould a piece of paste into an egg shape. Mould a smaller piece into an oval and place on top of the narrow end of the egg shape to form the head. Shape two large ears and attach them to the head. Shape a small ball of paste for the tail and attach it to the body with a dab of paste. Paint the inside of the ears with a little pink colouring. For the eyes, use pink royal icing and pipe on with a no. 1 writing nozzle.

Mouse

Mould a piece of pink (or white) icing into a cone shape for the body. Shape two pieces of icing into ears, working them like the petals of the rose. Stick the ears on to the pointed (head) end of the body with a dab of paste. Roll a small piece of icing into a thin tail and attach it to the rounded end of the body. For the eyes, use pink royal icing and pipe them on with a no. 1 writing nozzle, or use silver dragees.

Moulded Marzipan Decorations

Almond paste (marzipan) used for modelling must be supple enough to bend without cracking but firm enough to hold its shape. Bought ready-made marzipan is ideal to use for making decorations as you can simply break off the amount you need. If using home-made almond paste, make a large quantity and keep it in a polythene bag, breaking off small amounts as you need them; it will keep for several weeks. Care must be taken not to over-knead, as this will make the paste oily and difficult to handle.

To colour the paste, add food colouring a little at a time (see colour chart on page 57), kneading it in until it is evenly coloured. Keep the paste not being worked in a polythene bag, as it dries out quickly if exposed to air. Leave the decorations for 2–3 days to dry before positioning them on the cake. Alternatively make them up to 4 weeks in advance and store them in an airtight tin.

Simple Flowers

To make daffodils, use yellow marzipan. Curl round a small strip for the trumpet and attach four or five petals to the base, curving outwards. For violets, make five small circles from purple marzipan. Mould one into a cone. Attach three to one side, and place the last circle underneath to the other side. Use yellow marzipan for stamens.

Oranges and Lemons

Colour some paste orange or lemon. Roll into a ball for an orange and a plump oval for a lemon. Roll the shapes over the fine surface of a grater to get the texture of the skin. Press in a clove at one end for the calyx.

Apples

Colour some paste green and roll it into a ball, making a slight indentation at the top and the base. Cut a clove in half and use the top for the calyx and the rest for the stalk. Paint pink colouring on one side, gradually blending it into the green.

Bananas

Colour some paste yellow and form it into a banana shape. Paint with brown colouring to mark the characteristic stripes on the skin.

Cluster of Grapes

Colour some paste green or purple and shape into a cone. Roll out small balls for the grapes and stick them neatly on to the cone. Press in a clove for the stalk.

Carrots

Colour some paste orange and shape into small cones. Make stalks from a small piece of green-coloured paste. Mark the skin lightly with a pointed knife.

Cabbage

Colour some paste green. Shape about two thirds into a small ball for the heart. Shape the remainder into six or eight leaves. Arrange the leaves around the heart, overlapping each one. Press gently at the base to join them together.

Parsnips

Shape some natural-coloured paste into a cone. Paint with a little brown colouring and make a stalk from a small piece of green-coloured paste. If the shape is slightly imperfect it will look more realistic.

Peas

Shape tiny pieces of green-coloured icing into balls.

Pears

orm some natural-coloured marzipan into a pear shape. Use clove for the stem and calyx as r apples. Paint with green and ink colouring, gradually lending in the colours.

Strawberries

Colour some paste red and shape into a rounded cone. Roll over the surface of a grater or granulated sugar. Make a hull from a small piece of green-coloured paste and press on to the top of the strawberry.

Plums

Colour some paste purple, using pink and blue colouring. Roll into an egg shape and mark a line down one side. Press a clove into the top for the stalk.

Above: Moulded marzipan fruits and vegetables

Marzipan Cut-Outs

These are decorations made from flat cut-out shapes of marzipan and coloured and assembled as required. The designs below all use templates which can be found on page 62. You can also draw your own templates or use designs from greetings cards, wrapping paper, etc. And pastry cutters in unusual shapes will also make simple effective marzipan cut-out decorations.

Mistletoe	**Holly Leaves**	**Christmas Tree**	**Stars**

Mistletoe leaves are made from a paler green marzipan than that needed for holly leaves. Cut them into long thin tongue shapes with rounded ends. Mark a heavy vein down the centre with a knife and leave to dry. White mistletoe berries can be rolled from white or natural coloured marzipan.

Colour some marzipan deep green. Roll it out evenly on a piece of waxed paper. Cut each piece into rectangles. Use the template to cut out leaf shapes with a sharp pointed knife, or use the base of an icing nozzle to cut out the leaf shape. Mark veins on the leaf with the point of a knife. Leave to dry, laying some of the leaves over a spoon handle to give a curved shape. Colour a little marzipan red and roll into tiny balls for berries.

Using the template, trace the outline of the tree and tub on to greaseproof paper and transfer to a piece of card. Roll out a little green and a little red marzipan and place the templates on top. Cut out carefully around the pattern with the point of a sharp knife. Attach the tub to the tree and leave on waxed paper to dry. Pipe dots of icing on the points of the tree and place coloured sugar balls on top.

Make a template of a star. Roll out some natural or yellow marzipan evenly. Cut out stars using the template as a guide (or use a star-shaped pastry cutter). Leave to dry. Using white royal icing (see page 39) and a no. 1 writing nozzle, pipe lines round the edges of the stars. Decorate the points with silver dragees.

SUGAR-FROSTED FLOWERS AND FRUIT

Sugar-frosting is easy to do and gives a pretty finish to cakes covered with buttercream, glacé icing or frosting, or as a decoration on cheesecakes. Frosted fruits should be used within 2 hours, leaves and flowers may be kept for up to 6 weeks. Store between layers of tissue paper in an airtight container. Use small non-poisonous spring flowers, heathers, roses or violets, herb leaves such as mint and fruits such as currants, grapes, cherries, and segments of mandarin orange. Put 1 egg white in a small bowl with 2 teaspoons of cold water and whisk until lightly frothy. Make sure the flower heads or fruit are clean and dry, then paint all over with the egg white, or dip into the egg white, until evenly coated. Sprinkle with caster sugar, or roll in caster sugar, and leave to dry on greaseproof paper lightly dusted with sugar.

Crystallized Flowers

These attractive decorations keep well if made with care. Real flowers can be used as decorations at any time of year, instead of making them from marzipan or fondant moulding paste. Always make more than you need and avoid using any flowers which are poisonous.

Use fairly small flowers, such as primroses and violets, which are not quite fully open. Remove all bruised petals and leaves. With roses, the petals can be crystallized individually and rearranged into flowers again. Mint leaves crystallize well too. There are two methods of crystallization.

Method 1

Put 120 ml (4 fl oz) triple-strength rosewater into a screwtop jar with 50 g (2 oz) gum arabic (available from chemists) and leave overnight or longer, giving an occasional shake until the gum arabic crystals have dissolved. Hold the flower carefully by the stem (the stem can be removed when the flower is crystallized). Using a fine paintbrush, paint the rosewater mixture all over the petals on both sides. Quickly roll or dredge in caster sugar, making sure the flower is

Frosted flowers and leaves

mpletely covered, then shake f the surplus sugar. Place on a re rack or on greaseproof or on-stick silicone paper and ave to dry in a fairly warm ace for 1–2 days. Pack refully between layers of sue paper to store.

Method 2

Melt 450 g (1 lb) loaf or granu-lated sugar in a heavy-bottomed saucepan. Bring to the boil, then strain through scalded muslin into a clean pan to remove any impurities. Bring back to the boil and boil to 104°C (220°F) on a sugar thermometer. Leave to cool to about blood heat. Arrange the flowers on a wire rack over a shallow tin and pour the sugar syrup over each flower, using a fine paintbrush to ensure the whole flower is coated. Drain off excess syrup, then leave the flowers undisturbed in a warm place for 12–18 hours or until crystals begin to form on the surface. This means that crystallization is taking place. Pack away carefully as above.

CHOCOLATE

Whether used in elaborate cakes, rich puddings or simple confectionery, chocolate is one of the most versatile ingredients in baking and sweet-making. The most suitable chocolate for cooking is a plain or bitter chocolate with a minimum of 50 per cent cocoa solids (see page 11, storecupboard ingredients). Some chocolate bars are specifically made for baking, and are available at good stores and delicatessens. These are less sweet than eating chocolate and give a fine rich flavour for cakes and desserts.

The simplest way to use chocolate is to grate it on a fine, medium or coarse grater for the top and/or sides of cakes and small cakes, cheesecakes and creamy desserts. Chill the chocolate bar a little first, and rinse your hands in cold running water before you start. The warmth of your hands may make the chocolate melt as you work. Hold the chocolate in foil or greaseproof paper. Almost as simple is to make chocolate curls by peeling thin strips off a block of chocolate using a potato peeler. Peel the strips directly on to a cake or dessert, or chill after making and use to decorate the sides of a cream-covered or frosted gâteau.

Squares, Triangles and Circles

Spread a thin – 3 mm (⅛ inch) – even layer of melted chocolate on a sheet of greaseproof or non-stick silicone paper using a palette knife. Leave to set, but not completely hard.

Use a ruler and a sharp knife to mark out even-sized squares or rectangles. To make triangles, cut the squares in half. To make long-sided triangles, cut the rectangles in half. To make circles, cut the chocolate into small rounds using a pastry cutter. When they have set quite hard, carefully lift the tip of the

paper and peel it away from the chocolate. These shapes may be decorated with a piped chocolate design if desired. Fill a greaseproof paper piping bag with melted chocolate. Snip off the end and pipe straight or zig-zag lines directly on to the shapes. Leave them in a cool place to set.

Rose Leaves

Pick fresh, undamaged leaves with clearly marked veins. Wash them thoroughly and dry carefully. Melt 50 g (2 oz) cooking, plain or bitter chocolate in a *wide* heatproof bowl set over a pan of hot water. Stir until smooth, then cool to 36–43°C (92–110°F) or until the chocolate has a smooth, glossy appearance. Using a fine brush, spread it over the underside of each leaf. You can also draw the underside of each leaf across the surface of the melted chocolate. Make sure the leaf is evenly covered right to the edge. Leave to set, chocolate side up. When the chocolate is hard, carefully peel away the leaf, starting at the stem. Make more than you will need for the design, as these fragile shapes may break in handling.

See the Rose Leaf Gâteau, page 172, for a sumptuous use of chocolate leaves.

Caraque and Scrolls

Spread a thin layer of melted chocolate on to a marble slab or cold work surface using a palette knife. Leave until just firm but not hard. Using a sharp thin-bladed knife at an angle of about 45° push the knife across the chocolate with a slight sawing movement, scraping off a thin layer; this will form a long scroll. Take care not to cut too deeply into the chocolate or it will not curl. Place the curls on a plate and chill. Store in a

container between layers of waxed paper.

Chocolate Easter Eggs

These are fun to make and the small ones make good decorations for Easter cakes. Moulds are available in plastic, metal and china, and in various sizes. They can be obtained from kitchen hardware stores and specialist kitchen equipment and gadget shops. Brush the inside of the mould with melted chocolate to give it an even layer, then chill until set. Repeat with another coat on small eggs or two further coats on larger ones. Chill thoroughly, then remove the eggs from the moulds.

Paint melted chocolate on the underside of each leaf.

When the chocolate is set, carefully peel away the leaf.

Opposite: Simple home-made chocolate decorations

SIMPLE DECORATIONS

Melting Chocolate

To melt chocolate successfully, place the chocolate, broken into pieces, in the top of a double boiler or in a small heatproof bowl that will fit securely over the top of a saucepan. Partially fill the pan with hot water, making sure that the water does not touch the bowl or the top of the double boiler. Overheated chocolate becomes stiff and granular. Bring the water almost to the boil, then remove from the heat and place the bowl or top of the double boiler over the pan. Stir the chocolate with a wooden spoon until it is melted and smooth.

Chocolate can only be melted in a saucepan placed over direct heat when liquid is added at the beginning, for example when making some sauces. The minimum amount of liquid should be 150 ml (¼ pint) and the sauce should be stirred vigorously while the chocolate is melting.

Some of the most tempting cakes can be achieved with ease. The Lemon Cake on page 78, pretty as it is, is simply a sponge covered in glacé icing – the easiest icing to make – decorated with sugar flowers and the sides coated in coconut. There are a number of ready-made edible decorations available which you can use to good effect such as silver dragees, mimosa balls, chocolate mint sticks, miniature ratafia biscuits, delicate cornets and wafers, chocolate buttons, marrons glacés, glacé cherries, angelica and liquorice allsorts. The sides of a cake can be coated in chopped or flaked nuts, toasted or coloured desiccated coconut or chocolate strands. Use tiny foil-covered chocolate eggs for an Easter cake, and silver and gold chocolate 'money' for a children's party. For gâteaux, a few chocolate-dipped strawberries or pieces of chocolate-dipped crystallized ginger clustered on top make a stylish finish.

Other simple decorations you can make yourself, include chocolate shapes (pages 68–9), praline (page 49), crystallized flowers and frosted fruits (pages 66–7), and moulded figures (pages 63–5). Decorative extras can be a successful element in cake design if carefully used. These are the non-edible features such as ribbons, silver leaves and so on. The important thing to remember is to use them in moderation – a cake is ultimately to be eaten, not a sculpture, and non-edible decorations should be subsidiary parts of the whole. When buying ribbons, candle-holders, candles and cake frills, buy them before making the cake, so that if you need to colour the icing you can make sure it tones in well with the decorations. Paper cake frills come in various designs, ornate silver ones for weddings and anniversaries, printed ones for Christmas. If you make your own frill from fabric or broad lace remember to back it with a strip of greaseproof paper, to prevent staining from the cake. Silver horse-shoes and leaves are useful, especially if used in conjunction with piped or moulded flowers on a wedding cake. Tiered wedding cakes will need pillars to support them and a tiny silver vase for the top to hold a posy of fresh – they *must* be fresh – flowers on top. There is no reason why other celebration cakes should not also be decorated with a rosebud, a sprig of violets or primroses: but keep it light.

INTRODUCTION
PART 2

In the tempting variety of cakes in this section you are sure to find something for every occasion. The recipes – which range from those which are relatively quick and easy to prepare to others which are more demanding of time and effort – all prove that cakes are just as much fun to make as they are to eat. The first chapter in this section includes a selection of simply constructed Family and Traditional Cakes; it is here that you'll find well-established favourites – perhaps in an interesting variation such as Chocolate Battenburg or a Swiss Roll made luxurious with swirls of buttercream. Instructions for standard cake mixtures are given in full, here, while in subsequent chapters reference is made to the basic recipes in Part 1.

In the next chapter, Celebration Cakes, there are some stunning ideas for formal cakes for celebrations such as weddings, special birthdays, Christmas and many more. In this area of cake decorating the classic craft of piping with royal icing comes into its own. Novelty Cakes includes a number of fantastic ideas for children's parties – but there are also many adults who'd love to celebrate getting older with an unusual birthday cake such as a Clock, a Hat or a Basket of Chocolates. All the cakes in this book are delicious, but those in the continental Gâteaux chapter are made with particularly irresistible ingredients: fresh cream, chocolate, nuts and exotic fruits, conjured into glittering confections. And the chapter on Cheesecakes demonstrates the versatility of this popular type of cake.

Part 2 concludes with a selection of delectable Small Cakes and Pastries, deliciously pretty little mouthfuls just right for after-dinner coffee, Sunday tea or children's parties. Whatever its size, a cake makes every day special.

FAMILY & TRADITIONAL CAKES

A homemade cake at teatime is always a special pleasure. Included here are recipes to satisfy all tastes – from simple sponges to feather-iced and decorated cakes.

Most modern cooks are busy people, increasingly dependent on ready-made dishes which – though reliable – can be monotonous. There is no nicer way to brighten up your family's weekly menu than with a homemade cake, spoiling them a little and at the same time enjoying creating something that is both good to look at and delicious to eat.

An indispensable part of successful cake-making is the pleasure it gives to the cook as well as those who are lucky enough to eat the finished product. Perhaps this is because, however simple, every cake adds a touch of luxury to life. Luxurious they may be, but cakes can be easy to prepare, as is clearly shown in this chapter. Here are a range of recipes to satisfy everyone's idea of the perfect cake for Sunday tea, whether it's Apricot Butterscotch Cake (page 86) by the fireside or Lemon Cake (page 78) on a summer afternoon. Most are based on sponge mixtures, some with different flavours such as chocolate, coffee or orange. The icings used are easy to make and work with, and the decorations are uncomplicated but carefully applied. If you have never covered a cake with marzipan, make the Chocolate Battenburg (page 74) to get an idea of its texture and flexibility before progressing to its use on a rich fruit cake under royal icing. Make the Lemon Swiss Roll (page 76) one of your specialities and you will have mastered a skill which will enable you to make fragile roulades with ease. To get the feel of working with a piping bag, make a cake like Hazelnut Coffee Cake (page 80) that is decorated with swirls of buttercream. Practising in this way will build up your skills for the highly decorative effects that are achieved with piped royal icing. For an invaluable and versatile decoration, try Strawberry Feather Bar (page 82) with its attractive and stylish patterned glacé icing.

There is no mystery to making perfect cakes: the 'secret' is simply a combination of patience and confidence, two qualities that will increase the more cakes you make. As you try out these recipes, you will find that two or three become favourites with you and your family, the ones that you always enjoy making and which become part of your repertoire. Whatever your preference, there is an example here to fit the bill, whether it's a sticky Dark Ginger Cake (page 87), sophisticated Chocolate Mint Cake (page 84) or fruity St Clement's Ring (page 80). Delicious cakes like these can be relied on to transform a dull table, and yet are relatively straightforward to prepare. Morning coffee, afternoon tea, an unexpected visit from friends: all these occasions take on a festive air when a cake appears. Once you have enjoyed the delighted response a good cake always receives, you will be encouraged to experiment with your own variations and to progress to some of the more demanding recipes in the following chapters.

Although cakes have always been part of traditional family fare, the combination of busy modern life and the current emphasis on healthy living and a careful diet have tended to push them to the sidelines of the menu. This is a double misfortune, since life should not be so hectic that we cannot find time to practise the art of cookery as well as the joys of eating; and the indulgence of a fine homemade cake – especially if you use the Healthy Sponge recipe on page 22 – is scarcely harmful if it is occasional. If it is to be occasional, then let it be special, and that means homemade. Preparing traditional cakes for your family is the ideal way to develop confidence in the skills that can ultimately be displayed in the creation of wonderful celebration cakes and gâteaux.

Chocolate Battenburg

Battenburg is a firm favourite at family teatime or with morning coffee. Rectangular cakes like this are easy to serve, and the two-colour pattern is easy to achieve by halving two cakes lengthways and arranging them with the colours diagonally opposite.

100 g (4 oz) caster sugar
100 g (4 oz) butter or hard margarine
2 eggs
100 g (4 oz) self-raising flour, sifted
1 teaspoon coffee essence
2 teaspoons cocoa powder
Chocolate buttercream:
50 g (2 oz) butter, softened
100 g (4 oz) icing sugar, sifted
1 tablespoon cocoa powder, sifted
2–3 teaspoons milk
a few drops of vanilla essence
Topping:
175–225 g (6–8 oz) white marzipan
To decorate:
16 chocolate coffee matchsticks

Preparation time: about 40 minutes
Cooking time: about 30 minutes
Oven: 180°C, 350°F, Gas Mark 4

1. Grease and line a 20 cm (8 inch) square tin with greased greaseproof paper or use non-stick silicone paper. Make a pleat down the centre of the paper which stands up about 4 cm (1½ inches). This divides the tin so that the two flavours of cake can be baked at the same time but kept separate.

2. Use the sugar, butter or margarine, eggs and flour to make a Victoria sandwich cake (see page 18).

3. Divide the mixture in half and add the coffee essence to one portion and the cocoa to the other. Place one of the mixtures in one section of the tin and the other mixture in the other, and smooth the tops level with a round-bladed knife.

4. Place in a preheated oven and bake for about 30 minutes or until the cakes are well risen and firm to the touch. Turn them out carefully on to a wire rack without removing the paper. Leave until cold.

5. To make the chocolate buttercream, cream the butter, icing sugar and cocoa together, adding the milk a little at a time to give a spreading consistency. Add a few drops of vanilla essence to enhance the flavour.

6. Remove the paper from the cakes and stand them one on top of the other. Trim the cakes so that they are equal in size. Cut them in half lengthways and arrange the pieces so that the chocolate and coffee cakes are opposite.

7. Spread a little buttercream over the pieces of cake and stick them together. Spread a little buttercream around the sides – not at the ends – and set the remainder of the cream aside for decoration.

8. Roll out the marzipan to a rectangle just large enough to enclose the cake. Stand the cake on top of the marzipan. Wrap the marzipan around the cake, keeping the join underneath.

9. Trim the ends of the marzipan level with the cake and pinch a 'finger-and-thumb' design along the two top edges of marzipan. Mark a criss-cross pattern along the top of the cake with a sharp knife. Leave the marzipan to dry.

10. Place the remaining buttercream in a piping bag fitted with a star nozzle. Pipe a line of buttercream along the top of the cake. Decorate with chocolate matchsticks arranged in pairs.

Variations

Leave one half of the sponge mixture plain and tint the other half and the marzipan with a little pink food colouring. For a chocolate and lemon cake, flavour one half with cocoa powder and the other with grated lemon rind; sandwich the cakes with lemon curd and decorate with crystallized lemon slices.

Caribbean Rum Sandwich

This impressive cake is deceptively quick and easy to make. The sponge layers can be frozen, wrapped in foil, for up to 3 months, but once assembled the cake should be served on the same day.

175 g (6 oz) sugar
175 g (6 oz) soft margarine
3 eggs
175 g (6 oz) self-raising flour
1½ teaspoons baking powder
1 tablespoon rum

Filling:
1 × 375 g (13 oz) can crushed pineapple
1½ teaspoons arrowroot
150 ml (¼ pint) double or whipping cream
1–2 tablespoons rum
50 g (2 oz) flaked almonds, toasted
To decorate:
a few pieces of glacé pineapple

Preparation time: about 30 minutes
Cooking time: about 15 minutes
Oven: 190°C, 375°F, Gas Mark 5

1. Grease and base-line three 20 cm (8 inch) round sandwich tins.

2. Put the sugar, margarine and eggs into a bowl and sift in the flour and baking powder. Add the rum.

3. Beat the mixture by hand or with an electric mixer for 2–3 minutes, until it is quite smooth.

4. Divide the mixture between the tins and smooth the tops level with a round-bladed knife. Place in a preheated oven and bake for about 15 minutes or until the cakes are well risen and firm to the touch.

5. Turn the cakes out on to a wire rack to cool completely. When they are cold, remove the paper.

Left: Chocolate Battenburg
Right: Caribbean rum sandwich

6. To make the filling, strain off 1–2 tablespoons of pineapple juice into a small bowl and blend in the arrowroot. Heat the remaining crushed pineapple and juice to just below boiling point. Add the blended arrowroot and bring to the boil, stirring continuously until thickened and clear. Leave to cool.

7. Whip the cream and rum together. Fold half the flavoured cream into the cooled pineapple mixture with half the almonds.

8. Spread the cream and pineapple mixture over two layers of cake and place them one on top of the other. Place the third cake on top and spread the remaining cream over it, swirling it into an attractive pattern with the knife.

9. Sprinkle the remaining flaked almonds in the centre of the cake and arrange pieces of glacé pineapple around the edge.

Strawberry Gâteau

A cake with strawberries and cream is perfect for a summer tea party. Genoese sponge is a variant on the whisked mixture used for the Swiss roll which has better keeping qualities because of the added butter. The sponge can be made several days in advance of assembling the cake and will keep very well in an airtight tin.

Genoese sponge:
50 g (2 oz) butter or
*   margarine*
3 eggs
75 g (3 oz) sugar
75 g (3 oz) plain flour, sifted
*   twice*
Filling and decoration:
300 ml (½ pint) double cream,
*   lightly whipped*
225 g (8 oz) strawberries,
*   hulled*

Preparation time: 30 minutes
Cooking time: 25 minutes
Oven: 190°C, 375°F, Gas Mark 5

1. Grease and line two 18 cm (7 inch) sandwich tins with greased greaseproof paper or non-stick silicone paper.

2. Place the butter in a bowl set over a pan of hot water to melt without becoming hot. Set it aside for 2–3 minutes.

3. Put the eggs in a mixing bowl set over a pan of hot water and whisk for a few seconds. Add the sugar and continue whisking until the mixture is thick and pale in colour and forms a trail when the whisk is lifted. Remove from the heat and whisk until the mixture is cool.

4. Fold in half the sifted flour with a metal spoon. Pour in half the melted butter in a thin stream at the side of the bowl. Fold in the remaining flour and add the remaining butter in the same way.

5. Pour the mixture into the prepared tins and bake in a preheated oven for 25 minutes until the cakes are golden brown, well risen and firm to the touch. Turn out carefully and leave to cool on a wire rack. Carefully peel off the lining paper.

6. Slice the strawberries in half, keeping one strawberry whole for the centre of the cake. Mix together one third of the cream with half the fruit and spread over one of the cakes. Place the other cake on top.

7. Spread some of the remaining cream over the top of the cake and make a pattern with the tip of a knife. Place the remaining cream in a piping bag filled with a star nozzle and pipe swirls around the top edge. Arrange strawberry halves around the swirls of cream and place the whole strawberry in the middle of the cake.

Lemon Swiss Roll

Covering a Swiss roll with buttercream icing turns it into a Sunday treat. Roll the cake up the moment it comes out of the oven: if it is allowed to cool it will crack. Let it cool and set while rolled up before unrolling it to add the filling.

50 g (2 oz) sugar
2 eggs
50 g (2 oz) plain flour
½ teaspoon baking powder
grated rind of ½ lemon
caster sugar, for dredging
Lemon buttercream:
100 g (4 oz) butter, softened
175–225 g (6–8 oz) icing
*   sugar, sifted*
1–2 tablespoons lemon juice
Filling:
3–4 tablespoons lemon curd
To decorate:
chocolate triangles (see page
*   68)*

Preparation time: about 15 minutes
Cooking time: 10–12 minutes
Oven: 200°C, 400°F, Gas Mark 6

1. Grease and line a 28 × 18 cm (11 × 7 inch) Swiss roll tin with greased greaseproof paper or non-stick silicone paper.

2. Place the sugar and eggs in a mixing bowl set over a saucepan of hot, not boiling, water. Whisk until the mixture is thick and pale in colour and the whisk leaves a heavy trail when lifted. Remove the bowl from the saucepan and continue whisking until the mixture is cool. (If you use an electric mixer no added heat is necessary.)

3. Sift the flour and baking powder together. Sift them again over the whisked mixture. Fold the flour quickly into the mixture using a metal spoon.

4. Turn the mixture into the prepared tin and spread it out evenly, making sure the corners are filled. Place in a preheated oven and bake for 10–12 minutes or until the cake springs back when gently pressed with the fingertips and has begun to shrink slightly from the sides of the tin.

5. While the cake is in the oven, place a damp tea-towel on the working surface and lay a sheet of greaseproof paper or non-stick silicone paper on it. If using greaseproof paper, sprinkle it liberally with sugar.

6. When the cake is cooked, turn it out on to the sugared paper. Quickly peel off the lining paper and trim the edges of the cake with a sharp knife. Make an indentation with a round-bladed knife about 2.5 cm (1 inch) from the edge along the short side nearest to you. Starting at this end, roll up the cake loosely with the paper inside. Fold back the top of the paper so that it does not stick to the cake as it cools.

7. To make the lemon buttercream, cream the butter and icing sugar together, adding the lemon juice a little at a time to give a spreading consistency.

8. Unroll the cooled cake carefully and remove the paper. Spread the cake with the lemon curd and roll it up again.

9. Place the buttercream in a piping bag fitted with a star nozzle. Pipe rows of icing along the roll and one row of shells or rosettes on top. Decorate with chocolate triangles.

From the top: Strawberry gâteau, Lemon Swiss roll

Lemon Cake

175 g (6 oz) sugar
4 eggs
grated rind of 1 lemon
100 g (4 oz) plain flour, sifted
6 tablespoons lemon curd
Glacé icing:
300 g (10 oz) icing sugar
2–3 tablespoons warm water
a few drops of yellow food
    colouring
1 drop orange food colouring
To decorate:
25 g (1 oz) desiccated coconut
sugar flowers

Preparation time: 20 minutes
Cooking time: 30–35 minutes
Oven: 190°C, 375°F, Gas Mark 5

1. Grease and line a 23 cm (9 inch) round cake tin with greased greaseproof paper or non-stick silicone paper.

2. Place the sugar, eggs and lemon rind in a mixing bowl set over a saucepan of hot, not boiling, water. Whisk until the mixture is thick and pale in colour and the whisk leaves a heavy trail when lifted. Remove the bowl from the saucepan and continue whisking until the mixture is cool. (If you use an electric mixer no added heat is necessary.)

3. Sift the flour over the mixture and fold it in quickly using a metal spoon.

4. Turn the mixture into the prepared tin and place in a preheated oven. Bake for 30–35 minutes or until the cake springs back when lightly pressed and shrinks slightly from the sides of the tin. Turn out on a wire rack to cool.

5. When the cake is cool, remove the lining paper and cut the cake in half horizontally. Sandwich the two pieces together with 4 tablespoons of the lemon curd. Spread the remaining lemon curd around the side of the cake.

6. Place the desiccated coconut in a small bowl and add a drop of yellow food colouring. Stir until the coconut is evenly coloured.

7. Place the coconut on a sheet of greaseproof paper. Hold the cake between the palms of your hands and roll it lightly in the coconut until the sides are covered. Place the cake on a 23 cm (9 inch) round board.

8. To make the glacé icing, sift the icing sugar into a mixing bowl and very gradually add the water. The icing should be thick enough to coat the back of the spoon thickly. Add 2–3 drops of yellow food colouring. Immediately pour three quarters of the icing on to the top of the cake and spread it almost to the edge with a palette knife. Gently bang the cake two or three times on the table to help the icing flow to the edge. Leave for a few minutes to dry.

9. Add a few more drops of yellow and a drop of orange colouring to the remaining icing. Place in a greaseproof paper piping bag fitted with a No. 2 writing nozzle. Pipe parallel lines across the top of the cake, then more lines across them to form diamond shapes. Place a sugar flower in each diamond and leave to set.

Mocha Gâteau

Mocha is a delicious blend of chocolate and coffee flavours. This irresistible cake is equally good with coffee mid-morning or after dinner.

75 g (3 oz) sugar
3 eggs
50 g (2 oz) plain flour, sifted
1 tablespoon instant coffee
    powder
Chocolate buttercream:
100 g (4 oz) butter
225 g (8 oz) icing sugar, sifted
2 tablespoons cocoa powder
    blended with 2 tablespoons
    boiling water and cooled
1 tablespoon milk
To decorate:
75 g (3 oz) plain chocolate,
    grated
chocolate buttons

Preparation time: 20 minutes
Cooking time: 20–25 minutes
Oven: 190°C, 375°F, Gas Mark 5

1. Grease and line a 20 × 30 cm (8 × 12 inch) Swiss roll tin with greased greaseproof paper or non-stick silicone paper.

2. Place the sugar and eggs in a mixing bowl set over a saucepan of hot, not boiling, water. Whisk until the mixture is thick and pale in colour and the whisk leaves a heavy trail when lifted. Remove the bowl from the saucepan and continue whisking until the mixture is cool. (If you use an electric mixer no added heat is necessary.)

3. Sift the flour with the cocoa powder over the mixture and fold it in quickly using a metal spoon.

4. Turn the mixture into the prepared tin and place in a preheated oven. Bake for 20–25 minutes or until the cake springs back when lightly pressed and shrinks slightly from the sides of the tin. Turn out on a wire rack to cool.

5. To make the chocolate buttercream, cream the butter and icing sugar together, adding the cocoa powder dissolved in water and the milk a little at a time to give a spreading consistency.

6. When the cake is cool, remove the lining paper and cut the cake into 3 equal pieces. Sandwich them together using one third of the chocolate buttercream.

7. Spread more icing on the sides of the cake and coat with the grated chocolate. Place on cake board.

8. Spread more icing over the top of the cake and mark out lines lengthways with a palette knife. Place the remaining icing in a greaseproof paper piping bag fitted with a fluted nozzle and pipe a border along the edges of the cake. Decorate with chocolate buttons.

Variation

Make your own chocolate decorations such as triangles or leaves (see page 68). Caraque is a good choice for a rectangular cake, the strips laid closely side by side and lightly dusted with icing sugar.

From the top: Lemon cake, Mocha gâteau

St Clement's Ring

A light Victoria sponge mixture becomes extra special with the tangy flavour of citrus fruit and baked in an attractive ring shape.

175 g (6 oz) butter or
    margarine
175 g (6 oz) sugar
3 eggs
100 g (4 oz) self-raising flour,
    sifted
50 g (2 oz) ground almonds
grated rind of 1 orange
grated rind of 1 lemon
Glacé icing:
225 g (8 oz) icing sugar
2–3 tablespoons lemon juice
a few drops of yellow food
    colouring (optional)
To decorate:
shredded orange and lemon
    rind

Preparation time: 20 minutes
Cooking time: 40–45 minutes
Oven: 160°C, 325°F, Gas Mark 3

1. Grease and flour a 20 cm (8 inch) ring mould.

2. Cream the butter and sugar together until light and fluffy. Beat in one egg and mix well. Beat in the second egg, adding a little flour. Add the third egg with a little more flour and beat till smooth.

3. Fold in the remaining flour with the ground almonds and the grated orange and lemon rinds.

4. Pour the mixture into the prepared tin and bake in a preheated oven for 40–45 minutes until well risen and golden brown. Turn out carefully and leave to cool on a wire rack.

St Clement's Day Feast

Until recently the feast of St Clement, which falls on November 23, was a popular celebration in many parts of the British Isles. St Clement is the patron saint of blacksmiths. On their special day spiced cakes and apples were part of the traditional fare, and children would play apple-bobbing. There are a number of variations on clementing cakes. Among the simplest are little tarts made of shortcrust pastry. These pastry cases were filled with a creamed mixture of butter, sugar and egg yolk, into which the finely chopped flesh of an orange and a lemon were blended with the juice and strips of peel, and finally beaten egg white. The result is a light well-risen cake on a crisp pastry base – very popular with children at teatime.

5. To make the glacé icing, sift the icing sugar into a mixing bowl and gradually stir in the lemon juice. The icing should be thick enough to coat the back of the spoon thickly. Add 2–3 drops of yellow food colouring, if used.

6. Immediately pour the icing over the cake, allowing it to run down the sides. Strew the shredded orange and lemon rind over the icing and leave to set.

Hazelnut Coffee Cake

Piping the border of butter-cream rosettes as evenly and close together as you can gives this delicious cake its luxurious effect. It is a particularly easy mixture – and ideal for the food processor – as all the ingredients are combined simultaneously.

100 g (4 oz) butter or
    margarine
175 g (6 oz) soft brown sugar
2 eggs
6 tablespoons milk
1 tablespoon coffee essence or 1
    tablespoon instant coffee
    dissolved in 1 tablespoon
    boiling water and cooled
75 g (3 oz) hazelnuts, chopped
75 g (3 oz) raisins
225 g (8 oz) self-raising flour
1 teaspoon baking powder

Coffee buttercream:
75 g (3 oz) butter
225 g (8 oz) icing sugar
1 tablespoon milk
1 tablespoon coffee essence or 1
    tablespoon instant coffee
    dissolved in 1 tablespoon
    boiling water and cooled
To decorate:
toasted hazelnuts

Preparation time: 20 minutes
Cooking time: 30–40 minutes
Oven: 160°C, 325°F, Gas Mark 3

1. Grease and line two 20 cm (8 inch) sandwich tins with greased greaseproof paper or non-stick silicone paper.

2. Place all the ingredients in a mixing bowl and beat with a wooden spoon until well mixed.

3. Pour the mixture into the prepared tins and bake in a preheated oven for 30–40 minutes, or until well risen. Turn out and cool on a wire rack.

4. To make the coffee buttercream, cream the butter and icing sugar together, adding the milk and coffee essence a little at a time to give a spreading consistency.

5. Sandwich the cakes together with a little of the buttercream. Spread some more of the buttercream over the top of the cake and draw parallel lines across it with a palette knife.

6. Place the remaining buttercream in a greaseproof paper piping bag fitted with a star nozzle and carefully pipe a border of rosettes around the top edge of the cake. Top each rosette with a toasted hazelnut.

Variations

Make a little extra buttercream to coat the sides of the cake and cover with crushed hazelnuts. Substitute walnuts for hazelnuts in the recipe for a more sophisticated cake.

From the top: St Clement's ring, Hazelnut coffee cake

Strawberry Feather Bar

The delicate patterns of feather icing look best when there is a strong colour contrast between the icing and the base. The pink and white effect of this cake is particularly pretty, but dark chocolate feathers against coffee glacé icing are also attractive.

100 g (4 oz) sugar
100 g (4 oz) soft margarine
2 eggs
100 g (4 oz) self-raising flour
1 teaspoon baking powder
Filling:
75 g (3 oz) unsalted butter,
  softened
175 g (6 oz) icing sugar, sifted
1 tablespoon milk
red food colouring
2 tablespoons strawberry jam
To decorate:
100 g (4 oz) icing sugar
1–2 tablespoons boiling water
strawberry flavour dessert
  sauce

Preparation time: 15 minutes
Cooking time: 30–35 minutes
Oven: 160°C, 325°F, Gas Mark 3

1. Grease and line a 20 cm (8 inch) square cake tin with greased greaseproof paper or non-stick silicone paper.

2. Place all the cake ingredients in a mixing bowl and beat with a wooden spoon for about 2 minutes until light and fluffy.

3. Spoon the mixture into the prepared tin, making sure the corners are filled, and smooth the top. Bake in a preheated oven for 30–35 minutes until golden brown and firm to the touch. Turn out on to a wire rack, remove the lining paper and leave to cool completely.

4. To make the buttercream filling, place the butter, icing sugar and milk in a bowl. Beat together to give a light texture and spreading consistency. Tint the buttercream pink with a few drops of red food colouring.

5. Cut the cake in half and split each half horizontally. Sandwich the split cakes together with strawberry jam. Sandwich the two cakes together with a little buttercream to form a 20 cm (8 inch) bar.

6. To make the glacé icing, sift the icing sugar into a bowl and gradually beat in the water until the icing thickly coats the back of the spoon. Immediately spread the icing over the top of the cake, being careful not to let it drip over the sides (you can wrap a strip of greaseproof paper round the cake to prevent this).

7. Place a little strawberry flavour dessert sauce in a greaseproof paper piping bag fitted with a thin writing nozzle. Pipe lines of sauce widthways on the icing on top of the cake. Draw a fine skewer across the lines of sauce in alternate directions to form a feather pattern (see page 43).

8. Place the remaining buttercream in a piping bag fitted with a shell or star nozzle. Pipe a border around the top edge of the cake and leave to set.

Feather-iced cakes

When you have mastered the feather icing pattern you will find it an invaluable technique for quickly decorating simple sponge cakes of all sizes. Its most classic application is in a more complex but deservedly famous recipe. This is *Mille Feuilles*, which is made from layers of puff pastry sandwiched with whipped cream, or cream and crème pastissière, and glacé-iced on top feather fashion. The whole cake is then cut into fingers to serve as elegant pastries. The name means 'thousand leaves' from the numerous layers of fine pastry.

Lacy Sugar Cake

For the filigree pattern of sugar on top of the cake to have its full effect, the sides must be well coated with chopped nuts. Simple to achieve, this decoration is very impressive.

175 g (6 oz) sugar
175 g (6 oz) soft margarine
3 eggs
175 g (6 oz) self-raising flour
1½ teaspoons baking powder
finely grated rind of 1 orange
Filling and decoration:
6 tablespoons apricot jam,
  warmed and sieved
75 g (3 oz) chopped nuts
  (hazelnuts, almonds or
  walnuts), toasted
icing sugar, sifted

Preparation time: 15 minutes
Cooking time: 30–35 minutes
Oven: 160°C, 325°F, Gas Mark 3

1. Grease and line two 20 cm (8 inch) sandwich tins with greased greaseproof paper or non-stick silicone paper.

2. Place all the cake ingredients in a mixing bowl and beat with a wooden spoon for about 2 minutes until light and fluffy.

3. Divide the mixture equally between the prepared tins and smooth the tops level. Bake in a preheated oven for 30–35 minutes until golden brown and firm to the touch. Turn out on to a wire rack, remove the lining paper and leave to cool completely.

4. Sandwich the cakes together with two thirds of the apricot jam. Spread the remaining jam evenly around the side of the cake. Strew the chopped nuts on a sheet of greaseproof paper. Holding the cake between the palms of your hands, roll it carefully in the nuts to coat the sides.

5. Place the cake on a serving plate. Put a patterned doily on top of the cake. Dredge the cake with icing sugar using a fine sieve and covering the cake evenly. Very carefully lift off the doily to reveal the sugar pattern.

From the top: Lacy sugar cake,
Strawberry feather bar

Chocolate Mint Cake

If there's one cake which is by tradition everybody's favourite, it's chocolate. This chocolate sponge with two kinds of mint icing is sure to appeal to all the family.

225 g (8 oz) butter or
*   margarine*
225 g (8 oz) sugar
1 tablespoon cocoa powder
*   blended with 1 tablespoon*
*   hot water and cooled*
4 eggs
225 g (8 oz) self-raising flour,
*   sifted*
1 tablespoon hot water
Mint buttercream:
110 g (4 oz) butter
225 g (8 oz) icing sugar, sifted
2 tablespoons milk
a few drops of green food
*   colouring*
a few drops of peppermint
*   flavouring*
Glacé icing:
110 g (4 oz) icing sugar
1–2 tablespoons warm water
a few drops of green food
*   colouring*
a few drops of peppermint
*   flavouring*
To decorate:
75 g (3 oz) chocolate sugar
*   strands*
50 g (2 oz) plain chocolate

Preparation time: 30 minutes
Cooking time: 25–30 minutes
Oven: 180°C, 350°F, Gas Mark 4

1. Grease and line two 20 cm (8 inch) sandwich tins with greased greaseproof paper or non-stick silicone paper.

2. Cream the butter and sugar together until light and fluffy. Beat the cocoa powder paste in to the mixture.

3. Beat in one egg and mix well. Beat in the other eggs one at a time, adding a little flour with each one. Fold in the remaining flour with a metal spoon. Add the hot water.

4. Turn the mixture into the prepared tins and bake in a preheated oven for 25–30 minutes until well risen. Turn out carefully and leave to cool on a wire rack.

5. To make the mint buttercream, cream the butter and icing sugar together. Add the milk, green food colouring and peppermint flavouring and beat until creamy.

6. Use half the mint buttercream to sandwich the cakes together. Cover the sides with more buttercream. Place the chocolate strands on a sheet of greaseproof paper and holding the cake carefully between the palms of your hands, roll it in the chocolate strands until the sides are well covered. Place on a cake board.

7. Place the remaining buttercream in a nylon piping bag fitted with a 5 mm (¼ inch) fluted nozzle and pipe a border around the top of the cake.

8. To make the glacé icing, sift the icing sugar into a mixing bowl and gradually add the water. (You may find you do not not need as much as 2 tablespoons.) The icing should be thick enough to coat the back of the spoon thickly. Add 1–2 drops of green food colouring (the colour should be subtle). Immediately pour the glacé icing on top of the cake and spread it almost to the edge with a palette knife, taking care not to touch the piping. Gently bang the cake on the table two or three times to help the icing flow smoothly to the edge.

9. Melt the chocolate in a small bowl placed over a saucepan of hot water. Place the melted chocolate in a greaseproof paper piping bag, cut off the tip and dribble the chocolate across the top of the cake.

Frosted Fruit Cake

There's nothing complicated in the preparation of this cake, but it is mouthwateringly pretty, and the orange-flavoured liqueur sprinkled over the sponge gives it a special lift. Bake and serve this cake on the same day. The frosted decorations, however, can be made up to 2 weeks in advance if kept in an airtight container between layers of tissue paper.

75 g (3 oz) sugar
3 eggs
75 g (3 oz) plain flour
4 tablespoons Cointreau
450 ml (¾ pint) double cream,
*   whipped*
To decorate:
frosted grapes
frosted mint leaves

Preparation time: 15 minutes, plus frosting the fruit
Cooking time: 30–35 minutes
Oven: 190°C, 375°F, Gas Mark 5

1. Grease and flour a 23 cm (9 inch) ring mould.

2. Place the sugar and eggs in a mixing bowl set over a saucepan of hot, not boiling water. Whisk until the mixture is thick and pale in colour and the whisk leaves a heavy trail when lifted. Remove the bowl from the saucepan and continue whisking until the mixture is cool. (If you use an electric mixer no added heat is necessary.)

3. Sift the flour into the mixture and quickly fold it in with a metal spoon.

4. Turn the mixture into the prepared tin and place in a preheated oven. Bake for 30–35 minutes until the cake springs back when lightly pressed with the fingertips and has begun to shrink slightly from the sides of the tin. Turn out on a wire rack to cool.

5. Cut the cake in half horizontally and sprinkle with Cointreau. Sandwich the pieces together with a quarter of the cream. Place on a cake board. Cover the cake with the remaining cream and mark with a palette knife into a swirl pattern.

6. Decorate with clusters of frosted grapes and mint leaves. Keep the cake in the refrigerator until you are ready to serve it (because of the fresh cream).

Variation

For a luscious mocha variation, bake a chocolate Quick Mix Cake using the same size ring mould and following the instructions on pages 16–17. Sprinkle the horizontally cut halves with coffee liqueur. Sandwich and top with cream a above. Decorate with marrons glacés halves.

From the top: Chocolate mint cake,
Frosted fruit cake

Apricot Butterscotch Cake

This cake demonstrates the versatility of the basic Victoria sponge mixture. Adding black treacle and lemon juice enriches the flavour without making it excessively sweet, giving it a pleasant nuttiness that combines well with the apricots.

175 g (6 oz) butter or hard margarine
75 g (3 oz) light soft brown sugar
75 g (3 oz) dark soft brown sugar
3 eggs
175 g (6 oz) self-raising flour, sifted
1 tablespoon black treacle
1 tablespoon lemon juice
Filling:
1 × 425 g (15 oz) can apricot halves, drained
150 ml (¼ pint) double or whipping cream
3 tablespoons milk or medium white wine

Preparation time: 30 minutes
Cooking time: 20–25 minutes
Oven: 190°C, 375°F, Gas Mark 5

1. Grease and base-line two 20 cm (8 inch) square sandwich tins with greased greaseproof paper or non-stick silicone paper.

2. Place the butter or margarine in a mixing bowl and beat until soft. Add the two kinds of sugar and beat together until the mixture is very light and fluffy.

3. Beat in the eggs one at a time, following each with 1 table-spoon of the flour to prevent the mixture from curdling. Fold in the remaining flour. Beat in the black treacle and lemon juice, combining the ingredients smoothly.

4. Divide the mixture between the tins, levelling the tops and making sure the corners of the tins are filled.

5. Place in a preheated oven and bake for about 20–25 minutes or until well risen, golden brown and firm to the touch. Turn out on to a wire rack and leave to cool. Peel off the paper.

6. To make the filling, chop half of the apricots and cut the remaining half into quarters.

7. Whip the cream and milk or wine together until stiff. Put almost half into a greaseproof

paper or nylon piping bag, fitted with a 1 cm (⅓ inch) plain vegetable nozzle. Fold the remainder into the chopped apricots.

8. Use the apricot cream to

Dark Ginger Cake

ndwich the cakes together.
lace the cake on a serving
late.

. Pipe a lattice of cream over
ne top of the cake and fill
ternate squares with pieces of

apricot. Keep the cake in the refrigerator if it is not to be served immediately (because of the fresh cream).

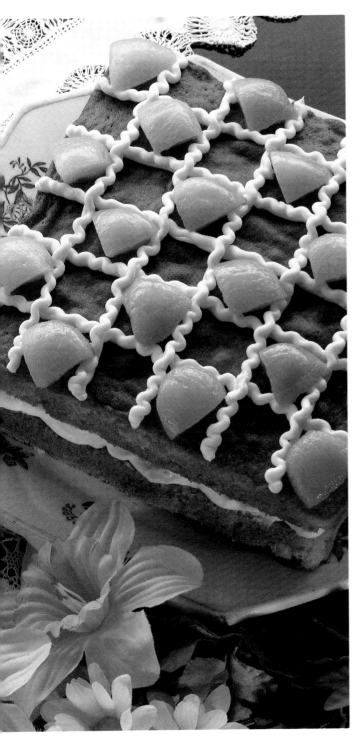

From the left: Dark ginger cake, Apricot butterscotch cake

The spiciness of this cake is well matched by its rich texture. It must be made 24 hours or more before eating for the flavours to blend.

175 g (6 oz) black treacle
40 g (1½ oz) demerara sugar
75 g (3 oz) butter or hard
  margarine
175 g (6 oz) plain flour
2 teaspoons ground ginger
1 teaspoon mixed spice
½ teaspoon bicarbonate of soda
2 eggs
100 ml (4 fl oz) milk or
  buttermilk
Ginger crème au beurre:
2 egg yolks
75 g (3 oz) sugar
4 tablespoons water
175 g (6 oz) butter
pinch of ground ginger or
  mixed spice
To decorate:
a few pieces of stem or
  crystallized ginger

Preparation time: 45 minutes,
plus standing
Cooking time: about 1¼ hours
Oven: 160°C, 325°F, Gas Mark 3

1. Grease and line a 23 × 13 cm (9 × 5 inch) loaf tin with greased greaseproof paper or non-stick silicone paper.

2. Put the treacle, sugar and butter or margarine into a saucepan. Heat gently until the ingredients have melted. Set aside to cool slightly.

3. Sift the flour, ginger, mixed spice and bicarbonate of soda into a bowl and make a well in the centre. Add the eggs and milk or buttermilk and the melted treacle mixture and beat until smooth.

4. Pour the mixture into the prepared tin and place in a preheated oven. Bake for about 1¼ hours or until a skewer inserted in the centre comes out clean. Turn out on to a wire rack and leave until cold. Wrap the cake in foil and store for at least 24 hours before eating.

5. To make the crème au beurre, beat the egg yolks in a bowl until smooth.

6. Place the sugar and water in a small heavy-bottomed saucepan and heat gently until the sugar dissolves. Boil steadily until the syrup reaches the thread stage, 107°C (225°F) on a sugar thermometer.

7. Remove the syrup from the heat and immediately pour it on to the beaten egg yolks, whisking well all the time. Continue to whisk until the mixture is very light and fluffy.

8. Cream the butter until it is soft, and gradually beat in the egg and sugar mixture. Flavour the cream with a pinch of ground ginger or mixed spice.

9. Place the crème au beurre in a piping bag fitted with a star nozzle and pipe a pattern of swirls on top of the cake (alternatively spread the cream on top of the cake with a palette knife and make a pattern with the knife). Decorate with pieces of stem or crystallized ginger.

Orange Gâteau

Like the Strawberry Gâteau on page 76, this cake is based on a Genoese sponge mixture (also known as a Torten) and so has good keeping qualities. This gives you the opportunity to make the sponge a few days ahead of assembling the cake. Use a small thin-skinned orange for making the glazed orange slices.

50 g (2 oz) butter
75 g (3 oz) self-raising flour
3 eggs
100 g (4 oz) sugar
finely grated rind of ½ orange
Filling and decoration:
225 g (8 oz) orange curd or
*   orange marmalade without*
*   peel*
450 ml (¾ pint) double or
*   whipping cream*
50 g (2 oz) flaked almonds,
*   toasted*
Glazed orange slices:
10 orange slices, 5 mm
*   (¼ inch) thick, or 5 slices*
*   cut in half*
75 g (3 oz) caster sugar

Preparation time: about 1 hour
Cooking time: about 30 minutes
Oven: 190°C, 375°F, Gas Mark 5

1. Grease and line a deep 20 cm (8 inch) round cake tin with greased greaseproof paper or non-stick silicone paper.

2. Heat the butter in a small saucepan until it has just melted. Remove the pan from the heat and leave to stand so that the sediment sinks to the bottom.

3. Sift the flour twice.

4. Place the eggs, sugar and grated orange rind in a mixing bowl set over a pan of gently simmering water. Whisk until light and creamy, so that the whisk leaves a heavy trail when lifted. Remove the bowl from the heat and continue whisking until the mixture is cool. (If you use an electric mixer no added heat is necessary.)

5. Fold the sifted flour lightly and evenly through the mixture.

6. Carefully pour in the butter, without the sediment, and fold it in lightly and carefully.

7. Turn the mixture into the prepared tin and bake in a preheated oven for about 30 minutes until well risen, golden brown and firm to the touch. Turn out and cool on a wire rack. Remove the lining paper.

8. Glaze the orange slices. Remove any pips from the slices and place them in a frying pan. Cover with cold water and set over a gentle heat. Poach for about 20 minutes or until the slices are tender, adding more water if necessary.

9. Lift the orange slices out of the pan with a slotted spoon and transfer them to a baking sheet.

10. Add the sugar to the water left in the pan and stir to dissolve. Bring the syrup to the boil and continue to boil until it is reduced to a thick glaze. Pour the glaze over the orange slices and leave them to cool.

11. Cut the cooled cake into three equal layers. Place the base layer on a serving plate and spread it with half the orange curd or marmalade.

12. Whip the cream until it is stiff and spread a thin layer over the orange curd. Place the second cake layer on top and spread with the remaining orange curd and a little cream. Top with the third cake layer.

13. Use most of the remaining cream to cover the top and sides of the cake completely. Put the rest of the cream into a piping bag fitted with a medium star nozzle.

14. Press the toasted almonds on to the sides of the gâteau, using a round-bladed knife or a palette knife.

15. Arrange the glazed orange slices in an overlapping circle on top of the gâteau. Pipe a border of shells around the top of the cake with the cream. A similar border can be piped round the base of the cake if you wish.

Variation

For a lemon gâteau, replace the orange rind in the sponge mixture with lemon rind; the orange curd with lemon curd, and glazed orange slices with glazed lemon slices.

Fruit Variety

Using a sponge mixture as the basis, build up a repertoire of cakes on the tried-and-tested combination of fruit, cream and nuts, adding a little liqueur to the whipped cream when serving cake as a dessert. In season, strawberries and raspberries are unbeatable. Alternatively, make a square cake and arrange closely packed rows of dark loganberries on top with a border of piped whipped cream and chopped hazelnuts on the side.

Orange gâteau

CELEBRATION CAKES

This selection of celebratory cakes provides the cake decorator with opportunities for dazzling display. Formal cakes with fine and intricate piping work and decoration feature here. Simpler, but equally effective, are cakes for Christmas and Easter with marzipan decoration.

All the important occasions in life – whether they are times of personal happiness, such as a wedding or special birthday, or great days in the calendar, like Christmas – are celebrated with a feast, and an essential part of that feast is a grand and formal cake. Although a number of conventions are associated with cakes in this category, the scope for an imaginative and skilful cake decorator is enormous.

Occasions of this kind will tend to be well-planned, so there is usually plenty of time to design and create the cake. Most formal cakes are based on a rich fruit mixture, because its flavour, firmness of texture and keeping quality is best suited to this type of icing and decoration as well to the occasion itself. Indeed a rich fruit cake should be made several weeks before it is to be iced and eaten, in order for the flavours to mature and blend.

Wedding cakes can be elaborately designed and decorated but sometimes an element of restraint is useful. What would look wonderful on a single layer may well be over fussy on a second and third. Don't be caught out making special decorations the night before! Tiny piped or run-out decorations can be made some time in advance and stored in an airtight container between sheets of tissue paper. Delicate items like this need to be handled with care. The separate tiers of the cake should also be well-packed before transporting them to be assembled before the reception.

With celebration cakes it is vital to know how many people the cake will feed. As a rough guide, a 450 g (1 lb) baked rich fruit cake without marzipan or icing should cut into about 10 portions when completed. Therefore, for every 45–50 people you will need about 2.25 kg (5 lb) basic cake. Square cakes usually weigh heavier than round ones of the same size, although the depths can vary slightly as well.

The diagram below shows how to cut a square and a round wedding cake.

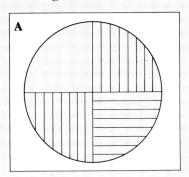
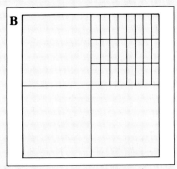

Because this chapter includes cakes for every significant occasion, the range of techniques involved is all-embracing. The finest piped royal icing work is used, for example, on the Hexagonal Wedding Cake – one of the most romantic designs imaginable – and the Eighteenth Birthday Cake. Pretty moulded flowers feature on many of the cakes – spectacularly on the American Wedding Cake – and marzipan fruits make a colourful display on the Harvest Festival Cake. A wide range of ideas for Christmas is included, expanding on the traditional white-iced cake with red and green decorations to take in an unusual Santa's Stocking and some delightful miniature designs. Easter is as important a feast day as Christmas, and has its own cake customs as well as the conventional chocolate eggs. The French Gâteau de Pâques is a marvellous cake for this springtime celebration.

Birthdays, anniversaries, engagements, retirement parties: these and many other occasions are milestones in life that deserve to be honoured with a cake. The beautiful designs in this chapter will give you inspiration for all of them.

WEDDING CAKES

A once-in-a-lifetime event calls for a beautifully crafted cake to match the occasion. Strictly traditional designs at their best are represented by these classic cakes which embrace a broad range of intricate techniques. Traditional or modern, wedding cakes represent the pinnacle of decorative skills as a vital part of an unforgettable day.

Hexagonal Wedding Cake

If you are able to buy or hire hexagonal cake tins, bake the cakes in sizes of 25 and 15 cm (10 and 6 inch). If you bake round cakes as directed in the recipe, cut them out as described on page 53. If you are unable to buy or make hexagonal cake boards, use round boards 33 and 20 cm (13 and 8 inches) in diameter.

1 × 28 cm (11 inch) and
  1 × 18 cm (7 inch) round
  Rich Fruit Cake (pages 24–5)
1 quantity apricot glaze (page
  38)
1.6 kg (3½ lb) marzipan (page
  37)
about 3 kg (6½ lb) sugar
  quantity royal icing (page
  39)
mauve liquid food colouring
a little egg white or lemon juice
about 120 piped fans (see
  below)
about 40 run-out heart shapes
  (page 61)
4 white cake pillars

Preparation time: icing and decoration of the cake, plus time for making and drying the fans and hearts

1. Brush the tops and sides of the cakes with apricot glaze and coat with marzipan (see page 38). Leave to dry.

2. Make up some royal icing. Attach each cake to the appropriate board with a dab of icing. Flat-ice the cakes with three coats all over and a further coat to the top of the larger cake. Leave to dry for 24 hours.

3. Tint a little of the icing pale mauve and put into a piping bag fitted with a fine writing nozzle (No. 1 or 0). To make the fans, take a sheet of card and draw a continuous line along the length of it, then draw a second line 1 cm (½ inch) below it broken into short lines of 2 cm (¾ inch) with about 1 cm (½ inch) gap between. Repeat these lines all over the card. Using each short line as a base, draw 5 petal shapes as a guide to making the fan. Repeat this 2–3 times (once you have piped two or three fans no extra guide lines will be necessary). Cover the card with a sheet of non-stick silicone paper, attaching it firmly with sticky tape.

4. To pipe the fans, start in the centre of one of the short lines, work round the petals, moving up to the tallest central point and back down again the other side, keeping to the short line for length and to the continuous line to give the height. Make some extra as some may break as they are moved. Leave to dry in a warm place. If you cannot get them all on one sheet, make another.

5. For the run-out hearts, draw heart shapes, each fitting into a 2.5 cm (1 inch) square, all over a sheet of card or stiff paper. Cover with a sheet of non-stick silicone paper and using a No. 1 or 2 writing nozzle and mauve icing, outline at least 40 heart shapes. Leave to dry. For 10 of the hearts, work a lattice pattern to fill the shapes. For the others, thin a little mauve icing with egg white or lemon juice until it flows, then put into a grease-proof paper icing bag without a nozzle. Cut off the tip and use to flood the hearts. Prick any air bubbles and leave to dry.

6. Make up the rest of the icing as and when necessary. Take a piping bag fitted with a No. 1 writing nozzle and white icing and pipe a series of dots all round the run-out hearts just in from the edge (but not on the lattice ones).

7. At the base of the large cake mark each section equally into four with small dabs of icing as markers. Divide the small cake into three sections in the same way. Fill a piping bag fitted with a medium star nozzle with white icing. Pipe twisted scrolls in a clockwise movement, graduated in size from small to large and back to small again, all around the base of both cakes between the markers. Leave to dry.

8. Attach three hearts (two run-outs and one lattice) centrally to each side of the large cake and two hearts (both run-outs) on the small cake. Use just a small dab of icing to attach each one.

9. On top of the large cake, prick out a 6 cm (2¼ inch) long line, 2.5 cm (1 inch) in from the edge of the cake on each section. Using tweezers, attach three fans upright to each of these lines with icing.

10. For the smaller cake, prick a line 4 cm (1½ inches) long and again 2.5 cm (1 inch) in from the edge. Attach two fans to each line and leave to dry.

11. Take a piping bag fitted with a No. 2 or 3 writing nozzle and filled with white icing. Pipe three dots centrally inside the fans on top of the cake, as shown. Next pipe one centrally on the outer side of the fans with a slightly smaller one each side of it. Finally take a No. 1 writing nozzle and white icing and complete the central design by piping four graduated dots towards the centre of the cake from the middle dot, and two graduated dots from the outer ones. On the outer side of the fan, pipe three more graduated dots to reach the end of the fans. On the smaller cake fewer dots will be required for only two fans, but keep to the same pattern.

12. Attach fans all around the top edge of the cakes, facing outwards. You need seven for each section on the large cake and five for the smaller cake.

13. Take the No. 1 writing nozzle and white icing and pipe a large dot at the bottom and in the middle of each fan on the top of the cake with a smaller one on each side. Do the same under the fans on the side.

14. Finally, using the same nozzle, pipe a squiggly white line of icing along the top of each scroll at the base of the cakes and attach a fan at each corner. Leave to dry.

15. Assemble the cake, positioning the smaller tier on top with the sides matching. Top with a silver vase of small flowers.

Hexagonal wedding cake

American Wedding Cake

American-style wedding cakes have the traditional three tiers, but there are no pillars supporting the middle and top tiers. This means that the icing on the base cake needs to be hard enough to take the weight of the other two cakes. Do not add glycerine to the icing which you use for the four coats on the base cake. The advantage is that designs for American wedding cakes can embrace the whole cake, like these cascading roses. For instructions on cutting the cake for ease of serving, see step 15.

One 33 cm (13 inch) thick round silver cake board
One 23 cm (9 inch) and one 18 cm (7 in) medium thick or thin but extra firm round silver cake boards
1 × 15 cm (6 inch) round, 1 × 20 cm (8 inch) round and 1 × 25 cm (10 inch) round Rich Fruit Cake (pages 24–5)
2 quantities apricot glaze (page 38)
1.75 kg (4 lb) marzipan (page 37)
about 2.75 kg (6 lb) sugar quantity royal icing (page 39)
cream and golden yellow liquid food colourings
about 50 white moulded roses of varying sizes (page 63)
about 60 cream moulded roses of varying sizes
about 60 pale golden yellow moulded roses of varying sizes
about 30 purchased silver or white moulded leaves

Preparation time: icing and decoration of the cake, plus making and drying of the roses

1. Brush the tops and sides of the cakes with apricot glaze and coat with marzipan (see page 38). Leave to dry.

2. Make up some of the royal icing and attach each cake to the appropriate board with a dab of icing. Flat-ice the cakes, giving three coats all over and a further coat to the top of the base cake. Leave to dry completely.

3. Make the roses, using about 450 g (1 lb) fondant moulding paste (see page 44) and leave them to dry. Also make the leaves if using moulded ones.

4. On the tops of the base and middle cakes, mark the size of the boards which will stand on them (for the next cake up) with pinpricks or dabs of icing.

5. Draw some scroll shapes on non-stick silicone paper to fit around the top space outside the cake boards on the middle and bottom tiers, the scroll for the base being rather more elongated. Place the paper patterns at four equal points on each cake and prick out the scroll design.

6. Make up the rest of the royal icing as necessary. Fill a piping bag fitted with a No. 2 writing nozzle with white icing and outline the scrolls, then pipe a second scroll shape beside the first. Leave to dry, then overpipe one line of the scrolls.

7. For the sides of all the cakes, draw vertical scroll shapes which work as a mirror-image pair on non-stick silicone paper. Prick these shapes on to the sides of the cakes.

8. Using the writing nozzle, pipe double lines in white icing as for the first scrolls, dry, then overpipe one scroll with white icing. Leave to dry.

9. Fill a piping bag fitted with a medium star nozzle with white icing. Pipe a fairly heavy shell border around the top edge of the three cakes. Leave to dry.

10. Fill a piping bag fitted with a fine writing nozzle (No. 1 or 0) with pale gold icing and pipe a continuous slightly looped line to fit around the shells both on top of the cake and on the sides. Leave to dry.

11. To assemble the cakes, stand the base on a flat surface, then put the middle tier carefully on top, so that the scrolls correspond.

12. Work a white shell border to match the one on the top edges of the cakes, to attach the base cake to the board and middle tier to the base cake. Do the same to the top tier.

13. With the fine writing nozzle and gold icing, pipe a slightly scalloped line above and below the shell borders as on the tops of the cakes.

14. Starting on top of the cake, arrange a cluster of roses of varying colours and sizes, attaching each one with a dab of icing. Continue attaching roses to build up a heavy swirling cascade of roses down the sides and over the tops of each of the cakes to the base. Keep the colours mixed and fill in the gaps with leaves. On each of the tiers, midway between the scrolls on the sides of the cake, attach one rose and three rose buds. Allow to dry.

15. To cut the cake, begin at the lowest tier. Run a knife vertically downwards all around where the lowest tier meets the bottom edge of the second tier. Take out a wedge from the bottom cake (see diagram) and cut it into slices. Continue this process with the middle tier, removing another wedge of slices until a cylindrical core remains. Cut the remainder in slices starting centrally from the top, working round and down.

American wedding cake

Traditional Wedding Cake

The lower tier of this handsome cake is unusually large, so that although there are only two tiers you can expect it to provide enough slices. Flat-ice the top of the lower tier before adding glycerine to the royal icing: it must be hard enough to take the weight of the top tier without cracking. For the best results, the cake must be kept at least 2–4 weeks, preferably up to 3 months, after baking.

One 33 cm (13 inch) and one 23 cm (9 inch) square silver cake board
1.5 kg (3 lb) currants
550 g (1¼ lb) sultanas
675 g (1½ lb) seedless raisins
350 g (12 oz) glacé cherries, quartered, washed and dried
225 g (8 oz) blanched almonds, chopped
300 g (10 oz) cut mixed peel
grated rind of 2 lemons
grated rind of 1 large orange
800 g (1¾ lb) plain flour
2½ teaspoons ground cinnamon
2 teaspoons ground mixed spice
½ teaspoon ground nutmeg or allspice
750 g (1 lb 10 oz) butter
750 g (1 lb 10 oz) dark soft brown sugar
12 eggs (size 1 or 2)
2 tablespoons black treacle
1 tablespoon gravy browning
about 150 ml (¼ pint) brandy
1 quantity apricot glaze (page 38)
1.6 kg (3½ lb) marzipan (page 37)

Royal icing:
7 egg whites
about 2.25 kg (5 lb) icing sugar, sifted
3 tablespoons lemon juice, strained
3–4 teaspoons glycerine
To decorate:
yellow and orange liquid food colouring
64 pale gold moulded roses (see page 63)
4 white square pillars

Preparation time: about 4 hours, plus making the roses
Cooking time: about 2¾ and 5 hours
Oven: 150°C, 300°F, Gas Mark 2

1. Grease and line an 18 cm (7 inch) and a 25 cm (10 inch) square cake tin (see page 14).

2. To make the cakes, put the currants, sultanas, raisins, cherries, almonds, peel and fruit rinds into a bowl and mix well.

3. Sift the flour with the spices into a separate bowl.

4. Cream the butter until soft. Add the sugar and cream again until the mixture is light and fluffy and pale in colour.

5. Beat in the eggs one at a time following each with 1 table-spoon of the flour mixture; fold in the remaining flour, then the treacle. Finally add all the fruit and mix well.

6. Put about two thirds of the mixture into the larger tin. Add the gravy browning to the remaining mixture and put it into the smaller tin. Level the tops and make a slight hollow in each.

7. Tie a treble thickness of brown paper or newspaper around the outside of the cake tins and place in a preheated oven. Bake (separately if necessary), allowing about 2½–2¾ hours for the smaller cake and 4¾–5 hours for the larger cake, or until a skewer inserted in the centre of the cakes comes out clean. Leave the cakes to cool in the tins and then turn them out carefully. Prick all over the surface with a skewer and pour over about half the brandy. Wrap in foil and leave for 2 weeks.

8. Repeat the dosing with brandy after 2 weeks and rewrap in foil. Leave for a further 2–4 weeks or up to 3 months before proceeding.

9. Prepare the apricot glaze. Use the glaze and the marzipan to cover both the cakes as described on page 38. A square cake is covered in just the same way as a round cake. Leave to dry for 3–4 days.

10. Make up the royal icing, in two batches for ease (see page 39). Place the icing in airtight polythene containers.

11. Position the cakes on the cake boards with a dab of icing. Put two flat coats of icing on the tops of the cakes (see page 40), omitting the glycerine from the first layer on the base cake. Leave to dry between coats.

12. Flat ice the sides of the cakes, working opposite sides at a time to get good square corners (see page 40). Spread some icing on to one side of each cake, making it as even as possible with a palette knife. Using an icing comb or palette knife draw the icing towards you, keeping it at an angle, and making sure the cake is stable to give it an even finish. Using a palette knife, cut off the icing down the corners in a straight line and also off the top edge and around the base of the cake. Repeat with the two opposite sides and leave to dry.

13. Add a second coat of icing to the sides in the same way and then give a final coat to the tops of the cakes. Leave to dry.

14. Draw a pattern for decorating the cakes. Cut a square of greaseproof paper the size of the top of each tier. Fold into quarters and then draw a parenthesis bracket sign on the paper across the corner (see diagram). Place this paper on the cake itself and prick out the shape with a pin on two opposite corners. Turn the paper round and prick out the other two corners. Half-fill a piping bag fitted with a medium writing nozzle with white icing and pipe over the outlines. Allow to dry and then overpipe.

15. For each corner draw a fancy 'W' shape on paper and prick out this shape on to the cake (see diagram). Pipe over the outlines and leave to dry, then overpipe.

Traditional wedding cake

5. On the sides of the large cake, make three evenly spaced marks along each side. On the small cake make just two marks. Using the writing nozzle and white icing, pipe two loops from each mark. When dry, overpipe. Attach three roses to the top of the centre loops on the large cake and two roses to the side loops and the loops on the small cake.

7. Using a small star nozzle and white icing, pipe a shell pattern all along the top edges of the cakes so it falls over the edge slightly. Leave to dry.

18. With the same nozzle and white icing pipe alternate small stars and elongated stars round the lower edges which reach about 2 cm (¾ inch) up the sides.

19. Tint a little icing a pale gold using yellow and orange food colourings and put into a piping bag fitted with a medium writing nozzle. Pipe loops between alternate shells all round the top edges.

20. Pipe a loop or double loop from the top of the elongated star to the next, round the base of the cakes. Leave to dry.

21. Attach a gold rose to the centre of each decorative 'W' on top of the cakes and another one or two at the lower corners of each cake.

22. To assemble the cake, place the pillars evenly on the lower tier and stand the smaller cake on top. Place a small flower arrangement of white freesias and/or small yellow roses in a tiny silver vase on top.

Use this template as a guide for drawing up the decorative pattern in step 14.

Three-Tier Wedding Cake

In purest white – apart from the centres of the daisies – and decorated with delicate lace-work, this magnificent cake is the perfect centrepiece for a grand wedding.

Three round silver cake boards 18 cm (7 inch), 25 cm (10 inch) and 35 cm (14 inch)
1 × 12.5 cm (5 inch) round, 1 × 20 cm (8 inch) round and 1 × 28 cm (11 inch) round Rich Fruit Cake (pages 24–5)
2 quantities apricot glaze (page 38)
2 kg (4½ lb) marzipan (page 37)
3.5–4 kg (8–9 lb) sugar quantity royal icing (page 39)
pink and green liquid food colourings
about 120 piped daisies with pink centres
about 25 white and pink butterflies
7 or 8 white cake pillars

Preparation time: icing and decoration of the cake, plus making and drying the daisies and butterflies

1. Brush the tops and sides of the cakes with apricot glaze and coat with marzipan (see page 38). Leave to dry.

2. Make up the royal icing in two batches for ease and place in airtight polythene containers. Attach each cake to the appropriate board with a dab of icing. Flat-ice the cakes giving three coats all over and a further coat to the tops of the cakes, especially the large one (see pages 40–41). Leave to dry for 24 hours.

3. Make the daisies (see p. 60) and butterflies (see opposite) and leave them to dry.

4. On thin card, draw three circles 2.5 cm (1 inch) smaller than the top of each of the cakes for templates and cut them out. Fold each circle into eighths, then draw a deep petal from the folded edge and a shallow curve shape (see page 51).

5. Place the templates centrally on each cake according to size. Carefully prick out the pattern with a pin on each cake. Remove the templates. Place some white royal icing in a piping bag fitted with a fine writing nozzle (No. 1) and use to outline the patterns. Pipe two further lines, one inside and one outside the first. Leave to dry. (Keep the piping bag in a polythene bag for later use; see step 7.)

6. Make templates for the sides of each cake. Take a strip of paper the depth and circumference of the iced cake and fold it into quarters, then in half again. Draw a shallow curve, then a deep curve to the folded edge keeping to about half the depth of the cake. Cut out, open up the papers and place them around the cake to correspond with the top design.

Prick out the pattern as before (step 5).

7. Using the white icing, pipe just inside the pattern using the writing nozzle. Pipe two further lines below the first.

8. To make the template for the cake boards, cut a circle the size of each board, then cut off 1 cm (½ inch) all round. Cut out a circle the size of each cake and discard. Fold the remaining rings into quarters, then eighths and draw a petal shape to correspond with that on the sides of the cakes but shallower. Cut out the pattern. Make one cut into each template and place them around the cakes on the boards. Outline the pattern with white icing. Leave to dry and remove the template.

9. Tint a little icing pale soft green or pink if preferred, and put into a piping bag fitted with a No. 1 nozzle. Use to overpipe all the centre outlines on the tops and sides of the cakes.

10. For the lacework, fill a piping bag fitted with a No. 0 nozzle with white icing. Work a lacework pattern (see page 58) to fill the spaces between the icing outlines on the tops and sides of the cakes and on the boards between the icing outline and base of the cakes. Leave to dry.

11. For the base border, fill a piping bag fitted with a large writing nozzle (No. 3 or 4) with white icing and pipe a border of plain large dots all around the base of the cakes to attach to the board.

12. To complete the decoration, on the small cake add one daisy to each point of the shallow curve on top of the cake, one at the join of deep curves on the sides and one centrally opposite the deepest part of each curve

on the board, attaching each with a dab of icing. Add two daisies in each matching place on the middle tier and three daisies on the large tier. Attach one butterfly (on each tier) on the top edge of the cake at the point of the curves and where the lacework joins the cake on the base. Leave to dry.

13. To assemble the cake, place four cake pillars evenly in the middle on the largest cake and place the middle tier on top. Place three or four cake pillars on the middle tier and put the small cake in place. Put a small arrangement of flowers in a silver vase on the top tier.

Simple butterflies

Draw the butterfly wings separately on a piece of stiff card, tracing from a picture if you can't manage freehand. Place a piece of non-stick silicone paper over the drawing and attach it firmly, so that it is quite flat. Using a writing nozzle and white icing, outline the wings. Thin a little royal icing with lemon juice or egg white until it just flows. Put into a paper icing bag without a nozzle, cut off the tip and pipe into the outline until it is filled. Prick any air bubbles and leave to dry. Repeat by moving the non-stick silicone paper over the pattern. Outline the wings in pale pink icing using a fine writing nozzle (No. 0) and pipe a little lacework over them. Leave to dry. To assemble: use pink icing and a No. 2 writing nozzle to pipe a squiggle the length of the wings on to non-stick silicone paper. Press on a pair of wings, one each side of the body, and leave to set.

Three-tier wedding cake

CHRISTENING CAKES

A christening is the happiest of family celebrations. Like a wedding, it's a time for champagne and a beautiful cake, one of the most welcome gifts you could make for the new arrival. An attractive way of adding the baby's name to the cake is to pipe the letters on little cubes of moulding icing like toy bricks and arrange them on top.

Christening Cake for a Girl

Christening cakes look best in pastel colours or in white. This pretty example with yellow roses is traditionally perfect for a baby girl. As the christening ceremony involves the bestowing of the baby's name, it should be a prominent feature of the cake.

One 25 cm (10 inch) round silver cake board
1 × 20 cm (8 inch) round Rich Fruit Cake (pages 24–5)
1 quantity apricot glaze (page 38)
575 g (1 ¼ lb) marzipan (page 37)
900 g (2 lb) sugar quantity royal icing (page 39)
yellow food colouring
100 g (4 oz) moulding paste (page 44)
about 40 piped yellow roses (page 60)
60 cm (24 inches) yellow ribbon about 4 cm (1 ½ inches) wide

Preparation time: icing and decorating the cake

1. Brush the top and sides of the cake with apricot glaze and coat with marzipan (see page 38). Leave to dry.

2. Make up the royal icing. Attach the cake to the cake board with a dab of icing. Flat-ice the cake, giving two coats all over and a third coat to the top if necessary (see pages 40–41). Leave to dry for 24 hours.

3. Make a template for an 8-point scallop (see page 51).

4. Tint about 2 tablespoons of the royal icing with yellow food colouring and put into a piping bag fitted with a medium writing nozzle.

5. Position the template on the cake and prick out the pattern. Outline the pattern using the yellow icing. Remove the template. Pipe two more outlines, each a little inside the former. Leave to dry, then overpipe the centre line, again using yellow icing.

6. Write the name of the child on a piece of paper and prick out the name a little above the centre of the cake. Pipe with yellow icing; when dry overpipe and leave to dry again.

7. Make the crib. Using about 50 g (2 oz) white moulding icing, mould the crib base. Use about 25 g (1 oz) white icing to mould the hood, and attach it to the base with a dab of water. Make a small pillow of white icing and place it in position. Tint the remaining icing pale yellow with a drop of yellow food colouring and roll it out to make a cover. Lay this over the base to cover it completely. Mark a criss-cross design on the yellow cover with a sharp pointed knife. Leave to dry.

8. Using a fine star nozzle and white royal icing, pipe a continuous twisted edging to the top of the cake so it begins on the side of the cake and just overlaps on to the top.

9. Using a medium star nozzle and white icing, pipe another continuous twisted edging to the base of the cake to attach it to the board.

10. While the base border is still wet, attach a yellow rose to every alternate twist. Leave to dry.

11. Attach a yellow rose to each point of the scallops on the top of the cake.

12. Tie the ribbon round the sides of the cake, finishing with or without a bow.

13. Finally, attach the crib with little icing so it stands inside the yellow outline just below the name.

Christening Cake for a Boy

If the child is being given a first name that is too long to fit attractively on the cake, use only the initials instead and design a monogram.

One 25 cm (10 inch) square silver cake board
1 × 20 cm (8 inch) square Rich Fruit Cake (pages 24–5)
1 quantity apricot glaze (page 38)
800 g (1 ¾ lb) marzipan (page 37)
1.4 kg (3 lb) sugar quantity royal icing (page 39)
green or blue food colouring
a little egg white, lightly beaten, or lemon juice, strained
silver dragees
1 metre (1 yard) white and/or mid-green or blue ribbon

Preparation time: icing and decorating the cake

1. Brush the top and sides of the cake with apricot glaze and coat with marzipan (see page 38). Leave to dry.

2. Make up the royal icing. Attach the cake to the cake board with a dab of icing.

3. Tint two-thirds of the icing pale green or blue with food colouring. Use to flat-ice the cake, giving two coats all over and a third coat to the top if necessary (see pages 40–41). Leave to dry for 24 hours.

4. Draw a small train with two or three carriages, or trucks, on non-stick silicone paper so it will fit on the cake. Place a little white icing in a greaseproof paper piping bag fitted with a fine writing nozzle. Outline the train and trucks and leave to dry. Thin a little icing with egg white or lemon juice until it flows. Spoon this into the outlines to fill them completely using a skewer to help guide the icing to the edge. Burst any bubbles which appear and leave until dry.

5. Write the child's name on a piece of non-stick silicone paper and prick out the letters in a gently curving line on the cake. Make a double outline using white icing and a medium writing nozzle. When the letters are dry, overpipe them and leave to dry completely. A neat row of tiny touching dots may also be piped on top of the outline of the name.

6. Position the train or trucks on the cake beneath the name and attach them carefully with a little icing. Outline it all with white icing, adding windows and wheels with simple spokes.

7. Pipe three straight lines in white icing in graduated lengths above the name and below the train, parallel to the edge of the cake. Pipe two small dots at the end of each line.

8. Using a fine star nozzle and white icing, pipe a zigzag border all round the top edge of the cake.

9. Work another zigzag on the side of the cake to join the first row and decorate the points with silver dragees.

10. Work a heavier zigzag border around the base of the cake, again decorating with silver dragees. Leave to dry.

11. Tie the ribbon or ribbons round the side of the cake, finishing with a bow, or attaching the ends of the ribbon with a dab of icing.

Christening cakes

VALENTINE CAKES

Whether it's tea for two or a romantic candlelight dinner, commemorate the day dedicated to lovers with a cake that is sure to melt the hardest heart. Here are two very different but equally delectable cakes designed to inspire undying affection from the object of your attentions – and what better reward for such a labour of love?

Chocolate Valentine Cake

This irresistible cake is made up of four layers sandwiched with strawberries, cream and grated chocolate, covered with melted chocolate cream, or *Crème ganache*. The crème should be poured over the cake while it is hot, so that it will set evenly. The Genoese sponge can be made several days in advance if kept in an airtight container, but once assembled the cake should be served on the same day.

One 23 cm (9 inch) round
    silver cake board
4 eggs
100 g (4 oz) caster sugar
100 g (4 oz) plain flour
25 g (1 oz) butter, melted
25 g (1 oz) hazelnuts, finely
    ground
300 ml (½ pint) whipping
    cream
50 g (2 oz) plain chocolate,
    grated
225 g (8 oz) firm strawberries
crème ganache:
300 g (10 oz) plain chocolate,
    broken into pieces
150 ml (¼ pint) double or
    whipping cream
To decorate:
chocolate leaves (page 68)
icing sugar, for dusting
    (optional)

Preparation time: 1 hour, plus cooling
Cooking time: 15–20 minutes
Oven: 180°C, 350°F, Gas Mark 4

1. Grease and flour two 18 cm (7 inch) heart-shaped tins, measured at the widest part.

2. Beat the eggs and sugar together in a bowl, then place the bowl over a saucepan of very hot (not boiling) water. Beat until the mixture becomes thick and creamy and leaves a

trail when a little of the mixture is pulled across the surface. Remove from the heat and continue to beat until the mixture is cold. (If using an electric beater, added heat is not necessary.)

3. Sift half the flour over the surface of the mixture. Add half the melted butter. With a metal spoon, fold in the flour using a cutting figure-of-eight action until all the flour has been incorporated. Repeat with the remaining flour, the hazelnuts and the remaining butter. Fold as lightly and as little as possible.

4. Pour the mixture into the prepared tins and tilt until the mixture spreads evenly over the tins.

5. Place in a preheated oven and bake for 15–20 minutes until the sponge is well risen and golden brown, and springs back when lightly pressed with

a finger. Turn out on to a wire rack to cool.

6. When the cakes are cool, split each heart into two layers. Whip the cream, fold in the grated chocolate and spread one third of the cream on one heart.

7. Reserve three strawberries with stalks for decoration. Slice some of the remaining even-sized strawberries to obtain 24 thin slices. Chop the remaining strawberries roughly.

8. Spread the chopped strawberries over the first layer of cream, smooth over a little more cream and sandwich with a second layer of sponge. Divide the remaining cream in two and sandwich the remaining sponges with the cream, ending with a layer of sponge. Stand the cake on a wire rack with a large plate underneath.

9. To make the *crème ganache*, place the chocolate in a heatproof bowl set over a pan of hot water. When the chocolate has melted, stir until smooth. Meanwhile, pour the cream into a separate pan and bring just to the boil. Gradually pour the cream into the melted chocolate, stirring vigorously until the mixture is smooth.

10. Pour the hot *crème ganache* over the cake and smooth it over quickly with a small palette knife. Leave to set for about 15 minutes.

11. Arrange the sliced strawberries in a row around the base of the cake. Place the three whole strawberries in a cluster on top and surround with chocolate leaves.

12. Leave the cake to set for about 2 hours. If liked, give it a very light sprinkling of icing sugar just before serving.

Above: Chocolate valentine cake

Sweetheart Cake

If the Chocolate valentine cake is dark and dangerous, this one is all sweetness and light! For a less formal effect, American frosting can be used for the icing. Swirl the frosting over the top and sides and make circular shapes with a palette knife.

One 30 cm (12 inch) round
*   silver cake board*
225 g (8 oz) caster sugar
225 g (8 oz) soft margarine
4 eggs
225 g (8 oz) self-raising flour
2 teaspoons baking powder
finely grated rind of 1 lemon
1 ½ quantities fondant
*   moulding paste (page 44)*
3 tablespoons raspberry jam
a few drops of red food
*   colouring*
icing sugar and cornflour, for
*   dredging*
To decorate:
royal icing for piping (page
*   39)*
frosted rose petals (page 66)
frosted mint leaves (page 66)

Preparation time: 35 minutes, plus setting time
Cooking time: 45–55 minutes
Oven: 160°C, 325°F, Gas Mark 3

1. Grease and line a 23–25 cm (9–10 inch) heart-shaped tin with greased greaseproof paper or non-stick silicone paper.

2. Place the sugar, margarine, eggs, flour, baking powder and lemon rind in a mixing bowl. Beat to combine the ingredients, then beat for a further 2 minutes until the mixture is light and fluffy. Turn the mixture into the prepared tin, making sure it is filled right to the edge. Smooth the top.

3. Place in a preheated oven and bake for 45–55 minutes, until the sponge is golden brown and firm to the touch. Turn out on to a wire rack, remove the lining paper and leave to cool before icing.

4. Split the cake in half horizontally and sandwich together with raspberry jam.

5. Tint the moulding paste pink with a drop or two of red food colouring. Roll out the paste on a work surface or a sheet of polythene dredged with a mixture of icing sugar and cornflour. Dredge the rolling pin with the same mixture. Roll to the width of the top of the cake, plus the sides, plus about 2.5 cm (1 inch) extra.

6. Support the icing on the rolling pin and place it centrally over the top of the cake. Press the icing on to the sides of the cake and down the sides, using a gentle circular movement to give an even covering. Dip your fingers in a mixture of icing sugar and cornflour while you work. When the finish is smooth, trim the base edge of the cake with a sharp knife. Place on a cake board and leave to dry for 24 hours.

7. Place two thirds of the royal icing in a greaseproof paper piping bag fitted with a small star nozzle and pipe a border round the top and base borders of the cake. Tint the remaining icing pink with a drop of red food colouring and overpipe the base border.

8. Decorate with frosted rose petals and mint leaves.

Above: Sweetheart cake

MOTHER'S DAY CAKES

A bouquet of flowers and breakfast in bed are essential gifts for Mother's Day, but it's a lovingly decorated cake that best conveys your affection. Whatever your skills, these two gâteaux – one simple, one splendid – provide you with the opportunity to say thank you in the sweetest way to the one who's at the heart of the family.

Daisy Cake for Mother's Day

This Mother's Day cake is decorated with an appropriately springtime air. The fondant and royal icings can be made in advance, as can the moulded daisies, but once assembled the cake should be eaten on the same day.

One 23 cm (9 inch) round
silver cake board
4-egg Victoria Sandwich Cake
mixture (page 18)
125 g (4 oz) strawberry jam
4 tablespoons apricot glaze
(page 38)
500 g (1 lb) fondant icing
(page 46)
125 g (4 oz) pink crème au
beurre (page 47)
50 g (2 oz) sugar quantity pink
royal icing (page 39)
To decorate:
18 moulded daisies (page 63)

Preparation time: 25 minutes
Cooking time: 25–30 minutes
Oven: 180°C, 350°F, Gas Mark 4

1. Grease and line two 20 cm (8 inch) sandwich tins with greased greaseproof paper or non-stick silicone paper.

2. Make up the cake mixture and pour it into the prepared tins. Place in a preheated oven and bake for 25–30 minutes. Turn out, remove the lining paper and leave to cool on a wire rack.

3. Sandwich the cakes together with the jam. Replace on the wire rack and brush the top and sides with apricot glaze. Place the wire rack over a large plate.

4. Place the fondant icing, divided into small pieces, in a basin set over a pan of hot water. Warm gently, stirring, until the fondant is smooth and has the consistency of thick cream. If the icing is too thick, add a little water.

5. Pour the icing over the cake, allowing it to run down the sides and tilting the cake a little if necessary to help coat it evenly – the icing should not be spread with a knife or the gloss will be spoiled. Leave to set, then trim off any excess icing. Place the cake on a board.

6. Place the crème au beurre in a nylon piping bag fitted with a 5 mm (¼ inch) fluted nozzle and pipe a decorative border around the base of the cake.

7. Place the royal icing in a greaseproof paper piping bag and snip off the end. Use the icing to write 'Mother' on the cake.

8. Arrange the daisies in clusters of three around the top edge of the cake. Using royal icing, pipe a looped border between the clusters.

Ideas for Children

A simplified version of the Daisy Cake can be made by children as a present for Mother's Day. A Quick-Mix sponge (page 16) is easier to prepare and rises well. Glacé icing is quickly made and easier than fondant icing, and can be tinted to a pale pink or lemon with food colouring. Instead of piping the name, 'Mother' can be written out with silver dragees and a border of sugar flowers arranged around the edge.

Mother's Day Cake

All the family will crave a slice of this sumptuous cake, even if it meant for mother. It incorporates a number of the techniques for using chocolate described on page 68. It's best to make a few extra rose leaves

One 23 cm (9 inch) cake board
4-egg quantity chocolate
Victoria Sandwich Cake
mixture (page 18)
2 quantities coffee buttercream
(page 46)
To decorate:
225 g (8 oz) plain chocolate
2–3 artificial flowers

Preparation time: about 45 minutes
Cooking time: about 20–25 minutes
Oven: 190°C, 375°F, Gas Mark

1. Make up the mixture and place in three greased 20 cm (8 inch) round sandwich tins, lined with greased greaseproof paper or non-stick silicone paper. Bake in a preheated oven for 20–25 minutes or until well risen and firm to the touch. Turn out and cool on a wire rack. Remove the lining paper.

2. Make up the coffee buttercream. Use some to sandwich the cakes together.

3. Spread a layer of coffee buttercream over the top of the cake and use a round-bladed knife to smooth the top with a backwards and forwards action. Turn the cake at right angles to the first lines and pull the same knife straight across in 7 or 8 equidistant lines to complete the pattern.

. Using a potato peeler, pare off mini chocolate curls from the block of chocolate, using about 150 g (5 oz) of it.

. Spread a thin layer of buttercream around the sides of the cake and carefully press on the chocolate curls, using a palette knife. Stand the cake on the board.

. Melt the remaining chocolate in a basin set over a pan of hot water. Take some clean, dry and unblemished rose leaves and paint the underside of each with melted chocolate. Leave to dry, add a second coat and chill thoroughly.

7. Attach a sheet of non-stick silicone paper to a board, then spread out the remaining melted chocolate on it. Leave until set but not quite dry, then, using a sharp knife and ruler, cut it into strips about 4 cm (1½ inches) wide. Quickly cut these into squares, then cut again to make into triangles. Leave to dry and set completely. Reserve the chocolate trimmings.

8. Melt the trimmings in a basin set over a pan of hot water and put into a greaseproof piping bag. Cut off the tip of the bag and carefully write 'Mother' across the cake.

9. Put the remaining butter-cream in a piping bag fitted with a large star nozzle and pipe a continuous twisted line of icing all around the top of the cake about 2.5 cm (1 inch) in from the edge.

10. Carefully separate the chocolate into triangles and place one between each of the buttercream whirls on top of the cake.

11. Peel the real rose leaves carefully from the chocolate ones. Arrange two chocolate leaves on either side of the artificial flowers in front of 'Mother'. Leave to set.

Opposite: Daisy cake for Mother's day
Below: Mother's day cake

CHRISTMAS CAKES

Of the many traditions observed at Christmas, few are as central as a suitably iced cake, bearing the season's symbols of holly, mistletoe and tidings of glad joy. Here are some inspiring variations on the green and red theme; but for a stunning new idea to ring the changes, see the delicately coloured cake with angels on page 114.

Square Christmas Cake

This impressive cake calls for a steady hand when applying the peaked icing on the side corners to make sure the ribbons stay clean. The rounded shape of the mistletoe leaves softens the angles of a square cake, but if you wished they could be replaced by the plaque bearing 'Season's Greetings' on the round cake.

One 25 cm (10 inch) square silver cake board
1 × 20 cm (8 inch) square Rich Fruit Cake (pages 24–5)
1 quantity apricot glaze (page 38)
800 g (1¾ lb) marzipan (page 37)
900 g (2 lb) fondant moulding paste (page 44)
a little egg white
icing sugar and cornflour, for dusting
To decorate:
about 20 green mistletoe leaves, 20 natural marzipan mistletoe berries and 4 green marzipan holly leaves (see opposite, step 5 and page 66)
450 g (1 lb) sugar quantity royal icing (page 39)
about 1.60 metres (1¾ yards) × 2 cm (¾ inch) wide red or green ribbon

Preparation time: to make, bake, marzipan and ice the cake and make the decorations plus about 45 minutes for the final decoration

1. Brush the cake with apricot glaze and use the marzipan to cover the cake (see page 38). Stand the cake on the board and leave for at least 24 hours for the marzipan to dry.

2. Brush the marzipan with egg white. Roll out the fondant paste on a surface dusted with icing sugar and cornflour and use to cover the cake (see page 44). Mould it to fit the cake and give a rounded edge on the top edge (not the sharp edge achieved with royal icing). Trim off around the base and smooth all over with fingers dipped in icing sugar and cornflour. Leave to dry for 24–48 hours.

3. Make the holly and mistletoe leaves and berries and leave to dry.

4. Make up the royal icing. Lay the ribbon diagonally over one corner of the cake, and then take it down to the base at the centre of the cake on the board and attach with a pin and a dab of icing. Take it up to the next corner and so on all round the cake. When you bring the ribbon back to the beginning, trim both ends evenly with an inverted 'V'.

5. Using a palette knife, add a thin layer of royal icing to the corners at the sides of the cake up to the ribbon, over the top edge corners of the cake and covering the cake board. Pull the icing up into peaks using the palette knife or a spoon handle. Take care not to get any icing on to the ribbon. Leave the icing to dry. (The rough icing may be added before the ribbon if preferred.)

6. Put the remaining royal icing into a piping bag fitted with a No. 2 writing nozzle and pipe a continuous looped border inside the ribbon on top of the cake. Leave to dry.

7. Attach a decoration of holly leaves and mistletoe berries and leaves to the centre of the cake with small dabs of icing.

8. Finally add bunches of three mistletoe leaves and some berries to the cake board where the ribbon meets it, attaching them with icing and removing the pins from the ribbon.

Variation

Make a marzipan Christmas tree cut-out to place in the centre of the cake and decorate around the cake with cut-out stars (see page 66). Press gold and silver dragees along the edges of the cut outs to emphasize their shape.

7. Carefully unroll the cooled cake and remove the paper. Spread all over with most of the whipped cream. Re-roll carefully and place on a foil-covered oblong board or a plate.

8. If you want a branch on the log, cut a 5 cm (2 inch) piece from the end of the cake at an angle and position it on one side of the cake.

9. To make the chocolate icing, put the chocolate and butter in the top of a double saucepan or heatproof bowl over a pan of gently simmering water, and heat until the chocolate melts. Remove the bowl from the heat and beat the mixture until smooth. Beat in the egg yolks and enough sugar to give a thick, smooth, spreading consistency. Spread the icing all over the cake, including the ends.

10. Mark with a fork or palette knife along the length of the roll and branch to resemble the bark of a tree and leave to set.

11. Put the remaining whipped cream in a piping bag fitted with a thick writing nozzle and pipe the filling on the ends to resemble rings. Leave to dry.

12. Sprinkle lightly with sifted icing sugar and decorate with holly leaves and berries and a robin or Christmas roses.

From the left: Chocolate Yule log, Ribbon and holly cake

Merry Christmas Cake

This enriched fruit cake mixture, with extra spices and brandy in the mixture, makes a Christmas cake to remember.

One 23 cm (9 inch) square silver cake board
225 g (8 oz) seedless raisins
225 g (8 oz) currants
225 g (8 oz) sultanas
100 g (4 oz) chopped mixed peel
50 g (2 oz) almonds, ground or finely chopped
50 g (2 oz) glacé cherries, quartered, washed and dried
grated rind of 1 lemon
225 g (8 oz) butter, softened
175 g (6 oz) light or dark soft brown sugar
4 eggs (sizes 1 or 2)
225 g (8 oz) plain flour, sifted
pinch of salt
1 teaspoon mixed spice
½ teaspoon ground cinnamon
good pinch of ground nutmeg
2 tablespoons brandy or sherry
3–4 tablespoons brandy for soaking (optional)
1 quantity apricot glaze (page 38)
800 g (1¾ lb) marzipan (page 37)
900 g (2 lb) sugar quantity royal icing (page 39)
To decorate:
red and brown food colourings
2 silver dragees
about 30 marzipan holly leaves and berries (page 66)

Preparation time: about 20 minutes plus icing and decorating the cake
Cooking time: 3½–3¾ hours
Oven: 150°C, 300°F, Gas Mark 2

1. Grease and double-line a 20 cm (8 inch) square cake tin with greased greaseproof paper or non-stick silicone paper.

2. Mix together the dried fruits, peel, almonds, cherries and lemon rind.

3. Cream the butter and sugar together until light and creamy.

4. Beat in the eggs one at a time, following each with a table-spoon of flour.

5. Sift the remaining flour with the salt and spices and fold into the creamed mixture, followed by the brandy or sherry. Add the fruit mixture and combine the ingredients well.

6. Turn the mixture into the prepared tin, level the top and make a slight hollow in the centre.

7. Wrap several thicknesses of brown paper or newspaper round the outside of the tin and bake in a preheated oven for 3½–3¾ hours or until a skewer inserted into the centre of the cake comes out clean.

8. Cool in the tin, then turn out on to a wire rack. Store in an airtight container or wrapped in foil until required. If using extra brandy, pierce the cake all over with a fine skewer and drizzle 3–4 tablespoons of brandy over it before storing.

9. To prepare the cake for decoration, brush the top and sides with apricot glaze, then cover with marzipan (see page 38), reserving about 100 g (4 oz) for the central decor-ation. Leave the marzipan to dry for a minimum of 24 hours.

10. Make up the royal icing and attach the cake to the board with a dab of icing. Flat-ice the cake all over, giving it two coats (see pages 40–41). Leave to dry.

11. To make the robin for the decoration, use 15 g (½ oz) of the reserved marzipan. Colour a small piece of it red and the remainder brown. Mould two small flat pieces for wings and mark feathers with a knife. Mould the remainder into a bird shape with head and pointed beak, and a tail. Use red

marzipan to mould over the robin's breast, up to his beak. Attach the wings, mark the tail feathers with a knife and add one silver dragee on each side of the head for the eyes. Leave to dry.

12. Roll out about 50 g (2 oz) of the remaining marzipan and cut to a rectangle measuring about 12.5 × 7.5 cm (5 × 3 inches). Position the rectangle on the cake diagonally across the centre and attach with a dab of icing at each corner.

13. Place some royal icing in a greaseproof paper piping bag fitted with a medium writing nozzle and pipe the words 'Merry Christmas' on the plaque. Pipe one or two outlines on to the cake to surround the plaque.

14. Colour the remaining marzipan red with food colouring. Roll it out thinly and cut out a small lantern. Attach the lantern to the plaque together with the robin, using a dab of icing.

15. Pipe three lines of 'corners on the cake making each a little shorter than the last one, using the medium writing nozzle. Ad dots to each corner and three more dots in a line towards the centre as shown.

16. Attach a set of three holly leaves with berries above and below the plaque.

17. Arrange a border of holly leaves and berries around the side of the cake, attaching each with a little icing.

18. Using a medium star nozzle pipe a sloping shell edging around the top edge of the cake, with each shell beginning on the top of the cake and ending on the side.

19. Use a thicker star nozzle to pipe a shell border around the base to seal the cake to the board. Leave to set.

Holly and Ivy Christmas Cake

The Christmas roses for this elegant cake can be made from bought fondant moulding paste (follow instructions on page 63) or piped freehand in royal icing, adapting instructions for Primrose, page 60.

One 20 cm (8 inch) round silver cake board
1 × 20 cm (8 inch) round Christmas cake (see Merry Christmas Cake, above)
1 quantity apricot glaze (see page 38)
700 g (1½ lb) marzipan (page 37)
900 g (2 lb) sugar quantity royal icing (page 39)
lemon juice or beaten egg white

To decorate:
5 Christmas roses (page 63)
4 marzipan ivy leaves (page 6. for template)
12 marzipan holly leaves and berries (page 66)

Preparation time: icing and decorating the cake

1. Brush the top and sides of the cake with apricot glaze, then cover it with marzipan (see page 38). Leave to dry for a minimum of 24 hours.

continued

From the top: Merry Christmas cake, Holly and ivy Christmas cake

2. Make up the royal icing. Attach the cake to the board with a dab of icing. Flat-ice the top of the cake only (see pages 40–41), giving it two coats. Leave to dry.

3. Draw a cross shape on a piece of paper the same size as the top of the cake, making the cross about 3 cm (1¼ inches) wide. Cut out the cross and place it on top of the cake.

4. Prick out the outline of the cross on top of the cake and remove the paper pattern.

5. Place some royal icing in a greaseproof paper piping bag fitted with a medium writing nozzle and outline the cross with royal icing. Leave to dry.

6. Thin a little of the royal icing with lightly beaten egg white or strained lemon juice until it just flows, then spoon it inside the lines of icing to fill the cross completely. Burst any air bubbles which appear with a pin. Leave to set.

7. Thicken the rest of the icing slightly with extra icing sugar, then use most of it to rough ice the sides of the cake. Pull the icing up into peaks all over, using a spoon handle or small palette knife. Let the peaks of icing just overlap on to the top of the cake to give it an edging.

8. Put the remaining icing into a piping bag fitted with a small star nozzle and pipe a narrow line of stars or shells to outline the cross.

9. Arrange a bunch of Christmas roses and ivy leaves in the centre of the cross, and holly leaves and berries along the spokes of the cross. Attach the decorations to the cake with a little icing. Leave to dry.

Santa's Stocking

This is an idea for a Christmas party cake for those who prefer a lighter Christmas cake but still favour marzipan. For a smaller stocking use a 28 × 18 × 4 cm (11 × 7 × 1½ inch) tin and a 4-egg quantity of Madeira Cake mixture. Bake for about 50 minutes.

1 × 5-egg quantity Madeira Cake mixture (page 19)
1 quantity apricot glaze (page 38)
450 g (1 lb) marzipan (page 37)
red and green food colourings
To decorate:
narrow gold, green and/or red Christmas ribbons
chocolate money
½ quantity vanilla buttercream (page 46)

Preparation time: decorating the cake
Cooking time: about 1 hour 15–20 minutes
Oven: 160°C, 325°F, Gas Mark 3

1. Grease and line a 30 × 25 × 5 cm (12 × 10 × 2 inch) tin with greased grease-proof paper or non-stick silicone paper.

2. Turn the mixture into the prepared tin and bake in a preheated oven for about 1 hour 15–20 minutes or until well risen and firm to the touch. Turn on to a wire rack and leave to cool.

3. Draw a 'stocking' on a sheet of paper the same size as the cake, following the diagram. Cut out and place on the cake.

4. Cut around the stocking shape with a sharp knife and place the stocking-shape cake on a cake board. Cut two or three parcels from the cake trimmings (see diagram).

5. Brush all over the stocking and parcels with apricot glaze.

6. Take three-quarters of the marzipan and colour it red with food colouring. Roll out between two sheets of poly-thene and use to cover the stocking completely. Make a few holly berries from the marzipan trimmings.

7. Colour half the remaining marzipan green. Roll out and cut out six holly leaves (see page 66). Use the remaining green marzipan to cover the largest of the cake parcels.

8. Roll out the remaining uncoloured marzipan and use to cover the other cake parcels. Tie the appropriate coloured ribbons round the parcels.

9. Position the parcels and chocolate money at the top of the stocking as if spilling out.

10. Put some of the butter-cream into a piping bag fitted with a thick writing nozzle and pipe 'Happy Christmas' along the stocking.

. Put the rest of the butter-
~~eam~~ into a piping bag fitted
~~th~~ a star nozzle and pipe
~~veral~~ rows of stars or shells at
~~e~~ top of the stocking to
~~present~~ fur.

. Attach the holly leaves and
~~rries~~ to the stocking with
~~ttercream~~. Leave to set.

Cut out stocking shape. Cut
'presents' from trimmings.

Snowman Christmas Cake

The evenly peaked rough icing
around the sides of this cake
provides a suitably wintry
looking setting for the little
snowman. The snowman and
the decorations for this cake are
made from fondant moulding
paste, not marzipan.

*One 25 cm (10 inch) round
silver cake board*
*1 × 20 cm (8 inch) round
Christmas cake (see Merry
Christmas Cake, page 110)*
*1 quantity apricot glaze (page
38)*
*700 g (1½ lb) marzipan (page
37)*
*1 kg (2¼ lb) sugar quantity
royal icing (page 39)*
*½ quantity fondant moulding
paste (page 44)*
*food colourings (red, green,
orange and brown)*
extra icing sugar, sifted

Preparation time: icing and
decorating the cake

1. Brush the top and sides of
the cake with apricot glaze, then
cover with marzipan (see page
38) Leave for a minimum of 24
hours to dry.

2. Make up the royal icing.
Attach the cake to the board
with a dab of icing.

3. Flat-ice the top of the cake
only with half the royal icing,
giving it two coats (see pages
40–41). Leave to dry.

4. Thicken the rest of the icing
with extra icing sugar, then use
most of it to rough-ice the sides
of the cake, pulling the icing up
into evenly spaced peaks with a
palette knife.

5. Tint one quarter of the
moulding paste green and use
to make into four cut-out holly
leaves (see instructions for
marzipan cut-outs, page 66).
Reserve the trimmings. Colour a
little of the remaining moulding

paste red and make some small
berries, reserving the remainder. Leave the holly and berries
to dry.

6. Shape some of the un-
coloured moulding paste into
two balls one larger than the
other, for the head and body of
the snowman. Press them gently
together. Make a hat with the
remaining red icing, and place
on the head. Tint a little of the
uncoloured moulding paste
orange. Make three thin ropes
of red, green and orange paste
and twist them together to form
a scarf, snipping the ends with
scissors for tassels. Wrap the
scarf around the neck of the
snowman. Make a nose with a
small piece of orange paste and
three buttons with red paste.
Colour a little of the uncoloured
paste brown and shape a
broomstick and eyes.

7. Place the snowman with the
broomstick in the centre of the
cake and make snowballs with
the remaining uncoloured
paste. Place the snowballs on
top of the cake in piles around
the snowman and arrange
groups of holly leaves and
berries around the top of the
cake. Dust the snowman with a
little icing sugar, for snow. Leave
to set completely.

Opposite page: Santa's stocking
Left: Snowman Christmas cake

Christmas Cake with Angels

It may depart from the traditional in shape and colour, but
this Christmas cake is still very
much in spirit with the season.
If you are unable to buy a cake
board of the correct size, cover
a board or a piece of thick card
with silver foil.

*One 33 × 18 cm (13 × 7 inch)
    silver cake board*
*1 × 20 cm (8 inch) square Rich
    Fruit Cake (pages 24–5)*
*1 quantity apricot glaze (page
    38)*
*900 g (2 lb) marzipan (page
    37)*
a little egg white, beaten lightly
*about 900 g (2 lb) fondant
    moulding paste (page 44)*
*icing sugar and cornflour for
    dusting*
*450 g (1 lb) sugar quantity
    royal icing (page 39)*
*yellow and blue liquid food
    colourings*
a little lemon juice (optional)
*90 piped snowflakes (see
    below)*
14 run-out angels (see below)

Preparation time: icing and
decorating the cake, plus
making and drying the angels
and snowflakes

1. Cut the cake in half, then cut
one piece in half crossways to
give two small squares. Stand
the larger strip of cake on the
cake board, brush one short
end with apricot glaze and
attach one of the small squares,
to give a cake of 30 × 10 cm
(12 × 4 inches). (Use the
remainder of the cake for tea as
it will not be needed here.)

2. Brush the top and sides of
the cake with apricot glaze and
cover with marzipan (see page
38). Leave to dry for 24 hours.

3. Brush the marzipan lightly
with egg white. Roll out the
moulding paste on a surface
dusted with icing sugar and
cornflour, and use to cover the
cake smoothly and evenly. Dip
your fingers in icing sugar and
cornflour as you smooth the
moulding paste over the cake.
Leave to dry.

. To make the snowflakes, make up the royal icing and, using a No. 1 writing nozzle and white icing, pipe out snowflake designs (they should have six sides but the patterns can differ) on non-stick silicone paper. Make about 90 and leave them to dry.

5. Make 14 angels (see right) and leave to dry completely.

6. Attach four angels with a little royal icing centrally to the top of the cake in a circle with the heads facing inwards, then attach one more at each end of the top. Next attach one angel on each short side and three

along each long side, all with their heads pointing in the same direction.

7. Using a No. 1 writing nozzle and white icing, pipe a series of slanting straight lines from the top of the cake over the edge, keeping them about 5 mm (¼ inch) apart. Leave to dry. When dry, pipe over the lines to give a trellis effect, taking them from the top of one line on the cake over two slanting lines and attaching to the base of the third one. Continue as evenly as possible all the way round the top edge and leave to dry completely.

8. For the base border, fill a piping bag fitted with a medium star nozzle with white icing and pipe alternate stars and elongated stars, which spread on to the cake board. At each corner pipe a very much larger pointed and elongated shape which reaches further up the corner of the cake and down on to the board.

9. Finally attach snowflakes with a little royal icing all around the angels on the sides and on top of the cake. Use tweezers to move the snowflakes and arrange them informally around the angel shapes. Leave to dry.

To make angels

Draw angel shapes using the template on page 62 on stiff card. Cover with non-stick silicone or waxed paper, then outline the various parts of the body with a piping bag fitted with a No. 2 writing nozzle and white icing. Fill in the hands. Leave to dry. Tint a little icing pale yellow with food colouring and put into a piping bag fitted with a No. 2 writing nozzle. Fill in the hair with a squiggly pattern and leave to dry.

Tint a little more of the icing pale blue with food colouring, then thin it down with a little egg white or lemon juice and put into a greaseproof paper piping bag without a nozzle. Cut off the tip and use to flood the dress. Leave to dry. Thin a little white icing with egg white or lemon juice and put into a paper piping bag without a nozzle. Cut off the tip and use to flood the face and wings. Leave to dry.

Christmas cake with angels

Miniature Christmas Cakes

*Four 18 cm (7 inch) round
   silver cake boards*
*1 quantity Christmas cake
   mixture (see Merry
   Christmas Cake, page 110)*
*1 quantity apricot glaze (page
   38)*
*700 g (1½ lb) marzipan (page
   37)*
*700 g (1½ lb) sugar quantity
   royal icing (page 39)*
*½ quantity moulding paste
   (page 44)*
*icing sugar and cornflour for
   dusting*
silver dragees
*food colourings (red, yellow
   and green)*
*1 metre (1 yard) Christmas
   ribbon*

Preparation time: icing and
decorating the cakes
Cooking time: 1¾–2 hours
Oven: 140°C, 275°F, Gas Mark 1

Gifts for Christmas

These little cakes – only
10 cm (4 inches) in diameter
– have a multiplicity of festive
uses. They make wonderful
presents for people living
alone, or to add to a
Christmas hamper full of
seasonal homemade fare. At
a special Christmas party for
all the family, why not make
a little cake for each pair of
guests? They are perfect for
Church bazaars too. Best of
all for the cake decorating
enthusiast, they give the
opportunity to try out a
number of designs on a
single theme.

1. To make the individual cake
cases, cut out 4 × 25 cm (10
inch) circles of double thickness foil and mould each
around the base and sides of an
850 g (1 lb 14 oz) can to make a
10 cm (4 inch) case. Remove
the can carefully and place the
cake cases on a baking sheet
covered with a double thickness
of brown paper.

2. Divide the cake mixture
evenly among the foil cases and
smooth the tops. Place in the
preheated oven and bake for
1¾–2 hours. Remove from the
oven and allow to cool slightly.
Remove the foil and leave the
cakes to cool completely.

3. Brush the tops and sides of
the cakes with apricot glaze,
then cover with marzipan (see
page 38), reserving the trimmings. Leave to dry for a
minimum of 24 hours.

4. Make up the royal icing.
Attach each cake to a board
with a little dab of icing.

5. Decorate cake 1: Flat-ice the
top of the cake (see page 40)

nd leave to dry a little. Rough-
ze the sides, swirling the peaks
vith a palette knife. Make a
emplate (see diagram) to fit the
op of the cake. From a sheet of
aper cut a circle 10 cm (4
nches) in diameter. Fold the
ircle evenly into 8 and cut off a
iagonal piece to form a star
hape. Open out the paper and
orick out the design on top of

the cake. Fill a greaseproof
paper piping bag fitted with a
star nozzle with royal icing. Pipe
along the outline of the star.
Press a silver dragee into each
point of the icing stars. Pipe a
star border around the edge of
the cake. Use moulding paste
trimmings from cake 3 to make
a Christmas rose (page 63).
Place in centre of the cake.

6. Decorate cake 2: Rough-ice
all over the cake with royal
icing. Use marzipan trimmings
to make holly leaves and berries
(page 66) and place three
clusters on top of the cake.

7. Decorate cake 3: Roll out half
the moulding icing on a surface
dusted with icing sugar and
cornflour to a circle large

enough to cover the top and
sides of the cake plus 2.5 cm (1
inch). Supporting the icing with
the rolling pin, place the icing
centrally on the cake and
smooth it into place with the
fingers, dipped in icing sugar
and cornflour. Trim the edges,
reserving the trimmings. Using
royal icing in a piping bag with
a plain nozzle, pipe 'Merry
Christmas' on top of the cake.
Colour a little royal icing red
and overpipe the letters. Use
the trimmings to make holly
leaves and berries. Tie a 50 cm
(20 inch) length of Christmas
ribbon around the cake.

8. Decorate cake 4: Roll out the
remaining moulding paste and
cover the cake as described for
cake 3. Use the trimmings to
make a red candle shape with a
yellow flame, and holly leaves
and berries. Finish by tying the
remaining length of ribbon
around the cake.

Variations

Some of the other Christmas
cakes in this chapter can be
adapted successfully to smaller
dimensions. Those that work
best in miniature are the
lacework round cake on page
98, the Holly and Ivy Cake on
page 100 and the Snowman
Cake on page 103.

Miniature Christmas cakes

EASTER CAKES

The festival of Easter brings to an end the sober days of Lent, heralding the spring with cakes for a great feast day. As well as a time-honoured Simnel Cake, try a delicious Gâteau de Pâques, glistening with crystallized fruits. And at summer's end, set a new tradition with a cake to celebrate the fruits of the field at Harvest Festival.

Simnel Cake

This cake derives its name from the Latin word for 'the best flour' used in it. Although long associated with Easter, in the seventeenth century this was the cake that young women in service made to take home on Mothering Sunday in March, showing off their culinary skills. The eleven small paste balls on top of the cake symbolize the faithful apostles of Christ.

225 g (8 oz) plain flour
pinch of salt
1 teaspoon baking powder
1 teaspoon ground cinnamon
¼ teaspoon ground nutmeg or
    mace
150 g (6 oz) butter or hard
    margarine
150 g (6 oz) soft brown sugar
3 eggs
2 tablespoons lemon juice
100 g (4 oz) raisins
150 g (6 oz) sultanas
50 g (2 oz) cut mixed peel
50 g (2 oz) glacé cherries,
    quartered, washed and dried
grated rind of 1 orange
450 g (1 lb) marzipan
a little apricot jam or egg white
To decorate:
about 1 metre (1 yard) of
    yellow ribbon about 2.5 cm
    (1 inch) wide

Preparation time: about 40 minutes
Cooking time: about 2 hours
Oven: 160°C, 325°F, Gas Mark 3

1. Grease and line an 18 cm (7 inch) round cake tin with greased greaseproof paper or non-stick silicone paper.

2. Sift together the flour, salt, baking powder, cinnamon and nutmeg or mace into a bowl.

3. Cream the butter or margarine and sugar together until very light and fluffy and pale in colour. Beat in the eggs, one at a time, adding 1 tablespoon of the flour mixture after each one. Fold in the remainder of the flour alternating with the lemon juice.

4. Combine the dried fruits, peel, cherries, and orange rind and stir into the mixture.

5. Spread half the mixture in the base of the prepared cake tin. Roll out one third of the marzipan and trim it to an 18 cm (7 inch) round to fit the cake tin. Lay the marzipan round on the cake mixture and cover with the remaining cake mixture.

6. Place in a preheated oven and bake for about 2 hours, or until cooked, and the cake has shrunk slightly from the sides of the tin. Leave to cool in the tin for 10 minutes, then turn on to a wire rack until quite cold.

7. Roll out just over half of the remaining marzipan to a round to fit the top of the cake. Brush the top of the cake with jam or egg white and position the marzipan on top. Mark a criss-cross pattern all over with a sharp knife and crimp the edge.

8. Roll the remaining marzipan into 11 even-sized balls. Attach them around the edge with a dab of jam or egg white.

9. Cut a strip of greaseproof paper the same width as the ribbon and circumference of the cake. Line the ribbon with the paper and tie it around the cake, securing the strip of greaseproof paper against the cake with a little jam and egg white to prevent the marzipan filling from staining the ribbon

Gâteau de Pâques

Pâques is the French word for Easter, but once you have tried this stunning cake you will want to use it for other special occasions.

2 quantities Genoese Sandwich mixture (page 22)
Filling:
450 g (1 lb) full or medium fat soft cheese
100 g (4 oz) caster sugar
finely grated rind of 1 lemon

300 ml (½ pint) double cream, whipped until stiff
To decorate:
Sifted icing sugar
a selection of crystallized or glacé fruits

Preparation time: about 40 minutes
Cooking time: 30–35 minutes or 1–1¼ hours
Oven: 190°C, 375°F, Gas Mark 5

1. Grease and line two deep 23 cm (9 inch) round sandwich or cake tins with greased greaseproof paper or non-stick silicone paper.

2. Make up the cake mixtures and put into the tins. Place in a preheated oven and bake for 30–35 minutes or until the cakes are well risen and just firm to the touch. Make up and bake the cakes separately if your oven shelf will not take both together.

3. Turn out on to a wire tray and leave until cold.

4. To make the filling, cream the cheese until soft. Add the sugar and continue to beat until light and fluffy. Beat in the lemon rind. Fold the whipped cream into the cheese mixture.

5. Split the cakes in half horizontally and use the filling to sandwich the four layers together.

6. Stand the cake on a plate and dredge the top heavily with sifted icing sugar. Arrange a ring of whole, sliced or pieces of crystallized or glacé fruits around the top of the cake and serve.

Variation

Flavour the cakes with the finely grated rind of 1 lemon or orange to each batch of mixture. For the filling: whip 600 ml (1 pint) double cream with 2–3 tablespoons orange liqueur until stiff. Peel 4 large oranges (free of white pith) and slice very thinly. Fill the split cakes with a layer of cream and then with orange slices. Assemble the gâteau and sprinkle the top with 2–3 tablespoons orange liqueur. Mask the cake in most of the remaining cream and press about 75 g (3 oz) toasted chopped hazelnuts round the sides. Pipe whirls of whipped cream on the top and decorate each with 3 toasted hazelnuts. Sprinkle a few chocolate mini curls (page 68) over the centre. Chill before serving.

From the left: Simnel cake, Gâteau de Pâques

Easter Egg Cake

These cakes are much more satisfying than hollow chocolate eggs! To make the smaller Easter egg use a 2-egg cake mixture and smaller dishes.

3-egg chocolate Quick Mix Cake mixture (page 16)
1½ quantities chocolate buttercream (page 46)
red, yellow or green ribbon
selection of marzipan flowers (page 64), e.g. daffodils, violets, and cut-out marzipan leaves

Preparation time: about 30 minutes, plus icing and decorating
Cooking time: about 45 minutes
Oven: 160°C, 325°F, Gas Mark 3

1. Divide the cake mixture between two greased and floured oval 600 ml (1 pint) ovenproof glass dishes.

2. Bake in a preheated oven for about 45 minutes or until well risen and firm to the touch. Turn on to a wire rack and leave to cool.

3. Use a little of the buttercream to sandwich the cakes together to give an egg shape. Stand the cake on a cake board.

4. Use the remaining buttercream to mask the whole cake. Smooth the surface with a palette knife.

5. Cut a strip of greaseproof paper the same width as the ribbon and lay across the cake, moulding it round as if the cake were tied up. Place the ribbon over the greaseproof paper. If preferred, complete with a ribbon bow on the side.

6. Arrange a spray of marzipan flowers and leaves on each side of the ribbon, attaching them to the buttercream. Leave to set.

Variations

The cake may be flavoured vanilla, coffee or any other flavour, if preferred, or a Madeira Cake mixture (pages 18–19) may be used.

For a children's party, make tiny individual egg cakes. Divide the Quick mix cake mixture between paper cake cases (see chart pages 16–17). After cooling, peel off the paper cake cases. Sandwich the cakes in pairs and coat them in chocolate buttercream.

Alternatively make up plain buttercream and tint it a bright shade of pink, green, blue or yellow. Then for a simple finish, roll the little eggs in coloured hundreds and thousands sweets or in chopped nuts. Brightly coloured sugar-coated chocolate sweets or white chocolate buttons could also be used as a covering to the buttercream, or use a mixture to make individual patterns on each egg.

The Healthy Sponge Cake recipe on page 22 could be subsituted for the Quick mix to give a more interesting texture to the little eggs.

Easter egg cakes

Easter Basket

The basketweave design on the sides of this cake looks complicated, and takes a little time to do, but once you get the rhythm of it it is relatively easy. Make the marzipan daffodils in advance if you wish.

100 g (4 oz) coffee Quick Mix Cake mixture (pages 16–17)
Chocolate buttercream:
2 tablespoons cocoa
2 tablespoons boiling water
100 g (4 oz) unsalted butter, softened
225 g (8 oz) icing sugar, sifted
To decorate:
75 g (3 oz) marzipan
a few drops of yellow food colouring
aluminium foil
1 metre (1 yard) narrow yellow ribbon

Preparation time: 20 minutes, plus making the decorations
Cooking time: 50 minutes
Oven: 160°C, 325°F, Gas Mark 3

1. Grease a 900 ml (1½ pint) pudding basin. Place the mixture in the basin and smooth the top. Bake in a preheated oven for 50 minutes until firm to the touch. Turn out on to a wire rack and cool.

2. To make the chocolate buttercream, blend the cocoa and boiling water to make a smooth paste. Leave to cool slightly. Place the paste in a bowl with the butter and icing sugar and beat to combine the ingredients. Continue to beat for 2 minutes, until the buttercream is light and fluffy.

3. Split the cake in half horizontally and sandwich the pieces together with a little buttercream. Place the cake, smallest end down, on a serving plate or board. Spread a little buttercream over the top and sides.

4. Place the remaining buttercream in a piping bag fitted with a ribbon nozzle. Pipe a basketweave design all round the sides of the cake (see page 59). Pipe a decorative border around the top edge of the cake.

5. Tint the marzipan yellow with a drop or two of food colouring and shape into daffodils (you will need about 20 – see page 64). Leave to dry a little and arrange on top of the basket.

6. To make the basket handle, take a strip of aluminium foil about 38 cm (15 inches) long and fold it over several times to form a thick strong band. Wrap with half the ribbon around the foil, securing it at each end with a little sticky tape. Curve the band into shape and place it on the cake, fixing each end to the icing. Make a bow on one side with the remaining length of ribbon.

Harvest Cake

Here is a splendid cake to celebrate one of the happiest festivals of the year. There's plenty of fruit inside, as well as the goodies on top.

One 25 cm (10 inch) square silver cake board
1 × 20 cm (8 inch) square Rich Fruit Cake (pages 24–5)
1 quantity apricot glaze (page 38)
800 g (1 ¾ lb) marzipan (page 37)
1 egg white
350 g (12 oz) fondant moulding paste (page 44)
a few drops of yellow food colouring
125 g (4 oz) sugar quantity royal icing (page 39)
icing sugar and cornflour, for dusting
To decorate:
an assortment of marzipan fruits and vegetables (pages 64–5)

Preparation time: icing and decorating the cake

1. Brush the top and sides of the cake with apricot glaze and cover with marzipan (see page 38). Place the cake on the cake board and leave to dry for a minimum of 24 hours.

2. Colour the moulding paste yellow with a drop or two of food colouring.

3. Roll out the moulding paste on a surface dusted with icing sugar and cornflour to make a 25 cm (10 inch) sqaure.

4. Brush the marzipan with a little egg white. Supporting the moulding paste with the rolling pin, place it centrally over the top of the cake. Smooth it over the top and down the sides with a circular motion, dipping your fingertips in icing sugar and cornflour as you work. Work the surplus to the base of the cake and trim the edges.

5. Colour the royal icing with a drop of yellow food colouring and place a little in a grease-proof paper piping bag fitted with a medium writing nozzle. Pipe the word 'Harvest' with a flourish across the top of the cake as shown (prick the letters out first if you wish).

6. Arrange the marzipan fruits and vegetables in a cluster in one corner. Place them carefully to occupy about a quarter of the cake, leaving about 2.5 cm (1 inch) clear at the sides to set them off. Group each type together balancing colour and size.

7. Place the remaining icing in a piping bag fitted with a 5 mm (¼ inch) fluted nozzle and pipe a shell border around the bottom edge of the cake to attach it to the board. Leave to dry before serving.

Opposite page: Easter basket
Below: Harvest cake

SPECIAL OCCASIONS

Many special days in life are made even nicer with a glorious cake. When you want to say congratulations on an anniversary, to wish a loved one good luck in a new venture or on retirement, or to celebrate a child's confirmation, choose one of these cakes. The designs can be adapted as you wish to suit a variety of different occasions.

Confirmation cake

*One 28 cm (11 inch) round
 silver cake board
1 × 23 cm (9 inch) round Rich
 Fruit Cake (pages 24–5)
1 quantity apricot glaze (page
 38)
800 g (1¾ lb) marzipan (page
 37)
1.4 kg (3 lb) sugar quantity
 royal icing (page 39)
deep purple or other food
 colouring
9 white piped roses (page 60)
6 silver leaves
white or silver and white
 4–5 cm (1½–2 inch) wide
 ribbon
For the Bible:
225 g (8 oz) marzipan (page
 37)
deep red food colouring*

Preparation time: icing and decorating the cake

1. Brush the top and sides of the cake with apricot glaze, then cover with marzipan (see page 38). Leave to dry.

2. Make up the royal icing and attach the cake to the cake board with a dab of icing. Flat-ice the cake, giving two coats all over and a third coat to the top if necessary (see page 40). Leave to dry for 24 hours.

3. To make the Bible, knead the marzipan and shape it into a rectangle. Place between sheets of polythene and roll out carefully into an open book shape, making a depression in the centre and at the ends as with an open book. This is done by pressing fairly firmly at each end, reducing the pressure until you come to the centre and then giving firm pressure in the centre again. Trim off the overhanging edges of the 'pages' and straighten the sides. Trim to give a border which represents the cover of the book. Make cuts into the sides of the book with a sharp knife to represent the pages.

4. Roll out the marzipan trimmings and cut them into a cross to fit one of the pages; position on the left-hand page and attach with a dab of icing. Using a fine paintbrush and deep purple food colouring, paint the cross and the 'cover' of the book. Transfer the book to a sheet of greaseproof paper and leave in a warm place to dry. If necessary, add a second coat of colouring.

5. Make a hexagonal template (see page 51), making the points about 2.5 cm (1 inch) from the edge of the cake. Place some royal icing in a grease-proof paper piping bag fitted with a medium writing nozzle and outline the hexagonal shape on top of the cake. Make two more outlines inside the first, leaving a small gap between them. Leave to dry, then overpipe the centre line.

6. Position the Bible a little above the centre of the hexagon and attach with icing. Using the writing nozzle, pipe words of your choice on the plain page of the book.

7. Write the name of the child on paper, then prick out the letters on the cake in front of the Bible. Outline this in white icing and overpipe when dry.

8. In front of alternate sides of the hexagon write the initials of the child; in front of the other sides, arrange a spray of roses and silver leaves, attaching them with icing.

9. Mark the top edges of the cake evenly into 12 or 18 portions, putting a small dot of icing on the cake and keeping it even with the lines of the hexagon on the top. Using a fine or medium star nozzle and white icing, pipe graduated twisted scrolls around the top edge of the cake between the dots (page 58) increasing pressure of icing in the centre of each scroll to make it larger and decreasing as you tail it off.

10. Work the same type of border round the base of the cake, making it a little heavier if preferred. Leave to dry.

11. Tie the ribbon round the side of the cake, with or without a bow.

Good Luck Cake

With its ornate icing patterns and delicate flower sprays, this handsome alternative to a horseshoe good luck cake could be used for other occasions with a change of wording (such as a 45th – sapphire – wedding anniversary).

*One 25 cm (10 inch) square
 silver cake board
1 × 20 cm (8 inch) square Rich
 Fruit Cake (pages 24–5)
1 quantity apricot glaze (page
 38)
800 g (1¾ lb) marzipan (page
 37)
1.6 kg (3½ lb) sugar quantity
 royal icing (page 39)
blue food colouring
little egg white, lightly beaten,
 or lemon juice, strained
length of 2–2.5 cm (¾–1 inch)
 wide blue ribbon
silver dragees*

Preparation time: icing and decorating the cake

1. Brush the top and sides of the cake with apricot glaze, then cover with marzipan (see page 38). Leave to dry.

2. Make up the royal icing and attach the cake to the cake board with a dab of icing.

3. Colour about three-quarters of the icing blue and use this to flat-ice the cake, giving two coats all over and a third coat to the top if necessary. Leave to dry for 24 hours.

4. On a piece of non-stick silicone paper write the words 'Good Luck'.

5. Place a little white or coloured icing in a greaseproof paper piping bag fitted with a medium writing nozzle and outline the words on the paper. Thin a little matching icing with egg white or lemon juice until it flows. Use this icing to flood the letters. Burst any bubbles that

appear and leave the words to dry.

. Place the ribbon over the cake as shown in the photograph and attach it to the board with a dab of icing.

7. Using a fine writing nozzle and white icing, work rows of lattice on the cake between the ribbon and the corners, taking care to start and end each row of icing neatly as it acts as a border.

8. Position the words of greeting on the cake and attach them with a little icing.

9. Using the medium writing nozzle and white icing, pipe sprays of lily of the valley on each side of the writing. This is done by piping slightly curved lines for both stems and leaves and then adding dots to each side of some of the lines to represent flowers.

10. Pipe two sprays of lily of the valley on each side of the cake in the same way.

11. Using a fine star or a rope or scroll nozzle, pipe a line of shells just inside the ribbons on top of the cake and along the top edge of the cake where there is no lattice. Place a silver dragee in between the shells on the lines across the top of the cake.

12. Pipe a heavier shell edging all round the base of the cake and down the corners. Leave to dry.

Good Luck Horseshoe Cake

This is a useful cake to include in your repertoire as it is appropriate for a number of occasions: a retirement party, a new job, moving house, an important exam or a new school term.

If you cannot find a horse-shoe cake tin, make a large round cake and cut it out as explained on page 53.

A lighter cake could be made with a sponge mixture and iced with buttercream or moulding icing. Such a cake would need to be eaten sooner than an iced fruit cake.

One 33 cm (13 inch) round silver cake board
1 × 25 cm (10 inch) round quantity Rich Fruit Cake mixture (pages 24–5), baked in a 25 cm (10 inch) horseshoe cake tin
1 quantity apricot glaze (page 38)
1 kg (2 lb) marzipan (page 37)
1.75 kg (4 lb) sugar quantity royal icing (page 39)
To decorate:
about 50 piped yellow roses (page 60)
24 small silver leaves

Preparation time: icing and decorating the cake

1. Brush the top and sides of the cake with apricot glaze and cover with marzipan (see page 38). Leave to dry for a minimum of 24 hours.

2. Make up the royal icing and attach the cake to the board with a dab of icing.

3. Flat-ice the cake, giving two coats all over and a third to the top, if necessary. Leave to dry. To cover the cake board, thin a little icing and place the cake on an icing turntable, smoothing the icing on to the board with a palette knife as you turn the cake. Leave to dry.

4. Fill a greaseproof paper bag fitted with a star nozzle with royal icing and pipe a coiled border round the top and base edges of the cake, stopping the base border at the inside straight edge.

5. Using a little royal icing, attach five clusters composed of three yellow roses and two silver leaves to the top of the cake at evenly spaced intervals. Attach pairs of roses and leaves to the sides of the cake, one cluster on the inside and a single rose with a pair of leaves at each end. Leave to set completely.

Good luck horseshoe cake

Golden Wedding Cake

All wedding anniversaries call for celebration, but 50 years is something special – and this cake rises to the occasion. The piped and run-out decorations are as delicate as they are beautiful, so make extra in case some of them crack in handling.

One 30 cm (12 inch) square gold cake board
1 × 25 × 15 cm (10 × 6 inch) rectangular Rich Fruit Cake (pages 24–5) or a 25 cm (10 inch) square cake trimmed to the correct size
1 quantity apricot glaze (page 38)
about 2.25 kg (4 lb) sugar quantity royal icing (page 39)
a little egg white or lemon juice
100 g (4 oz) fondant moulding paste (page 44)
gold dragees
about 1 metre (1 yard) narrow gold ribbon (optional)

Preparation time: icing and decoration of the cake, plus making and drying of the collars, plaque, numbers and fans

1. Brush the top and sides of the cake with apricot glaze and coat with marzipan (see page 38). Leave to dry for 24 hours.

2. Make up some of the royal icing and use a good dab to attach the cake to the board.

3. Flat-ice the cake giving it two coats all over and a third coat to the top if necessary (see pages 40–41). Leave to dry. Make up the rest of the royal icing as needed.

4. Meanwhile make the collars. On a sheet of paper, cut out a corner to fit the corners of the cake exactly. Draw a curved shape as in the picture which measures 4 cm (1½ inches) along each side. Cut this shape out and transfer the shape to a sheet of card. Also draw shapes for the collars for the long sides of the cake, which should be 5 cm (2 inches) long.

5. Lay a sheet of non-stick silicone paper over the collar templates. Using a No. 2 writing nozzle and white icing, outline them, making at least eight collars for the corners and four for the sides to allow for breakages.

6. Next place the paper collar templates around the base of the cake on the board and outline with white icing and the same writing nozzle.

Making the decorated run-out collars and numbers.

Golden wedding cake

Draw the figures 5 and 0 on
e card, cover with silicone or
axed paper and outline,
aking three of each, again to
low for breakages. (You only
ed one of each for the cake.)

Thin a little of the icing with
g white or lemon juice and
ut into a greaseproof paper
ing bag without a nozzle. Cut
f the tip and use to flood the
llars and numbers. Prick any
r bubbles that come to the

surface and leave undisturbed
until quite dry.

9. At the same time flood the
collar shapes on the cake
board, prick any air bubbles
and leave to dry.

10. Roll out the fondant
moulding paste thinly on non-
stick silicone paper and trim
evenly to a rectangle of approximately 12.5 × 5 cm (5 × 2
inches). Leave to dry
completely.

11. To make the fans, using
white icing and a No. 1 or 0
writing nozzle, follow the
directions for fans on the
Hexagonal Wedding Cake (page
92) but make the shape
different by piping four shallow
loops for the first row; three for
the second row; two for the
third and one final loop to
complete it, keeping the basic
pattern the same size and
shape. Make at least 40 fans to
allow for breakages. Leave to
dry.

12. When the collars are dry,
carefully pipe a series of dots all
around the outer edge using the
fine writing nozzle, and add
gold dragees to every other dot.
When dry, attach the collars
carefully to the corners and
sides of the cake with icing and
stand something underneath
them to hold in position while
they dry.

13. Pipe dots around the collars
on the board, again adding gold
dragees to every alternate dot.
Do the same to the 5 and 0,
adding gold dragees to every
alternate dot.

14. Using the medium writing
nozzle, pipe 'Happy An-
niversary' on the fondant
plaque. When dry, overpipe.
Leave to dry completely, then
attach the plaque centrally to
the cake with icing. (Measure
up first and prick out marks to
help you place the plaque
centrally.)

15. Stand the 50 up at the back
of the plaque and attach with
icing, holding it in position until
dry.

16. On a piece of paper, draw a
semicircle a little wider than the
side collar on the board and
prick it out on the side of the
cake. Take a piping bag fitted
with a No. 2 writing nozzle and
pipe a series of dots to outline
this shape. Also pipe a series of
dots all around the plaque on
top of the cake, adding a few
gold dragees if liked.

17. Using a piping bag fitted
with a No. 3 writing nozzle, pipe
a border of dots all round the
base of the cake except over the
run-outs. Next pipe a series of
small dots just each side of the
outlined semicircle above three
alternate dots, with two
graduated ones each side and
three in the centre. Pipe
another series of dots centrally
on the short sides of the cake.

18. Pipe a smaller border of
dots around the top edge of the
cake and a series of three, four
and three graduated dots on the
long sides under three alternate
main dots between the two
collars and centrally on the
short sides of the cake.

19. Finally attach three icing
fans in each corner of the cake
as shown, and three by each
central collar. Attach five fans
around each semicircle and one
fan at each corner, pointing
outwards.

20. Add a small bow of gold
ribbon at each corner on top of
the cake, if liked.

Variations

For a silver wedding, simply
change the numbers to 25 and
substitute silver dragees and
ribbon for the gold, placing the
cake on a silver board. To get a
good red for a ruby wedding
you will need to colour the icing
for the plaque, collars and fans
with a paste colour. Add a few
frosted red rose petals. The list
of wedding anniversaries and
corresponding materials is as
follows (though not all of them
are equally inspiring!).

Wedding anniversaries

1st	Paper
2nd	Cotton
3rd	Leather
4th	Fruit
5th	Wood
6th	Candy
7th	Wool
8th	Bronze
9th	Pottery
10th	Tin
11th	Steel
12th	Linen
13th	Lace
14th	Ivory
15th	Crystal
20th	China
25th	Silver
30th	Pearl
35th	Coral
40th	Ruby
45th	Sapphire
50th	Gold
55th	Emerald
60th	Diamond

BIRTHDAY CAKES

Everyone enjoys birthdays, no matter what their age, and seizes the opportunity for a party where the centrepiece is a beautifully decorated cake, such as the pretty one opposite.

The Sporting Birthday Cake on page 134 can easily be adap for a different purpose, while the most elaborate decoratio are reserved for special celebrations like an 18th birthday.

Square Birthday Cake

The fondant moulding paste used to cover this cake and to make the frill round the edge gives a soft finish so that the cake looks like a satin cushion with flowers embroidered on top.

One 25 cm (10 inch) or 28 cm (11 inch) square silver cake board
1 × 20 cm or 23 cm (8 or 9 inch) square Rich Fruit Cake (page 24–5)
1 quantity apricot glaze (page 38)
800–900 g (1¾–2 lb) marzipan (page 37)
a little egg white
900–1 kg (2–2½ lb) fondant moulding paste (page 44)
about 50 piped royal icing pink tea roses with white or pale green centres (step 3)
about 24 piped royal icing small pale green leaves (page 60)
225 g (8 oz) sugar quantity royal icing (page 39)
pink and green liquid food colourings

Preparation time: icing and decoration of the cake, plus time for making and drying the flowers, leaves and frills

1. Brush the top and sides of the cake with apricot glaze and coat with marzipan (see page 38). Stand on the cake board and leave to dry for 24 hours.

2. Brush the marzipan lightly with egg white. Roll out most of the fondant moulding paste and use to cover the cake smoothly and evenly (see page 44). Leave to dry.

3. Make the royal icing pink roses adapting freehand from the instructions for primrose (page 60) to give an open petal shape. Make the leaves. Allow to dry.

4. Make a template for the design of the flowers on top of the cake. Fold a 19 cm (7½ inch) square into a triangle, fold the triangle in half, then in half once again. Draw a small curve from the folded edge, then a deep petal shape to within about 2 cm (¾ inch) of the top of the paper. Cut out. Position the template on the cake and prick out the design.

5. Tint the royal icing pink to match the flowers and put into a piping bag with small writing nozzle. Outline the template.

6. Prick out the words 'Birthday Greetings' and the name of the person inside the piped line. Pipe over with pink or green icing. Let dry, then overpipe.

7. Arrange the pink flowers and green leaves over the outlined shape made by the template, attaching with a dab of icing.

8. Make a template for the sides of the cakes. Cut out a strip of paper the length of the side and two-thirds of the depth of the side. Fold into quarters and draw a shallow curve on it. Don't make this too deeply curved or it will be difficult to add the frills without breaking them.

9. For the frilling on the side of the cake, tint the remaining fondant paste the same pink or a little paler than the flowers and roll out thinly. Cut into strips about 2 cm (¾ inch) wide, then mark a line along the length of each strip about 5 mm (¼ inch) down from the top edge. Next, take a wooden cocktail stick and roll it gently from side to side below the marked line, to thin out the icing. This should make the frilling. Do not attempt to make the frills too long or they will break when you pick them up.

10. Fit the template round the sides of the cake and pipe a line of pink icing on to the side of the cake to follow the scallop lines. Attach the frilling to this line. Make joins as and when necessary by slightly moistening the ends of the frills, pressing together and rubbing over the joins with the fingertips. The frilling must be added while still soft or it will become brittle and be difficult to handle.

11. Using a medium writing nozzle and pink icing, pipe a series of dots all round the base of the cake to attach it to the board. Next, pipe another dot directly under the point of the curved frill just above the base dot, then a smaller one still above that. Add a fourth dot with the fine nozzle. Add two dots of graduating sizes above the dots each side of the central one; and one dot over the one each side beyond that. Repeat under all the points of the frills.

12. Add a pink rose and two small leaves by every other dot decoration on the board, so that the flower tilts slightly up the cake but the leaves are on the board. Leave to dry.

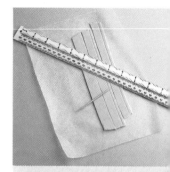

Strips of fondant moulding paste cut and ready to make the frills for the cake.

Gently rolling a tooth pick along the strips below the marked line to 'frill' them.

Square birthday cake

Eighteenth Birthday Cake

This elegant cake will delight the most sophisticated teenager. The effect is achieved with subtle colouring and extremely delicate piping of the trellis-work on top of the cake and the curtainwork attaching it to the board.

One 28 cm (11 inch) round silver cake board
1 × 20 or 23 cm (8 or 9 inch) round Rich Fruit Cake (pages 24–5)
1 quantity apricot glaze (page 38)
800 g (1¾ lb) marzipan (page 37)
1.25 kg (2½ lb) sugar quantity royal icing (page 39) or 350 g (12 oz) sugar quantity royal icing and 900 g (2 lb) fondant moulding paste (page 44)
peach liquid food colouring

Preparation time: icing and decoration of the cake, plus time for drying the run-out numbers

1. Brush the top and sides of the cake with apricot glaze and cover with marzipan (page 38). Stand the cake on the board and leave to dry.

2. Tint the royal icing a pale peach and use to give two coats all over the cake *or* tint the moulding paste pale peach and use to cover the cake (page 44). Leave to dry.

3. Draw the number '18' eight times on a piece of card, cover with non-stick silicone or waxed paper and run-out the figures. To do this, tint all the remaining icing a deeper shade of peach and put some into a piping bag fitted with a No. 0 or 1 fine writing nozzle. Outline the figures carefully. Next, thin a little of the icing with lemon juice or egg white, fit into a paper icing bag, snip off the end and use to flood the figures

(see picture, top right). Leave the numbers undisturbed to dry completely.

4. Make a template for the cake (see page 52). Draw a 19 cm (7½ inch) circle on thickish paper and cut it out. Fold the circle in half and draw a pencil line across the length of the semicircle 2 cm (¾ inch) up from the edge on each side. Next, fold the paper evenly to give three even portions. Open out and make a mark 1 cm (½ inch) each side of the folded line at the curved edge. Number these 1 to 4 working from left to right. Draw lines from points 1 and 4 to where the folds meet the pencilled line. Next mark the centre of the pencilled line and draw two lines from here to the curved edge to join points 2 and 3. Repeat on the other side. Position on the cake and prick out these shapes with a pin.

5. Using the writing nozzle, pipe out the name in the centre of the cake in the space between the pricked-out shapes. Leave to dry, then overpipe. When dry again, decorate the letters with a series of tiny dots, if liked.

6. Pipe two long lines under and above the name, making the one nearest the writing about 2.5 cm (1 inch) shorter at each end.

7. Using the finest writing nozzle you have, work a 5-row trellis to fill the shapes pricked out on top of the cake. To do this, first pipe a series of parallel lines beginning with the two outer shapes of each set of three and keeping in line with the lines already piped on top of the cake, just over 5 mm (¼ inch) apart. For the central shape outline it, then pipe lines parallel with the left-hand side. Turn the cake round and work the remaining three shapes in the same way.

8. Turn the cake back again and when the first piping is dry, pipe lines parallel to the other side of the shape, again spacing them evenly 5 mm (¼ inch) apart. Complete all the trellis in the same way. When dry continue to work the trellis up until you have five rows. If you find it very difficult to keep it neat and even, stop after completing three layers.

9. Fill a piping bag fitted with a small writing nozzle with deep peach icing. Pipe a series of small dots all around the top edge at about 2 cm (¾ inch) intervals to make a border. Pipe a loop from each of these dots.

10. Pipe a second row of small dots all around in between the first ones. Again work a row of loops from each dot, with slightly deeper curves than the first ones.

11. For the curtain decoration base, first make a template for the curves. Cut a strip of stiff paper for about 2 cm (¾ inch) deep. Fold into 4 cm (1½ inch) widths and cut out shallow curves. Open out the strip and place around the sides of the cake, so that it touches the board. Using the writing nozzle pipe a series of almost touching tiny dots all round to outline the curves. Remove the template and with a medium writing nozzle, pipe a border of dots around the cake to attach it to the board. Next with the small writing nozzle, pipe a series of dots all round the cake board about 1 cm (½ inch) from the end of the dots, matching one for one with those on the side of the cake.

12. With the fine writing nozzle work straight lines from the dots on the cake to the corresponding dots on the board keeping it very neat and even. Leave to dry.

13. Attach either six or eight number 18s evenly all round the sides of the cake with tiny dabs of icing. Leave to dry.

Drawing, piping and filling the outlines for the run-out 18s for the Eighteenth Birthday Cake.

Piping straight lines from the dots on the side of the cake to the dots on the board, to create a curtain effect.

Eighteenth birthday cake

Sporting Birthday Cake

This design makes a good general birthday cake for men and boys, but it is distinguished enough to be adapted for a 21st birthday or a clubhouse celebration when your team's won the cup!

One 25 cm (10 inch) square silver cake board
1 × 20 cm (8 inch) square Rich Fruit Cake (pages 24–5)
1 quantity apricot glaze (page 38)
800 g (1¾ lb) marzipan (page 37)
1.25 kg (2½ lb) sugar quantity royal icing (page 39)
yellow food colouring
a little egg white, lightly beaten, or lemon juice, strained

Preparation time: icing and decorating the cake

1. Brush the top and sides of the cake with apricot glaze, then cover with marzipan (see page 38). Leave to dry for 24 hours.

2. Make up the royal icing and attach the cake to the cake board with a dab of icing. Tint two thirds of the icing yellow with food colouring. Use to flat-ice the cake, giving it two coats all over and a third coat to the top if necessary (see pages 40–41).

3. Draw the outline of two crossed cricket bats and two crossed tennis rackets, a yacht or other type of boat, or a car about 5 cm (2 inches) high on a sheet of paper. These sporting motifs can be drawn freehand, or by tracing a picture of the correct size. Place the drawings under a sheet of non-stick silicone paper.

4. Fill a greaseproof paper piping bag fitted with a medium writing nozzle with white icing and outline the drawings five times each for bats and rackets or nine times for boats or cars, moving the pattern under the paper each time.

5. Thin about 6 tablespoons of the icing with a little egg white or lemon juice until it flows, then use to flood the outlines. Burst any air bubbles that appear and leave the run-out motifs to dry.

6. When dry, pipe details such as racket-strings, sails or car windows with white icing.

7. Using white icing and a piping bag fitted with a medium nozzle pipe two square outlines on the top of the cake about 2.5 cm (1 inch) in from the cake's edge. When dry, overpipe the inner square.

8. With the same nozzle pipe 'brackets' in each of the corners of the cake, making two lines of graduated lengths.

9. Midway between the brackets, along the sides, pipe five dots in a straight line. Then pipe three dots in front of these and finally two dots, one in front of the other in the centre.

10. Write the name or greeting on a piece of paper. Prick the words on to the cake and outline three times with white icing. When dry, overpipe and complete with dots. Leave to dry.

11. Using white icing and a thick writing nozzle, pipe a row of dots round the top edge of the cake. Pipe a second row on the side of the cake in between the first ones but so they just touch.

12. Pipe a row of large dots with a smaller one on top (by depressing the nozzle after piping the first part of the dot) all round the base of the cake.

13. Carefully stick a pair of bats and rackets or two boats on each side of the cake with a dab of icing. Leave to dry.

Draw the outlines for the tennis rackets or other sporting motifs. Pipe onto squares of non-stick silicone paper. Fill handle and frame outlines.

When you have filled in the outlines of the frames and handles, pipe in the racket strings working lengthways and across the frames.

Sporting birthday cake

NOVELTY CAKES

Everyone loves a surprise cake, while for the cake maker novelty cakes provide a wonderful opportunity to create imaginative cake designs. Most novelty cakes are based on a sponge cake mixture, but for simple shapes you could use a fruit cake mixture instead.

When the occasion calls for fun, a novelty cake is the right choice. This chapter shows that there is nothing that cannot be represented in the form of a cake: all it takes is a sense of adventure and a lively imagination.

The focus of attention at children's parties is always a cake, the more amazing the better, and their delight in a special creation is particularly rewarding to the cook. The range of ideas is limitless: a well-loved nursery rhyme character, perhaps, like Humpty Dumpty (page 148), a Fairy Castle (page 141) or a friendly Lion (150). Children particularly enjoy the results of your inventiveness when you choose a theme that is a special favourite of the birthday girl or boy, such as Ballet Shoes (page 146) or a Spaceship Rocket (page 156) – and the cakes are great fun to make.

There are many other occasions, not only for children, on which a cake that is out-of-the-ordinary adds a sparkle to the proceedings. The Flower cake on page 152 could be made for a garden party, mother's day or the summer meeting of your local horticulatural society. The Hat cake in the same page would also be fun for mother's day, or as a birthday cake for a teenage girl. While most men like cakes, they might not appreciate being presented with one that's covered with moulded roses. The Executive Case on page 145 would be much more appropriate.

The most versatile novelty cakes are in the shape of numerals, which can be used for birthdays at any age, for wedding and other anniversaries and any occasion at which a number is significant. By using different icings and decorations you can achieve any effect you please.

Most of the cakes in this section are based on the Quick Mix mixture (page 16, or use the Healthy Sponge recipe on page 22), with one or two Madeira and Whisked Sponge recipes. The cakes are baked in a variety of tins and moulds with the minimum amount of trimming needed to achieve a particular shape. As you work your way through the recipes you will realize how easy it is to construct special cakes from a few basic shapes. A butterfly, for example, could easily be made by cutting a round cake in half and turning each semi-circle round so that the curved edges are side by side. The Peppermint Racer (page 157) is one example of the transport theme which is perennially popular: fire engines, tractors, trains and boats can all be constructed on the same principle.

Soft cakes are easier to cut and shape if they are made one or two days before required. It is easier to cover with icing if apricot glaze is applied over the whole cake and left to set overnight. The most versatile icing is fondant moulding paste, which can be coloured in any shade and used to cover cakes and make models and fancy shapes. Buttercream provides a good surface for small decorations and is also used for the basketweave pattern shown on the Basket of Chocolates (page 142) and the Summer Straw Hat (page 153). If you want to give buttercream a smooth surface, use a small palette knife dipped into hot water.

If you cannot buy a cake board of the size and shape you need, cut several thicknesses of cardboard to the required size and cover the built-up board with foil. You can also use a wooden board or chopping block, covered with foil.

The techniques in this chapter can easily be adapted to other novelty ideas – a cake that looks like a book or a golf-course, a maypole or a bottle of champagne. Half the fun lies in thinking up the ideas. And once you have discovered the delights of making novelty cakes, your talents are sure to be much in demand.

Numeral Birthday Cakes

These cakes are especially fun for children and can be decorated in many ways to incorporate a hobby or child's special fancy. For a formally iced cake using marzipan and royal icing, a Rich Fruit Cake (page 24) can be used. Numeral cakes are fun for jubilee celebrations, length of service parties, retirements, or the number of a new house. They make good anniversary cakes, especially for 25, 40 and 50 years. For a 40th or ruby wedding cake, decorate with chocolate butter cream, glacé cherries and grated chocolate or chocolate curls.

Quick Mix Cakes (pages 16–17) or Madeira Cakes (page 19)
225 g (8 oz) jam or ¼ quantity buttercream, if necessary, for sandwiching cakes together
1¾–2 quantities buttercream (page 46)
food colouring and flavouring (optional)
candles and candle holders (optional)
jelly sweets (optional)
marzipan flowers (page 64)
marzipan leaves (page 63)

Preparation time: icing and decorating the cakes

1. If using pairs of cakes sandwich them together with the jam or buttercream. Place on a cake board of the appropriate size.

2. Tint the buttercream and add flavouring, if using. Use to mask the whole cake, perhaps finishing with a swirling design all over or backwards and forwards lines made with a round-bladed knife.

3. Tint the remaining buttercream a darker shade and put into a piping bag fitted with a star nozzle. Use to pipe a shell or star edging round the top edge and base of the cake.

4. Stick candles at intervals on the top of the cake. Alternatively, put seedless or sieved jam into a greaseproof paper piping bag (see page 56), without a nozzle, then cut off the tip. Pipe a message on the top of the cakes.

5. Stick jelly sweets in a line round the sides, or pipe stars of buttercream.

6. Finally, position the marzipan flowers and leaves on top of the cakes, attaching with buttercream. Leave to set.

Shaping Numeral Cakes

Nought: bake one 23–30 cm (9–12 inch) round cake. When cold cut a 7.5–12.5 cm (3–5 inch) diameter hole in centre.

One: bake one 15 cm (6 inch) square sandwich cake. Cut in half and position one piece above the other.

Two: bake one 29 × 21 × 4 cm (11½ × 8½ × 1½ inch) slab cake or a 30 × 25 × 5 cm (12 × 10 × 2 inch) cake. Cut a pattern, transfer to the cake and cut out.

Three: bake two 20 cm (8 inch) round sandwich cakes. Cut out a pattern, transfer to the cakes and cut out. Stick the two cakes together with jam or butter cream.

Four: bake one 18–25 cm (7–10 inch) square sandwich cake. Cut out a pattern, transfer to the cake and cut out, taking care when removing the middle piece.

Five: bake one 29 × 21 × 4 cm (11½ × 8½ × 1½ inch) slab cake or one 30 × 25 × 5 cm (12 × 10 × 2 inch) cake. Cut a pattern, transfer to the cake and cut out.

Six or Nine: bake one 29 × 21 × 4 cm (11½ × 8½ × 1½ inch) slab cake or one 30 × 25 × 5 cm (12 × 10 × 2 inch) cake. Cut a pattern, transfer to the cake and cut out.

Seven: bake one 18–25 cm (7–10 inch) square cake, or bake one 29 × 21 × 4 cm (11½ × 8½ × 1½ inch) or one 30 × 25 × 5 cm (12 × 10 × 2 inch) slab cake. Cut out a pattern, position on the cake and cut out.

Eight: bake two 20 cm (8 inch) round sandwich cakes. Cut out a pattern with a 7.5–9 cm (3–3½ inch) circle out of the centre. Transfer to the cakes and cut out. Trim a piece off the side of each cake and sandwich together with jam or butter-cream to make an eight.

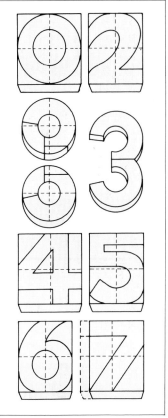

Numeral birthday cakes

Pirates' Treasure Chest

This cake sums up the best of 'novelty' cakes in that it is as much fun to make as it is to serve – it won't be long before the party guests have run off with the treasure!

One 25 cm (10 inch) square gold cake board
3-egg quantity orange-flavoured Quick Mix Cake mixture (pages 16–17)
100 g (4 oz) chocolate dots
50 g (2 oz) chocolate and hazelnut spread
gold dragees
1 chocolate-covered mini Swiss roll
jelly diamond cake decorations
2 tablespoons apricot jam, warmed and sieved
coffee sugar crystals, for sprinkling
assorted sweets, including foil-covered chocolate coins, sweet 'jewellery' and gold 'bullion'
pirates' treasure map (optional)

Opposite page: Sugar plum fairy castle
Below: Pirates' treasure chest

Preparation time: icing and decorating the cake
Cooking time: about 55 minutes
Oven: 160°C, 325°F, Gas Mark 3

1. Grease and line a 1 kg (2 lb) or 1.5 litre (2½ pint) loaf tin with greased greaseproof paper or non-stick silicone paper.

2. Make the cake mixture and stir in the chocolate dots. Pour into the prepared tin and bake for about 55 minutes, until golden brown and firm to the touch. Turn out on to a wire rack. Remove the lining paper and leave the cake the right way up to cool.

3. Cut a horizontal slice about 1 cm (½ inch) deep from the top of the cake to make the lid of the chest, and trim a narrow strip off one long side. Spread the sides of the base of the chest with chocolate and hazelnut spread. Place on the cake board.

4. Spread the top of the lid with chocolate and hazelnut spread, leaving the underside un-covered. Using clean tweezers, arrange a row of dragees around the top and bottom edges of the base and the lid and down each corner.

5. Cut a thick slice from the flat side of the Swiss roll, then place the roll lengthways on top of the base, towards the front of the centre. Place the lid on the base, with the trimmed side at the back. (The Swiss roll will help to keep it open.) Decorate the top of the lid with rows of jelly diamonds.

6. Spread the area around the base of the cake with jam and sprinkle with sugar crystals. Stuff the chest with chocolate coins and sweet 'jewellery'. Place a pile of coins, bullion and sweets around the base of the chest. Place the map, if using, on the board with a gold coin or two to hold it in place.

Sugar Plum Fairy Castle

One 30 cm (12 inch) fluted round silver cake board
6-egg quantity Whisked Sponge Cake mixture (pages 20–21)
6 tablespoons apricot glaze (page 38)
1½ quantity fondant moulding paste (page 44)
pink food colouring
50 g (2 oz) quantity Quick Mix Cake mixture (pages 16–17)
400 g (14 oz) sugar
2 teaspoons cold water
cornflour for sprinkling
pink food colouring pen
225 g (8 oz) sugared almonds

Preparation time: 1 hour, plus cooling and drying
Cooking time: 40 minutes
Oven: 180°C, 350°F, Gas Mark 4

1. Place two thirds of the whisked sponge mixture in a greased, greaseproof paper-lined 33 × 23 cm (13 × 9 inch) Swiss roll tin, and one third of the mixture in a greased, greaseproof paper-lined 28 × 18 cm (11 × 7 inch) Swiss roll tin. Bake in a preheated oven for 15–20 minutes until well risen and firm to the touch.

2. Use some of the apricot glaze as filling and roll up following the instructions for making a Swiss roll (page 20) but roll the smaller Swiss roll lengthways to make a long thin roll.

3. Make the fondant moulding paste and tint it very pale pink with a few drops of food colouring, then wrap it in cling film.

4. Place the quick mix cake mixture in a greased, grease-proof paper-lined 20 cm (8 inch) sandwich tin and bake in a preheated oven for 15–20 minutes until well risen and firm to the touch. Turn out and cool on a wire rack.

5. Place the sugar in a bowl and add a drop of pink food colouring to tint it the same colour as the fondant moulding paste. Reserve one third of the sugar and add the water to the remainder. Mix well together so that the sugar becomes damp.

6. Make three cone shapes out of paper (see small photograph opposite). Fill the large cone with the dampened sugar and press firmly down. Place a piece of card over the top and invert the sugar cone, then remove the paper shape. Use the other two papers to make one medium and two small cones and leave in a warm place to dry hard.

Trim the ends of each Swiss roll, so that they are level. Cut one third off each roll to make your towers all of different heights (see diagram).

Unwrap the moulding paste and cut it into five pieces. Roll out one piece thinly on a surface well sprinkled with cornflour, the width of the largest roll and long enough to roll completely around it.

Brush the roll with some of the remaining apricot glaze. Place it on the moulding paste, trim the moulding paste to fit, then roll up, carefully sealing the join by rubbing over it with fingers dipped in cornflour. Repeat to cover the remaining rolls. Knead and re-roll the trimmings.

0. Place the reserved sugar on a piece of greaseproof paper and roll each iced roll in it to coat evenly. Leave to dry.

1. Place the round cake on the cake board and, using plain cutters the same size as the base of each roll, cut out and remove four rounds (these will not be needed).

2. Brush the cake with some more of the apricot glaze and roll out the remaining moulding paste to a circle large enough to cover the round cake. Place the moulding paste over the cake, and gently press it into the holes. Smooth over and trim off the excess at the base. Sprinkle the moulding paste and cake board with the remaining pink-tinted sugar.

3. Place each pink tower in position in the cut-out holes and carefully place the sugar ones on top of each.

4. Make the windows and doors for the towers with the fondant moulding paste trimmings (as in the main photograph) and use the pink pen to mark the lattice work

and door panels. Place these in position and secure with the remaining apricot glaze.

15. Arrange the sugared almonds like a path and steps into the castle.

Using a paper cone to make the castle's sugar towers.

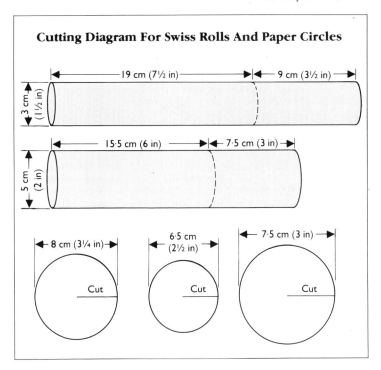
Cutting Diagram For Swiss Rolls And Paper Circles

Basket of Chocolates

Here is a sure way to a chocolate-lover's heart. Take your time building up the basketweave pattern and you will find it easy once you have done three or four lines.

One 28 cm (11 inch) round or heart-shaped heavy gold board
1 × 20–23 cm (8–9 inch) heart-shaped Quick Mix Cake (pages 16–17) or Madeira Cake (page 19) (baked in a heart-shaped tin or cut to shape, see page 53)
brown food colouring
about 175 g (6 oz) fondant moulding paste (page 44)
1 quantity apricot glaze (page 38)
1–2 tablespoons coffee essence (optional)
2 quantities buttercream (page 46)
about 350 g (¾ lb) assorted luxury chocolates
1 large gold bow
1 artificial flower

Preparation time: to make the cake, icing etc. and about 1 hour for the final decoration

1. Add a touch of brown food colouring to the fondant paste to tint it to a pale coffee colour. Roll out the paste on a surface dusted with cornflour and icing sugar and cut to a heart shape the same size as the cake. Cut in half down the centre, place on a sheet of non-stick silicone paper and leave to dry in a warm place.

2. Stand the cake on the board. Brush the cake all over with apricot glaze.

3. Add a touch of brown food colouring or coffee essence to tint the buttercream a pale coffee colour to match the lid. Spread a thin layer of buttercream over the top of the cake and neaten with a palette knife.

4. To work the basketweave, fit one piping bag with a basketweave nozzle and another with a No. 2 writing nozzle and fill both with buttercream. Beginning at the indentation at the back of the cake and holding the basketweave nozzle at an angle to the cake, pipe three or more horizontal lines about 2.5 cm (1 inch) long, one above the other and with the width of the nozzle left between them. Next, with the writing nozzle pipe a straight vertical line down the edge of the horizontal ribbon lines. Take the basket nozzle again and pipe more lines the same length as the first ones to fill the gaps but beginning halfway along those already piped and covering the straight lines. Pipe another straight vertical line down the edge and continue to build up the basketweave around the sides of the cake in this way, taking care to keep it even.

5. Work basketweave in the same way on the dried fondant paste heart pieces for the lid, and pipe a squiggly line with the writing nozzle around the edge. Leave to dry.

6. Arrange the chocolates (in their paper cases if preferred) around the top edge of the cake. Build up with more chocolates on the front half of the cake, but leave the centre empty.

7. Carefully place the lids on the cake sticking the cut edge into the centre and allowing the lids to rest on the chocolates as if they are peeping out. Place the gold ribbon bow and the flower in the centre of the lid.

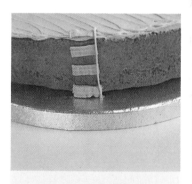

The first step in making the basket weave pattern.

Building up the basket weave pattern round the cake.

Basket of chocolates

Hickory Dickory Dock Cake

If you cannot find a cake board of the right size for this large cake, cover a tray or chopping board with silver foil.

One 50 × 25 cm (20 × 10 inch) silver cake board
4-egg quantity Quick Mix Cake mixture (pages 16–17)
1 quantity fondant moulding paste (page 44)
a few drops of red food colouring
3 tablespoons bramble jelly, warmed and melted
225 g (8 oz) icing sugar, sifted
boiling water
chocolate buttons
2–4 silver dragees (optional)
cornflour and icing sugar, for dusting
75 g (3 oz) desiccated coconut

Preparation time: icing and decorating the cake, plus drying time
Cooking time: 35–40 minutes
Oven: 160°C, 325°F, Gas Mark 3

1. Grease and line a 20 cm (8 inch) round sandwich tin and an 18 cm (7 inch) square cake tin with greased greaseproof paper or non-stick silicone paper. Divide the cake mixture between the tins. Place in the preheated oven and bake for 35–40 minutes, until golden brown and firm to the touch.

2. Turn the cakes out on to a wire rack, remove the lining paper and leave to cool completely.

3. Knead the moulding paste to make it pliable. Reserve a piece to make a mouse (or two small mice if you want to show the mouse running down the clock as well as up). Tint the remainder of the moulding paste pale pink with a drop or two of red food colouring.

4. Using a 20 cm (8 inch) round cake tin or plate as a guide, cut a curved edge from one side of the square cake so that it fits snugly against the round cake. Separate the cakes and brush the top and sides of each with warm bramble jelly.

5. Divide the pink fondant moulding paste in half. Roll out each half on a surface dusted with cornflour and icing sugar and use to cover both cakes, fitting it carefully around the sides. Place the two cakes on the tray and fit together.

6. Spread a little warm bramble jelly on the board and sprinkle desiccated coconut evenly over.

7. To make the piping icing, put three-quarters of the icing sugar into a bowl with a little boiling water and stir to give a stiff piping consistency. Beat until smooth. Place the icing in a greaseproof paper piping bag fitted with a star or shell nozzle and pipe shells around the top of the round cake and the three edges of the square cake. Pipe a border of shells around the base of both cakes.

8. Attach a chocolate button to the centre of the round cake and place 12 buttons around the edge. Mix the remaining icing sugar with a little water to give a piping consistency and place in a piping bag fitted with a thin writing nozzle. Pipe numbers on the buttons and clock hands set at one o'clock.

9. Pipe two zigzag lines of icing on the lower cake to form the pendulum and finish it with two chocolate buttons.

10. Shape the reserved un-coloured piece of moulding icing into the mouse or mice. Press in silver dragees (if using) for eyes. Place on the lower cake as shown.

Hickory Dickory dock cake
Opposite page: Executive case

Executive Case

e 20 cm (8 inch) square thin
silver cake board
egg quantity Coffee Quick Mix
Cake mixture (pages 16–17)
quantity fondant moulding
paste (page 44)
od colourings (red, green,
blue and gold)
tablespoons apricot glaze
(page 38)
oblong wafer biscuit
ck food colouring pen
blackcurrant candy stick
sheets of rice paper

eparation time: 40 minutes,
us setting
ooking time: 50–55 minutes
ven: 160°C, 325°F, Gas Mark 3

Place the cake mixture in a
eased and lined 26 × 19 × 5 cm
0½ × 7½ × 2 inch) oblong tin
d bake in a preheated oven
r 50–55 minutes until well
en and firm to the touch.
rn out of the tin, remove the
per and cool on a wire rack.

Make the moulding paste.
serve a small piece and
lour the remainder a deep
own colour by adding red,
een and a touch of blue food
lourings.

Cut the cake in half across
e width, sandwich together
th apricot glaze and trim the
p square. Brush with apricot
aze and place upright on the
ke board.

Roll out one third of the dark
rown coloured moulding
aste to a 13 cm (5 inch)
quare. Cut the square in half
d place each piece down the
de of the case. Carefully trim
ong the edges to fit.

Roll out the remaining piece
f dark brown paste large
ough to cover the front, top
d back of the case. Carefully
t the paste over the case and
im to fit, neatly joining the
ges together.

6. Mark a line across the top
and down the side for the
opening seam.

7. Cover the biscuit with
trimmings of brown moulding
paste for the handle. Roll,
cut and trim a 4 cm (1½ inch)
square for the label.

8. Roll out the white moulding
paste and cut out two locks,
two handle supports and the

initials and paint with gold food
colouring. Leave to set. Cut out
the name tag from white paste.
Reserve the trimmings. (See
diagram, bottom.)

9. Secure the locks, the handle
and supports in place with a
little glaze. With a food colouring pen, write the name and
address of the person on the
white plaque then stick together
with the label.

10. Fix the label in position
under the handle.

11. Re-roll the dark brown
moulding paste trimmings into
a 15 cm (6 inch) round. Place
the candy stick in the centre,
then pleat the remaining paste
around like an umbrella (see
pictures, right).

12. With the remaining white
icing, make a handle and top for
the umbrella and trim with gold
food colouring. Leave to set,
then place on the cake board.

13. Using the rice paper and
colouring pen, make a newspaper and write the day and
date of the celebration,
favourite newspaper title and a
few lines written in columns.
Place by the case.

Set out the candy stick, brown
moulding paste round, and
white handle and top.

Pleating the circle of fondant
moulding paste for the
umbrella.

**Cutting Diagram For Locks
And Handle**

Handle

7·5 cm (3 inches)

4·5 cm (1¾ inches)

Lock × 2

2 cm
(¾ in)

Ballet Shoes

As the Swiss roll is very fragile when it is made, leave it to settle for a day first.

When rolling out the fondant moulding paste, take care not to roll it out too thinly, otherwise the cake may show through and the moulding paste will be difficult to handle when it is being moulded into shape.

One 20 cm (8 inch) round thin silver cake board
3-egg quantity Whisked Sponge Cake mixture (pages 20–21)
3 tablespoons apricot glaze (page 38)
1 quantity fondant moulding paste (page 44)
cornflour and icing sugar, for dusting
pink and yellow food colourings
4 ice cream wafers
1 metre (1 yard) peach ribbon, 1 cm (½ inch) wide

Preparation time: 30 minutes
Cooking time: 10–15 minutes
Oven: 180°C, 350°F, Gas Mark 4

1. Place the cake mixture in a greased and lined 33 × 23 cm (13 × 9 inch) Swiss roll tin and bake in a preheated oven for 10–15 minutes until well risen and firm to the touch.

2. Turn the cake out on to a piece of sugared greaseproof paper. Remove the lining paper. Trim off the edges of the cake.

3. Quickly spread with some of the apricot glaze and roll up from the long edge. Cool on a wire rack. Store for a day before making the shoes.

4. Make the moulding paste and add a few drops of pink and yellow food colourings to make it peach-coloured.

5. Cut the wafers out to form the soles of the shoes. Cut the Swiss roll in half and press one end of each half into a point.

6. Cut out a shallow oval shape from the centre of each roll, then brush both all over with most of the remaining glaze.

7. Cut the icing in half. On a surface dusted with cornflour and icing sugar, roll out one half large enough to cover one roll. Use this icing to cover one of the rolls completely, join on the undersides, and neaten the edges. Shape the heel and toe of the shoe until smooth.

8. Brush the wafer sole with glaze and press into position on the ballet shoe, trimming to fit if necessary. Using well-cornfloured hands, press the icing into the oval depression in the centre of the shoe and form a sharp edge all around the top with the fingers.

9. Make an icing bow from the peach icing trimmings. Make into a pencil-thin roll, fold into two loops, trim and place in position on the toe with glaze. Repeat steps 7 to 9 for the other shoe.

10. Cut the ribbon into 4 pieces; press in position at the back of each shoe and secure with icing. Arrange the ballet shoes on the cake board.

11. Petal candle holders, made from icing trimmings, may be made for this cake, if liked. Take a small ball of icing and press into a petal shape, curling the edge of the petal inwards to form a centre. Press out another petal shape and wrap around the centre petal; repeat with a third petal, then cut off the stem. Press the candle into the centre. Repeat to make as many candle holders as required, then place beside the ballet shoes.

Ballet shoes

Humpty Dumpty

This idea could be adapted to make a clown or a witch; or you could place two cakes side by side for Tweedledum and Tweedledee.

Two 20 cm (8 inch) thin silver cake boards
3-egg quantity Chocolate Quick Mix Cake mixture (pages 16–17)
1 quantity buttercream (page 46)
1 tablespoon cocoa powder
2 teaspoons boiling water
food colourings (pink, blue, green and yellow)
50 g (2 oz) desiccated coconut
4 tablespoons apricot glaze (page 38)
25 g (1 oz) liquorice allsorts
1 tablespoon chocolate-flavoured toasted rice
50 g (2 oz) marzipan (page 37)
black food colouring pen
1 sheet rice paper

Preparation time: 40 minutes
Cooking time: 25–45 minutes
Oven: 160°C, 325°F, Gas Mark 3

1. Grease and base-line a 1 litre (2 pint) pudding basin, an 18 cm (7 inch) round sandwich tin and a 500 g (1 lb) loaf tin.

2. Place 2 tablespoons of the cake mixture in the basin, and divide the remainder between the two tins.

3. Bake in a preheated oven for about 30 minutes for the basin and round cake, and 40–45 minutes for the loaf tin, until well risen and firm to the touch.

4. Turn out of the basin and tins and remove the paper; cool on a wire rack.

5. Make the buttercream and divide it into three portions. Blend the cocoa and water together and cool, then beat it into one third of the butter-cream icing. Colour another third of the icing pink and the remaining third blue with the appropriate food colourings.

6. Reserve 1 tablespoon of the coconut. Divide the remainder into three and colour one third blue, one third green and one third yellow by adding a few drops of each food colouring to a portion of coconut and mixing until well blended.

7. Brush one cake board with apricot glaze and sprinkle over the coloured coconut to make a background picture, green for the grass, blue for the sky, white for clouds and yellow for the sun.

8. Spread the top and sides of the oblong cake with the chocolate buttercream icing. Place on the cake board 1 cm (½ inch) from the bottom and mark the icing with a knife to resemble a brick wall.

9. Sandwich the round and pudding basin cakes together with apricot glaze and spread half with pink icing and half with blue icing. Place on the board against the top of the wall.

10. Arrange the sweets across the middle of the cake to form a 'belt', and use different-shaped sweets for the eyes, nose and mouth. Press the toasted rice in position for hair.

11. Colour half the marzipan pink and half blue with food colourings and shape the pink into arms and the blue into legs. Place in position on the cake.

12. The second cake board may be used, if liked, to add the Humpty Dumpty nursery rhyme to the cake. Brush a 7.5 cm (3 inch) border of apricot glaze on the board and sprinkle with tinted desiccated coconut. Use a food colouring pen to write the rhyme on the rice paper and secure it to the cake board, inside the coconut border, with a little glaze.

Characterful Cakes

The basic idea for the Humpty Dumpty Cake can be extended to other characters from nursery rhymes or children's stories. The round face can also be made from white marzipan or fondant moulding paste colourfully decorated to look like a circus clown with the toasted rice 'hair' arranged at the sides so that the 'head' looks bald. For a teddy bear, cover the round cake with chocolate buttercream.

Covering the cake board with coconut to make the background.

Making the clouds and sun in the sky behind Humpty Dumpty.

Lion Cake

This is one of the simplest cakes to decorate for a children's party, yet provides an extremely effective centrepiece for the table with its cheerful colours.

One 25 cm (10 inch) round silver cake board
2 × 20 cm (8 inch) Chocolate Victoria Sponge Cakes (page 18)
175 g (6 oz) sugar quantity chocolate buttercream (page 46)
175 g (6 oz) chopped nuts (hazelnuts or almonds)
225 g (8 oz) marzipan (page 37)
food colourings (yellow and pink)
a little egg white, lightly beaten
1 dessertspoon cocoa
2 chocolate buttons or beans
2 chocolate flakes
2 or 3 pieces of thin spaghetti

Preparation time: icing and decorating the cake

1. Sandwich the cakes together with chocolate buttercream. Cover the top and sides of the cake with buttercream.

2. Cover the sides of the cake with 75 g (3 oz) of the chopped nuts and place it on the board.

3. Tint 175 g (6 oz) of the marzipan yellow. Roll it out and cut out one circle 13 cm (5 inches) in diameter and two circles 5 cm (2 inches) in diameter. Reserve the trimmings.

4. Tint a small amount of marzipan pink. Roll it out and cut out two 2.5 cm (1 inch) circles. Attach the pink circles to the centre of the small yellow circles with egg white, pressing the edges down firmly and evenly. Curve each piece inwards and place them in position on either side at the top of the cake as ears.

5. Position the largest circle in the centre of the cake for the lion's face. Gently press around the outer edge of the marzipan to curve downwards.

6. Knead the cocoa in 25 g (1 oz) of marzipan. Roll it out thinly and cut out two 4 cm (1½ inch) squares. Place these in position as eyes. Attach a chocolate button or bean to each with a dab of buttercream. Place a little buttercream in a greaseproof paper piping bag fitted with a medium writing nozzle and pipe pupils on each eye.

7. Form a wedge shape from the remaining brown marzipan and press it into place for the nose. Roll a small piece of pink marzipan into a ball. Flatten the ball and curve it into a mouth shape. Put the mouth in place on the lion's face.

8. Roll the yellow marzipan trimmings into two even-sized balls, each weighing about 15 g (½ oz). Flatten the balls and attach with a spot of butter-cream to either side of the mouth. Prick them over with a fork.

9. Carefully break up the chocolate flakes and spread them in a neat circle around the face as a mane. Break the spaghetti pieces into 10 cm (4 inch) lengths and place four on either side of the mouth as whiskers.

10. Finally spread a layer of buttercream round the edge of the cake board and sprinkle with the remaining chopped nuts.

Lion cake

Flower Cake

This exceptionally pretty cake is easy to serve as it is already cut into six wedges.

One 25 cm (10 inch) round silver cake board
Madeira cake:
250 g (10 oz) butter
250 g (10 oz) caster sugar
5 eggs
250 g (10 oz) self-raising flour, sifted
125 g (5 oz) plain flour
grated rind of 2 lemons
5 teaspoons lemon juice
cornflour and icing sugar, for dusting
To decorate:
1 quantity apricot glaze (page 38)
450 g (1 lb) fondant moulding paste (page 44)
food colourings (pink, yellow and mauve)
1 quantity buttercream (page 46)
mimosa balls
artificial butterflies and/or bees

Preparation time: about 1¼ hours
Cooking time: about 1 hour 30–40 minutes, plus cooling
Oven: 160°C, 325°F, Gas Mark 3

1. Grease and line a 23 cm (9 inch) round cake tin with greased greaseproof paper or non-stick silicone paper.

2. Cream the butter and sugar together in a mixing bowl until light and fluffy and pale in colour. Beat in the eggs one at a time following each with 1 tablespoon of self-raising flour.

3. Sift the remainder of the two types of flour together and fold into the mixture followed by the lemon rind and juice. Turn into the prepared tin, place in a preheated oven and bake for about 1 hour 30–40 minutes or until well risen, firm to the touch and a skewer inserted in the centre of the cake comes out clean. Turn out on to a wire rack and leave until cold.

4. Draw a circle on a piece of paper the same size as the cake and cut it out. Fold it in half and then carefully into three. Trim 'petals' out of the top edge so each one comes to a rounded point (above right). Unfold and place the template on the cake. Cut the cake through into six wedges to fit the pattern and trim round the 'petals'.

5. Remove the six pieces of cake and brush the top and sides of each one with some of the apricot glaze.

6. Colour the fondant icing a pale pink by kneading in liquid food colouring until evenly blended. Roll it out thinly on a surface dusted with cornflour and icing sugar and cut into six pieces. Use each one to mould around a cake 'petal'. Trim the surplus from around the base.

7. Re-assemble the flower on the cake board. Tint about one quarter of the buttercream yellow and put into a piping bag fitted with a star nozzle. Pipe a series of yellow stars over the centre of the cake to make a circle of about 6 cm (2½ inches) across. Position mimosa balls to represent the centre of a daisy.

8. Tint the remaining buttercream a deeper pink than the icing and put about three-quarters into a piping bag fitted with a small star nozzle. Use to outline the petals with a shell edging and then outline round the base of the cake to attach it to the board.

9. Tint the remaining pink buttercream a mauvish-pink and put into a piping bag fitted with a medium writing nozzle. Pipe lines of varying lengths protruding from the centre of the flower part-way along the petal like stamens. Leave to set.

10. Attach butterflies and/or bees to the cake as required.

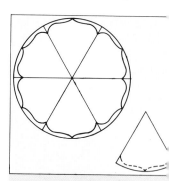

Cutting a petal template from the folded paper.

Summer Straw Hat

This fanciful creation makes a perfect birthday cake for a girl or for any summer tea party. If you want it to look more like a man's boater, increase the cake quantity by one-sixth (50 g/2 oz each of flour, sugar and margarine plus an extra egg) and bake the second cake in a straight-sided 20 cm (8 inch) cake tin. Use a navy blue and red striped ribbon and omit the roses.

One 28 cm (11 inch) round silver cake board
300 g (12 oz) self-raising flour
3 teaspoons baking powder
300 g (12 oz) soft (tub) margarine
300 g (12 oz) caster sugar
5 eggs
grated rind of 2 oranges or lemons
20 g (¾ oz) cornflour

To decorate:
about 100 g (4 oz) jam or lemon curd
2 quantities vanilla buttercream (page 46)
yellow liquid food colouring, or another colour
about 1 metre (1 yard) heavy ribbon, 2.5–4 cm (1–1½ inches) wide
1 artificial flower or 1 real flower or a few moulded roses (page 63)

Preparation time: about 1½ hours, plus setting
Cooking time: 50 minutes
Oven: 160°C, 325°F, Gas Mark 3

1. Grease and line a 25 cm (10 inch) round cake or sandwich tin with greased greaseproof paper. Grease a 900 ml (1½ pint) basin and dredge it with flour.

2. Sift the flour and baking powder into a bowl. Add the margarine, sugar, eggs and grated orange or lemon rinds and beat well for about 2 minutes until smooth.

3. Pour about two thirds of the mixture into the prepared tin and level the top. Beat the cornflour into the remaining mixture and pour into the prepared basin.

4. Place in a preheated oven and bake the round cake for about 40 minutes and the basin for about 50 minutes or until the cakes are well risen and firm to the touch and a skewer inserted in the centre comes out clean. Turn out on to wire racks and leave to cool.

5. Stand the round cake on a cake board. Spread the base of the basin cake with jam or lemon curd and stand it centrally on the first cake to make a hat shape.

6. Colour the buttercream lightly with yellow food colouring to give a deep shade of cream (or any other colour you like).

7. Beginning in the centre of the hat, work a basketweave pattern (page 59) using a medium writing nozzle and ribbon or basket nozzle. The size of the weave will have to be adjusted to follow the shape of the hat. Leave to set.

8. Tie a ribbon (with a strip of non-stick silicone paper or greaseproof paper inside it to prevent grease-marks) around the hat and finish with long streamers. Add a large, real or artificial flower or a few moulded roses to the side of the hat.

From the left: Flower cake, Summer straw hat

Gingerbread House

*One 35 cm (14 inch) square
  cake board*
450 g (1 lb) plain flour
1 tablespoon ground ginger
1 tablespoon mixed spice
8 tablespoons golden syrup
*75 g (3 oz) margarine or
  butter*
*75 g (3 oz) soft light brown
  sugar*
*1 tablespoon bicarbonate of
  soda*
2 tablespoons water
1 egg
1 egg yolk
For the icing and decoration:
boiled sweets
*450 g (1 lb) sugar quantity
  royal icing (page 39)*
2 packets small jelly sweets
2 round liquorice allsorts
1 tube chocolate beans
*100 g (4 oz) liquorice allsorts
  dolly mixtures, coloured
  dragees, sugar flowers
  miniature torch*

Preparation time: 30 minutes,
plus decorating the cake
Cooking time: 20 minutes
Oven: 190°C, 375°F, Gas Mark 5

1. Line two baking sheets with
non-stick silicone paper.
Following the diagram right, cut
out thin card shapes for the
roof, base, side and end walls of
the house.

2. Sift the flour with the ginger
and spice into a mixing bowl.
Place the syrup in a saucepan
with the margarine and sugar.
Stir over a low heat until melted.
Dissolve the bicarbonate of
soda in the water in a bowl,
then add to the dry ingredients
with the syrup mixture, egg and
egg yolk. Mix well together with
a wooden spoon to form a soft
dough.

3. Roll out the dough to a 5 mm
(¼ inch) thickness on a floured
board or work surface. Using
the card shapes as a guide, cut
the pieces required, and cut
two 4 cm (1½ in) × 1 cm (½ in)

chimney rectangles from the
trimmings. Place the dough
shapes on the baking sheets.
Cut out windows and doors and
trim them, if necessary, to the
exact size of the cards.

4. Roll out a small strip of
dough and place it along the
base of one door. Place a boiled
sweet in the centre. (This will
melt to produce a glass effect.)
Place a sweet in each window
space.

5. Bake the dough in the oven
for 10 minutes, switching the
baking sheets after 5 minutes.
Remove from the oven and
allow to cool on the baking
sheets for 10 minutes. Transfer
to a wire rack and leave to cool
completely.

6. Roll out the dough trimmings
and cut into a 1 × 2.5 cm
(½ × 1 inch) piece for the
fence. Bake in the oven as
before.

7. Place the base piece of the
house on the cake board or a
tray covered with foil and
spread the edges with icing.
Spread a thin layer of icing on
all edges of the side and end
walls. Join the side and end
walls around the base, press
together to secure and hold
gently in place for a few
minutes until the icing has set a
little.

8. Spread a little icing around
the edges of the roof, where it
will join the walls and carefully
place the roof in position. Leave
to set for at least 1 hour before
decorating.

9. Spread icing over the tray and
stick the small baked pieces
around the house for the fence.
Spread icing on the ridge of the
roof and around the edges of
the roof to form snow. Sandwich the chimney pieces
together with icing. Cut a
triangle from one corner so that

the chimney will sit on the
sloping roof. Stick in position
with icing and spread a little
icing around the top. Cover the
chimney side of the house
completely with icing.

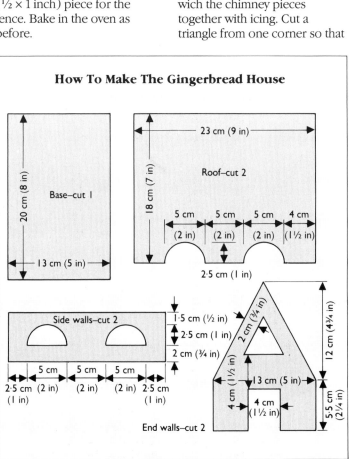

How To Make The Gingerbread House

Base–cut 1
20 cm (8 in)
13 cm (5 in)

Roof–cut 2
23 cm (9 in)
18 cm (7 in)
5 cm (2 in) 5 cm (2 in) 5 cm (2 in) 4 cm (1½ in)
2.5 cm (1 in)

Side walls–cut 2
5 cm (2 in) 5 cm (2 in) 5 cm (2 in)
2.5 cm (1 in) 2.5 cm (1 in)

End walls–cut 2
1.5 cm (½ in)
2.5 cm (1 in)
2 cm (¾ in)
2 cm (¾ in)
12 cm (4¾ in)
4 cm (1½ in)
13 cm (5 in)
4 cm (1½ in)
5.5 cm (2¼ in)

. Fix two liquorice allsorts on the chimney. Fill a grease-oof paper piping bag with ng and snip off the end. Pipe es of icing across the un-iced le of the roof. Attach rows of sweets to the icing. Pipe icing around the windows and doors and decorate with sweets. Fix a dragee in place for the door handle. Pipe around the garden and fix dragees on the piping.

Place sugar flowers in the garden. Pipe 'snow' on top of the fence.

11. Leave the icing to set completely. When ready to serve, switch on the torch and place it in the house, through the back door.

Gingerbread house

Rocket Cake

Food for budding astronauts, this streamlined cake is precisely decorated with little stars. To get a good red colour like this, you will need to use a paste rather than a liquid colouring.

One 15 cm (6 inch) round
* silver cake board*
4-egg quantity Quick Mix Cake
* mixture (pages 16–17)*
4 small bars white chocolate
225 g (8 oz) red jam, warmed
* and sieved*
225 g (8 oz) sugar quantity
* buttercream (page 46)*
red food colouring
1 ice cream cone
1 candle (red or white)

Preparation time: about 15 minutes, plus assembling and decorating the cake
Cooking time: 1 hour
Oven: 160°C, 325°F, Gas Mark 3

1. Grease and line a 20 cm (8 inch) square cake tin with greased greaseproof paper or non-stick silicone paper.

2. Pour the mixture into the tin and bake in a preheated oven for about 1 hour or until the cake is golden brown and firm to the touch. Turn out on to a wire rack and remove the lining paper. Leave to cool.

3. Draw a 10 × 10 cm (4 × 4 inch) square on a sheet of kitchen foil or non-stick silicone paper. Melt the white chocolate in a bowl set over a saucepan of hot (not boiling) water and spread it out within the marked square with a palette knife. Shake gently to level the surface and leave until just set. Using a ruler and a sharp knife, trim the edges of the chocolate square, then cut it in half to make two rectangles. Cut each in half diagonally to make a total of four triangles. Chill until hard.

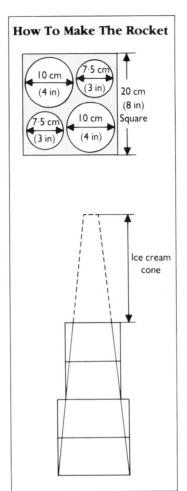

How To Make The Rocket

4. Following the diagram, cut the cake into two 10 cm (4 inch) rounds and two 7.5 cm (3 inch) rounds. Assemble the rocket placing the large rounds on top of each other and trimming the edges to slope the sides. Do the same with the smaller rounds. Sandwich all the rounds together with the jam. Place the cake on the board.

5. Make up the buttercream and tint two thirds of it red, leaving the remainder white. Spread the lower half of the cake with red buttercream and the top half with white, using vertical strokes to smooth the surface.

6. Cut the tip of the ice cream cone (just large enough to hold the candle). Spread the cone with red buttercream. Place the

iced cone on top of the cake. Place the remaining red buttercream in a nylon piping bag fitted with a small star nozzle and pipe a few evenly spaced stars over the white section. Pipe a border of stars at the top of the cone, where the cone meets the cake, where the red and white cakes meet and at the base of the cake on the board.

7. Place the remaining white buttercream in a piping bag fitted with a small star nozzle and pipe the outline of a door on the red part of the cake and a number above it on the cone

8. Arrange the chocolate triangles around the base and place a candle in the top.

Peppermint Racer

One 28 cm (11 inch) round cake board
3-egg quantity Chocolate Quick Mix Cake mixture (pages 16–17)
75 g (3 oz) sugar quantity buttercream (page 46)
peppermint essence
a few drops of green food colouring
2–3 tablespoons apricot jam, warmed and sieved
Demerara sugar, for sprinkling
2 mini Swiss rolls
5 liquorice catherine wheels
4 round mints
silver or green dragees
white and green soft mints
rice paper
food colouring pen
1 green plastic cocktail stick

Preparation time: about 15 minutes, plus decorating the cake
Cooking time: 55 minutes
Oven: 160°C, 325°F, Gas Mark 3

1. Grease and line a 1 kg (2 lb) or 1.15 litre (2½ pint) loaf tin with greased greaseproof paper or non-stick silicone paper.

2. Pour the cake mixture into the prepared tin and bake in the preheated oven for 50–55 minutes or until firm to the touch. Turn out on to a wire rack, remove the lining paper and leave to cool completely.

3. Make the buttercream and add peppermint essence to taste. Tint the buttercream pale green with a drop or two of green food colouring.

4. Cut the cake as shown in the diagram and trim the front corners to shape the body of the car. Brush the cut surfaces with a little of the jam. Spread buttercream all over the cake and smooth with a palette knife dipped in hot water.

5. Spread the cake board with jam and sprinkle it thickly with Demerara sugar. Place the two Swiss rolls on the cake board about 10 cm (4 inches) apart to make the axles. Place the cake on top.

6. Replace the sweets in the centre of each liquorice wheel with a round mint. Press a wheel on to the sides of the car in front of each axle. Use dragees to outline the front and rear 'windscreens', putting them in place with a pair of tweezers. Arrange a semicircle of dragees above each wheel.

7. Unwind the remaining liquorice wheel and cut four strips to make the front and back bumpers. Cut small strips of liquorice, split in half lengthways and make the windscreen wipers. Make door handles from small bits of liquorice and stick dragees on either side of the handle.

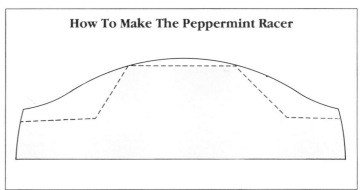

How To Make The Peppermint Racer

8. Stick soft white mints at the front and rear end of the car for the lights. Place a row of green and white soft mints along one side of the bonnet, roof and boot. Make an exhaust from two pieces of the trimmings, if liked.

9. To make the number plates, cut two small oblongs of rice paper and write the child's name and age on the paper using a food colouring pen. Stick on the front and back ends of the car, and place a soft white mint to either side. Use the green cocktail stick for an aerial.

Opposite page: Rocket cake
Above: Peppermint racer

Willie Wasp

*One 25 cm (10 inch) square
  cake board
4-egg quantity Chocolate Quick
  Mix Cake mixture (pages
  16–17)
225 g (8 oz) sugar quantity
  chocolate buttercream (page
  46)
25 g (1 oz) chocolate vermicelli
350 g (12 oz) yellow marzipan
3 tablespoons cocoa
2 tablespoons boiling water
icing sugar, for kneading
175 g (6 oz) white chocolate
25 g (1 oz) plain cooking
  chocolate (optional)
2 cocktail sticks*

Preparation time: 45 minutes,
plus cooling
Cooking time: 45 minutes
Oven: 160°C, 325°F, Gas Mark 3

1. Grease a 600 ml (1 pint)
pudding basin and line the base
with a disc of greaseproof
paper. Grease a 450 g (1 lb) loaf
tin measuring about
9 × 19 × 5 cm (3½ × 7½ × 2
inches). Fill both containers
two thirds full with the cake
mixture. Smooth level.

2. Bake in a preheated oven for
45 minutes or until the cakes
are well risen and spring back
when lightly pressed with the
finger. Turn out and cool on a
wire rack.

3. Cut the loaf along its length
and sandwich the pieces
together with a little buttercream. Place diagonally on the
cake board.

4. Flat base down, cut the
pudding cake from top to
bottom into two thirds and one
third. Use buttercream to
sandwich the cut edge of the
large piece against one end of
the loaf, and the smaller piece
against the other. Trim the sides
level with the loaf cake.

5. Reserve 2 tablespoons of
buttercream and cover the cake

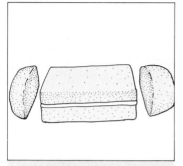

Dividing the pudding cake.
Assembling to make body.

Making the wings from
melted white chocolate.

with the remainder. Coat the
large rounded end with the
vermicelli to represent the head.

6. Divide the marzipan into
150 g (5 oz) and 200 g (7 oz)
portions. Blend the cocoa with
the water, then cool. Mix the
cocoa into the larger quantity of
marzipan and knead with icing
sugar until smooth.

7. Roll 2 small balls of the
yellow marzipan to make eyes
and a fine strip for a mouth. Roll
the remainder into a rectangle
measuring 10 × 20 cm (4 × 8
inches). Roll 100 g (4 oz) of the
chocolate marzipan into a
rectangle measuring 7.5 × 20 cm
(3 × 8 inches). Cut each
rectangle into four and three
2.5 × 20 cm (1 × 8 inch) strips
respectively. Lay these bands
alternately from the head join,
beginning and ending with a
yellow band.

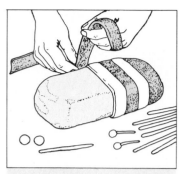

Covering with the strips
of marzipan.

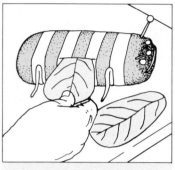

Putting the wings into
lengthways cuts in the body.

8. Mould 50 g (2 oz) of the
remaining chocolate marzipan
over the small rounded end, so
that the body is covered. Tuck
the uneven edge under the last
yellow band. Brush the marzipan body with a little water.

9. Half cover two cocktail sticks
with a little of the remaining
marzipan and place a small ball
on each to represent antennae.
Push the cocktail sticks into the
head. **Note**: if the cake is for
younger children it might be
better to replace the sharp
cocktail sticks with chocolate
'matchstick' sweets.

10. Fix the eyes and mouth in
place with buttercream.

11. Roll the remaining chocolate marzipan into a long
sausage and cut it into six 15 cm
(6 inch) lengths. Dab a little
buttercream on each end. Stick
one end on to the body and
bend the leg, sticking the other
end on to the cake board.
Repeat with all the legs.

12. Melt the white chocolate in
a bowl set over a pan of hot
water. Draw two wing shapes
about 18 cm (7 inches) long
and 7.5 cm (3 inches) wide on
greaseproof paper. Spread the
melted chocolate on the paper.
Cool until set.

13. If liked, melt the plain
chocolate, fill a small greaseproof paper icing bag and pipe
fine lines on the wing shapes to
look like veins. Cool until set,
then lift off the paper.

14. With a sharp knife, cut a line
lengthways either side of the
top of the striped body. Open
slightly with the knife and gently
push in the wings. Keep chilled
in warm weather.

Willie wasp

ÂTEAUX

Luxurious and irresistibly tempting these gâteaux can be served on their own, with tea or coffee, or as an impressive dinner party dessert. Despite their elegant finished appearance they can be easy and quick to make, especially if you do the baking a little in advance.

Gâteau is simply the French word for cake, but the English have adopted it to mean a special kind of cake – luxurious, frivolous and mouthwatering, fit to grace a party table or be served with coffee at the end of a superb dinner party. As befits a cake of such high standing, the ingredients are often rich and sophisticated. While the basis of many gâteaux is a light sponge mixture, it is often flavoured with chocolate, coffee or spices, or sprinkled with liqueur after cooking and cooling. Chocolate is frequently used to decorate gâteaux as well as flavouring the mixture, often simply grated and used to coat the sides, but occasionally to make a *pièce de résistance* like Rose Leaf Gâteau (page 172).

Almonds, walnuts and hazelnuts appear frequently in and on luxurious cakes. Their crunchiness contrasts nicely with light cake and smooth cream, and the flavour offsets the sweetness of sugary icings. Almonds are also the basis of praline, one of the most delectable flavouring in the cake-maker's repertoire. Useful in many recipes, it comes into its own with Praline Gâteau (page 178). Chocolate, cream and nuts are widely used in continental cakes, and a fourth important ingredient is fruit, often in conjunction with a suitable liqueur. Of elegant fruits the plump black cherry reigns supreme, having the necessary qualities of juiciness, delicate size and natural – but not excessive, for these are sophisticated cakes – sweetness. Raspberries, grapes and tiny strawberries are the cherry's rivals. A number of classic cakes and desserts include citrus fruits: this book includes a refreshing idea for a pretty Lime Gateau (page 164).

A collection of gâteaux would be incomplete without the classics such as Black Forest Gâteau (page 162), Sachertorte (page 170), Gâteau Japonaise (page 165) and Paris-Brest (page 168). These recipes and other delights such as Marron

Tuile Gâteau (page 166) and Franzipan Tart (page 184)
demonstrate the variety of techniques involved in this branch
of cake-making: meringue, choux paste, crème patissière,
sweet pastry and other basic recipes are called upon, and
here more than elsewhere the art of decorating with
chocolate excels. As you try out the various gâteaux you will
learn to make a range of separate components that can be
combined in innumerable ways to make an impressive range
of stunning cakes.

Often the separate elements of a particular cake can be
made in advance, so that it can be assembled at leisure on
the day it is to be eaten. A Whisked Sponge will keep for
2 days in an airtight container, but can be frozen for
2 months. A Quick Mix cake can be made up to 1 week
ahead and can be frozen for 1–2 months. Meringues keep
for 7–10 days in an airtight container. Crème pâtissière can
be stored in the refrigerator for 2 days before use.
Chocolate decorations can be stored in an airtight container
for several weeks. Once you have assembled a gâteau that
includes fresh cream, it must be kept chilled until the
moment of serving and eaten on the same day.

It is the way in which these separate items are put together
that determines whether a cake can properly be called a
gâteau. There is little of the laborious icing and fine piping
work used for celebration cakes here: the art of the gâteau
lies in the precision and care with which a few well-chosen
and top-quality ingredients are arranged. Slices of fruit
exactly matching in size; chocolate leaves in a perfect circle;
swirls of cream just touching on the border of the cake: these
decorative finishes, deceptively simple as they appear, cannot
be skimped or rushed. As the cakes on the following pages
show, the results are irresistibly tempting.

Black Forest Gâteau

Bavaria is famous for its mouthwatering cakes, and this must be the most famous of all. The sponge layers may be made a day in advance, but once assembled the cake must be eaten on the same day, and kept cool until serving.

3 eggs
175 g (6 oz) caster sugar
175 g (6 oz) plain flour
2 tablespoons cocoa powder
2 teaspoons baking powder
4 tablespoons hot water
To fill and decorate:
450 ml (¾ pint) fresh double or
*   whipping cream*
3 tablespoons Kirsch
1 × 425 g (15 oz) can black
*   cherries, drained or 450 g*
*   (1 lb) fresh black cherries,*
*   stoned*
100 g (4 oz) plain chocolate,
*   coarsely grated*
extra whole cherries

Preparation time: 30 minutes plus cooling
Cooking time: 40 minutes
Oven: 190°C, 375°F, Gas Mark 5

1. Grease and line a 23 cm (9 inch) round cake tin with greased greaseproof paper or non-stick silicone paper.

2. Place the eggs and sugar in a bowl set over a saucepan of hot water. Whisk until the mixture is thick and pale and leaves a trail when the whisk is lifted. Remove the bowl from the pan and continue to whisk for 2 minutes while the mixture cools a little.

3. Sift the flour with the cocoa and baking powder on to a plate. Carefully fold the flour into the egg mixture, using a large metal spoon. Gently stir in the hot water.

4. Pour the mixture into the prepared tin and bake in a preheated oven for 35–40 minutes until well risen and firm to the touch. Carefully turn the cake out on to a wire rack. Remove the lining paper and leave to cool completely.

5. Split the cake into three equal layers. Whip the cream stiffly and place one quarter in a piping bag fitted with a large star nozzle. Sprinkle the first layer of cake with a little Kirsch and pipe a band of whipped cream around the edge. Spread the stoned cherries evenly around the edge, inside the band of cream.

6. Place the second sponge layer on top of the cherries and sprinkle with a little Kirsch. Spread with a layer of cream. Sprinkle the underside of the top layer of sponge with the remaining Kirsch and invert it on to the middle layer.

7. Spread the top and sides of the cake with the rest of the cream and coat the sides with grated chocolate. Scatter the remaining grated chocolate on top of the cake.

8. Use the remaining cream in the piping bag to pipe whirls around the top edge. Decorate with the extra whole cherries.

A Continental Touch

Many of the most luxurious continental gâteaux come not from France but from Germany and Austria, where the tradition of going out to an elegant café for coffee in the mid-morning or afternoon is long established. Each region has its own specialities: the Black Forest Gâteau of Bavaria is one that makes full use of the local black cherries and the liqueur – Kirsch – distilled from them. This principle can be adapted to other variations, for example sprinkling an orange gâteau with Grand Marnier. Buttercream can be flavoured with liqueur if liked, substituting the liqueur of your choice for the milk and vanilla essence. German cakes that do not include cream nevertheless are traditionally served with *Schlagsahne*, 150 ml (¼ pint) of whipped cream into which 1 stiffly beaten egg white is folded just before serving. Serve this with, for example, Sachertorte (page 170) and Cranberry and Apple Strudels (page 218).

Black Forest gâteau

Fresh Lime Gâteau

The luscious cream of this pretty cake is lightened by the tangy flavour of lime.

2 eggs
50 g (2 oz) caster sugar
50 g (2 oz) plain flour
grated rind of 1 lime
caster sugar, for sprinkling
To fill and decorate:
300 ml (½ pint) double cream
juice of ½ lemon
slices of fresh lime

Preparation time: 15 minutes, plus cooling
Cooking time: 10 minutes
Oven: 200°C, 400°F, Gas Mark 6

1. Grease and line a 28 × 18 cm (11 × 7 inch) Swiss roll tin with greased greaseproof paper or non-stick silicone paper.

2. Place the eggs and sugar in a bowl set over a saucepan of hot water. Whisk until the mixture is thick and pale in colour and the whisk leaves a trail when lifted. Remove the bowl from the heat and continue whisking until the mixture is cool.

3. Sift the flour twice and fold into the whisked mixture with the grated lime rind. Place the mixture in the prepared tin and smooth the top, making sure the corners are filled. Place in a preheated oven and bake for 8–10 minutes, until the cake springs back when lightly pressed with the fingertips and has begun to shrink slightly from the sides of the tin.

4. While the cake is in the oven, place a clean damp tea-towel on a working surface, lay a sheet of greaseproof paper on top and sprinkle it very lightly with caster sugar. Immediately the Swiss roll is cooked, turn it out on to the sugared paper. Remove the lining paper and trim off the crusty edges. Make a shallow indentation with a knife blade on the short side nearest to you. Immediately roll up the cake with the paper inside (do not delay or the cake will crack if it is allowed to cool any more than is necessary). Lay a sheet of clean greaseproof paper on top of the roll and leave it to cool completely.

5. Whip the cream with the lime juice until it is stiff. Carefully unroll the cake and spread it with a little of the cream. Roll it up again and cover it with more cream. Use a palette knife to mark evenly spaced lines around the roll. Place the cake on a serving plate.

6. Place the remaining cream in a nylon piping bag fitted with a medium star nozzle. Pipe a line of rosettes along the top of the cake and a decorative border on both bottom edges. Decorate with quartered slices of lime arranged like butterfly wings along the top.

Variation

Substitute grated orange rind for lime in the sponge mixture and use a tablespoon of orange juice instead of the lemon juice in the cream. Decorate with slices of fresh kiwi fruit.

Gâteau Japonaise

50 g (12 oz) strawberries,
 hulled and sliced
-egg quantity Quick Mix Cake
 mixture (pages 16–17)
aponaise:
5 g (3 oz) ground almonds
00 g (4 oz) caster sugar
* egg whites*
o decorate:
00 ml (½ pint) double cream
* tablespoons Kirsch*
* tablespoons crunch nut*
 topping
* tablespoons strawberry jam*
 teaspoon water

reparation time: 25 minutes
ooking time: about 60
iinutes
ven: 160°C, 325°F, Gas Mark 3

. Grease and line a 20 cm
8 inch) sandwich tin. Stir 100 g
4 oz) of the strawberries into
ie cake mixture, pour into the
n and bake for 20–25 minutes
ntil well risen and firm to the
ouch. Turn out to cool on a
/ire rack.

. To make the japonaise, mix
ie almonds and 50 g (2 oz) of
ie sugar together in a bowl.
/hisk the egg whites until stiff,
ien whisk the remaining sugar
ito them until the mixture
olds soft peaks. Add the
lmond mixture and fold in
ell.

. Line two baking sheets with
on-stick silicone paper and
raw a 19 cm (7½ inch) circle
n each. Place the japonaise
iixture in a piping bag fitted
vith a 1 cm (½ inch) plain
ozzle. Pipe the mixture over
ie circles.

. Place one baking sheet just
bove and one just below the
entre of the preheated oven
nd bake for 30–35 minutes
ntil lightly browned and firm
) the touch. After 20 minutes
emove one layer and mark it
ito 10 wedges, then return it to
ie oven for 10–15 minutes.

5. Cool the layers on the paper.
Cut through the wedges on one
and remove the lining paper.

6. Place the cream and 1
tablespoon of the Kirsch in a
bowl and whip until stiff. Place
one third in a piping bag fitted
with a small star nozzle.

7. Spread the uncut layer with a
layer of cream, then place the
strawberry cake on top. Spread
the sides with cream and coat
evenly with crunch nut topping.
Place on a serving plate.

8. Heat the jam and water
together until melted. Sieve and
cool.

9. Spoon the remaining Kirsch
over the top of the cake and
spread the remaining cream
evenly over the top.

10. Pipe 10 thin lines of cream
radiating out from the centre
and pipe a shell edging around
the top.

11. Position the japonaise
wedges in the cream on top of
the gâteau and fill in between
with the remaining strawberry
slices.

12. Brush generously with
strawberry glaze and pipe a
swirl of cream in the centre.
Keep cool until ready to serve.

*Opposite page: Fresh lime gâteau,
Gâteau japonaise*

Marron Tuile Gâteau

100 g (4 oz) plain flour
100 g (4 oz) icing sugar, sifted
2 eggs, separated
4 tablespoons milk
1 teaspoon vanilla essence
300 ml (½ pint) double cream
250 g (9 oz) chestnut purée
3 oranges
25 g (1 oz) pistachio nuts,
*   skinned and chopped*

Preparation time: 20 minutes
Cooking time: 15–20 minutes
Oven: 180°C, 350°F, Gas Mark 4

1. Place the flour, icing sugar, egg yolks, milk and vanilla essence in a bowl. Mix together with a wooden spoon, then beat to form a smooth batter.

2. Whisk the egg whites until stiff, then fold gently but thoroughly into the batter with a large metal spoon.

3. Trace eight 9 cm (3½ inch) circles on a baking sheet lined with non-stick silicone paper. Spread a level tablespoon of the mixture on to each.

4. Bake in the preheated oven for 5 minutes, then quickly loosen each round with a palette knife and return to the oven for 2–3 minutes until golden brown at the edges.

5. Working quickly, roll each round into a cone shape and carefully insert the pointed end of each into a wire rack, so that they will cool standing away from the rack.

6. Line the baking sheet with a fresh piece of non-stick silicone paper and draw three 20 cm (8 inch) circles on it. Spread the remaining mixture over them.

7. Bake for 10–15 minutes until golden brown at the edges. Leave to cool on the paper before removing.

8. Place the cream in a bowl and whip until stiff. Reserve 2 tablespoons, then fold the chestnut purée into the remaining cream.

9. Halve one orange and cut one half into seven thin wedges. Peel, segment and chop the remaining oranges.

10. Place one tuile layer on a serving plate. Spread with one quarter of the chestnut cream and half the chopped oranges. Place another tuile layer on top and cover with chestnut cream and oranges as before. Place the remaining tuile layer on top and spread with chestnut cream.

11. Place the remaining chestnut cream in a piping bag fitted with a medium star nozzle. Pipe the cream into each cone and arrange them on top of the gâteau, radiating out from the centre. Add a swirl of chestnut cream in the middle.

12. Use the reserved cream to pipe a swirl at the end of each cone, and one in the centre, and sprinkle a few pistachio nuts over the cream. Arrange orange wedges in between the cones.

Making tuile cones

Ensure the mixture is spread thinly over each marked circle and cook until the mixture is just beginning to turn a pale golden colour. Remove the baking sheet and loosen each tuile round from the paper, then return to the oven to soften for a few minutes.

Quickly remove only one tuile round at a time and form into a cone shape. If the mixture sets too quickly, return to the oven to soften.

Austrian Meringue Basket

6 egg whites
¾ teaspoon cream of tartar
425 g (15 oz) caster sugar
To fill and decorate:
600 ml (1 pint) double or
*   whipping cream*
3 tablespoons brandy or sherry
40 g (1½ oz) ratafia biscuits,
*   crushed*
350 g (12 oz) strawberries,
*   sliced*
350 g (12 oz) raspberries
sugar-frosted flowers (page 66)
*   or crystallized rose petals*
*   (pages 66–7)*

Preparation time: 35 minutes
Cooking time: 1¾–2 hours
Oven: 110°C, 225°F, Gas Mark ¼

1. Line four baking sheets with non-stick silicone paper and draw an 18 cm (7 inch) circle on each.

2. Place 4 egg whites and half a teaspoon of cream of tartar in a bowl. Whisk until very stiff, then gradually whisk in 275 g (10 oz) of the sugar. Whisk well after each addition until the meringue is thick and stands in peaks.

3. Place the meringue in a piping bag fitted with a 1 cm (½ inch) plain nozzle. Pipe two rings of meringue on the circles on two baking sheets and place on the second and third shelves of the preheated oven.

4. Pipe another two rings of meringue on the marked circles on the remaining two baking sheets, but continue piping to give closed coils, ending in the centre. These will be the basket's lid and base.

5. Pipe a second ring on top of the outer ring of the base layer and place in the oven with the two rings. Bake the meringues for 20 minutes, or until firm enough to lift.

6. Loosen the two circles from the paper. Pipe a few dots of meringue at intervals around the top edge of the base and place one ring on top. Pipe dot on to the ring and place the second ring on top.

Return to the oven with the
l and bake for 20 minutes.
emove the basket and spread
e remaining meringue
noothly over the sides. Return
the oven for 20 minutes.

Use the remaining egg
hites, cream of tartar and
gar to make some more
eringue. Place this in a piping
g fitted with a small star
ozzle.

9. Remove the basket from the
oven and pipe a double row of
scrolls around the top and base
of the basket. Remove the lid
and return to the oven.

10. Pipe the remaining meringue in scrolls around the edge
and over the top of the lid.
Return to the oven for 45
minutes to 1 hour until the
mixture has set. Leave on the
paper until cold.

11. Whip the cream and brandy
or sherry together until thick.
Fold in the ratafias and fruit
until evenly blended.

12. Place the basket on a flat
serving plate and carefully
spoon in the fruit and cream
mixture. Place the lid in
position.

13. Use whipped cream to
attach sugar-frosted flowers or
crystallized rose petals to the
side and lid of the basket.

*From the left: Marron tuile gâteau,
Austrian meringue basket*

Paris-Brest Aux Fraises

This cake gets its name from a famous bicycle race from Paris to the town of Brest, its shape imitating a wheel. It must be eaten within two hours of assembly, while the choux pastry is still light and dry. If strawberries are not in season, replace them with 225 g (8 oz) halved and depipped black grapes and 2–3 sliced nectarines, soaked in liqueur in the same way as the strawberries.

1 quantity choux paste (page 34)
1 quantity crème pâtissière (page 48)
450 g (1 lb) strawberries, all but a few hulled
3 tablespoons orange liqueur or brandy
300 ml (½ pint) double cream icing sugar, for dusting

Preparation time: about 1 hour, plus standing
Cooking time: 45–50 minutes
Oven: 200°C, 400°F, Gas Mark 6

1. Grease a large baking sheet and stand a greased 25–30 cm (10–12 inch) flan ring on it. Spread the choux paste in a 5 cm (2 inch) edging inside the flan ring.

2. Place the baking sheet in a preheated oven and bake for about 40 minutes or until well risen, golden brown and firm to the touch. Either make a few holes in the sides of the choux ring to allow the steam to escape or turn it carefully over so that it is upside-down on the baking sheet, and return it to the oven for a few minutes for the inside to dry out. Leave to cool on a wire rack.

3. Reserve a few unhulled strawberries for decoration and slice the remainder. Put the sliced strawberries in a bowl with the liqueur or brandy and leave to stand for 2–4 hours.

4. Make up the crème pâtissière. Whip the cream until thick and fold it into the crème pâtissière. Fold the strawberries and any juice in the bowl into the cream mixture.

5. Split the choux ring carefully horizontally so that the piece for the lid is about one third of the whole. Scoop out any soft pastry on the inside. Stand the base on a large serving dish or board. Fill it with the strawberry cream and replace the lid.

6. Dredge the top of the ring with icing sugar and place the whole strawberries in the centre.

Variations

The original Paris-Brest is sprinkled with flaked almonds before being baked, and is filled either with Crème au Beurre (see page 46) or double cream whipped until stiff and flavoured with icing sugar and vanilla essence. Dust with more icing sugar before serving.

Paris-Brest au Chocolat: Sprinkle the choux pastry ring with flaked almonds before baking. To make the filling, blend 75 g (3 oz) of melted plain chocolate with Crème Patissière (page 48) and fold in 250 ml (8 fl oz) whipped double cream. If you do not have time to prepare Crème Patissière, make a custard with 150 ml (¼ pint) milk and 1 tablespoon instant custard powder, following the packet instructions. Transfer the cooked custard to a bowl to cool, covering with cling film to prevent a skin from forming.

All versions of Paris-Brest can have a little crushed praline (see page 49) folded into the filling. If you do not wish to use a piping bag for the choux paste, spoon it carefully into the flan ring. If you do not have a flan ring, draw a circle 20–23 cm (8–9 inches) in diameter on a large piece of greaseproof paper. Turn the paper over and lay it on the baking sheet. Spoon or pipe the pastry into the circle.

Individual choux rings can be made from the above recipes. Make them about 10 cm (4 inches) in diameter. Prepare, bake and fill in the same way.

Paris-Brest aux fraises

Sachertorte

This is one of Vienna's most famous cakes, renowned for its lightness, which is achieved by the high proportion of egg whites.

165 g (5½ oz) unsalted butter, softened
165 g (5½ oz) sugar
7 eggs, separated, whites stiffly beaten
165 g (5½ oz) plain chocolate
100 g (4 oz) plain flour, sifted
40 g (1½ oz) ground almonds
100 g (4 oz) apricot jam
Chocolate icing:
100 ml (3½ fl oz) double cream
2 teaspoons brandy
100 g (4 oz) plain chocolate, broken into pieces
To decorate:
chocolate leaves (page 68)

Preparation time: 40 minutes, plus cooling
Cooking time: about 1¼ hours
Oven: 180°C, 350°F, Gas Mark 4

1. Butter and line an 18 cm (7 inch) round cake tin with greaseproof paper. Brush the paper with melted butter and dust with flour.

2. Beat the butter in a mixing bowl, until it is pale and soft. Add the sugar and beat until light and fluffy. Add the egg yolks, one at a time, beating well after each addition.

3. Place the chocolate in a bowl set over hot water. When it has melted, pour it into the cake mixture and blend it in.

4. Sift the flour and almonds into the bowl and fold into the butter mixture. Gently fold in a third of the beaten egg whites, then fold in the rest.

5. Pour the mixture into the tin and bake in a preheated oven for 45–55 minutes or until a skewer inserted into the centre comes out clean. Remove from the oven and leave the cake in the tin for 10 minutes before turning it out to cool completely.

6. Warm the apricot jam and spread it over the top and sides of the cake. Leave it to set.

7. To make the icing, place the cream in a saucepan with the brandy and bring just to the boil. Add the chocolate pieces and stir until the chocolate melts and is thick and smooth. Pour the chocolate mixture evenly over the cake and leave to set, about 15 minutes.

8. Decorate with chocolate leaves, dusted with icing sugar.

Variation

When the cake is cool, split it in half horizontally and sandwich the two layers with apricot preserve. Sachertorte is served with whipped cream in Vienna.

Dark Raspberry Cake

6 eggs, separated, whites stiffly beaten
100 g (4 oz) caster sugar
50 g (2 oz) vanilla sugar (page 11)
65 g (2½ oz) plain flour, sifted
65 g (2½ oz) cocoa powder
Filling:
450 ml (¾ pint) double cream
50 g (2 oz) vanilla sugar
65 ml (2½ fl oz) rum or Kirsch
75 g (3 oz) redcurrant jelly
225 g (8 oz) raspberries
225 g (8 oz) strawberries, halved
To decorate:
chocolate scrolls (optional)
icing sugar

Preparation time: 45 minutes
Cooking time: 40–45 minutes
Oven: 180°C, 350°F, Gas Mark 4

1. Butter and line a 20 cm (8 inch) round cake tin with greaseproof paper. Brush the paper with melted butter and dust with flour.

2. Whisk the egg yolks with the sugars in a mixing bowl until the mixture falls off the whisk in a thick ribbon.

3. Sift the flour and cocoa powder together on to a sheet of greaseproof paper. Gently fold a third of the flour into the mixture, then a third of the beaten egg whites and repeat until all of the flour and egg whites are incorporated.

4. Pour the mixture into the prepared tin and bake in a preheated oven for 30–40 minutes or until the cake is springy to the touch. Remove from the oven and leave the cake in the tin on a wire rack for 5 minutes before turning it out to cool completely.

5. Whisk together the cream and vanilla sugar in a mixing bowl, until the mixture forms light, firm peaks.

6. To assemble the cake, slice the sponge into three layers. Warm 1½ tablespoons of the rum or Kirsch together with the redcurrant jelly in a small saucepan, stirring constantly, until the mixture forms a syrup. Brush the warm syrup over the bottom layer, arrange the raspberries on top and spread over a layer of the whipped cream.

7. Cover with another layer of the cake and brush with the remaining rum or Kirsch. Arrange the strawberries on top and spread over a thick layer of the whipped cream.

8. Place the third layer of cake on top and spread the top with the whipped cream. Decorate with a piped border of the remaining whipped cream and chocolate scrolls (if using) dusted with icing sugar.

From the top: Dark raspberry cake, Sachertorte

Rose Leaf Gâteau

The moule à manque tin in which this cake is baked has slightly sloping sides which helps the cake to rise but a 20 cm (8 inch) deep cake tin can be used instead.

75 g (3 oz) self-raising flour
25 g (1 oz) cocoa
100 g (4 oz) caster sugar
4 eggs, separated
2 tablespoons vegetable oil
3 tablespoons boiling water
Chocolate icing:
300 ml (½ pint) double cream
225 g (8 oz) plain chocolate
4 tablespoons black cherry jam, warmed
icing sugar, to dredge

Preparation time: 30 minutes, plus setting
Cooking time: 45–50 minutes
Oven: 180°C, 350°F, Gas Mark 4

1. Grease and lightly flour a 20 cm (8 inch) moule à manque tin.

2. Sift the flour and cocoa into a bowl and add the sugar, egg yolks, oil and water. Mix together with a wooden spoon, then beat until smooth.

3. Whisk the egg whites until very stiff and fold one third into the chocolate mixture using a large metal spoon. Add the remaining egg white and fold in until the mixture is evenly blended.

4. Pour the mixture into the prepared tin and bake in the preheated oven for 45–50 minutes until well risen and firm to the touch. Turn out on to a wire rack and cool.

5. To make the chocolate icing, place 150 ml (¼ pint) of the cream and 175 g (6 oz) of the chocolate in a saucepan. Heat very gently, stirring occasionally, until the chocolate has melted.

6. Remove from the heat and cool until the icing is thick enough to coat the back of the spoon. Whip the remaining cream until it is stiff.

7. Cut the cake into three equal layers. Place the bottom one on a wire rack with a plate underneath and spread with half the jam and one third of the whipped cream.

8. Place the second layer on top and spread with all the remaining jam and half the remaining cream. Cover with the top layer.

9. Pour the chocolate icing over the top of the cake, making sure it runs down the sides, covering them completely. The excess icing should be caught by the plate. Leave the cake for about 30 minutes to set the icing.

10. Mix the chocolate icing on the plate with the remaining whipped cream. Place in a piping bag fitted with a small star nozzle and chill.

11. Melt the remaining chocolate in a heatproof bowl set over a saucepan of hot water, stirring occasionally.

12. Use the chocolate to coat 14 large, 10 medium, 8 small and 5 tiny rose leaves (see page 68).

13. Place the gâteau on a serving plate. Pipe shells of chocolate cream around the base. Arrange the rose leaves in circles on top, starting at the outer edge with the largest leaves. Dredge lightly with icing sugar.

Variation

There are many different shapes that can be made from chocolate and used to decorate this cake instead of rose leaves. Melt the chocolate and spread it in a thin even layer on a sheet of waxed, greaseproof or non-stick silicone paper. When it is set, but not completely hard, mark out the shapes with a sharp knife and then cut them out. Elongated triangles arranged like the spokes of a wheel look good on a round cake, but for a rosette design smaller shapes such as circles are best. Make half the circles from plain chocolate and half from white chocolate for a contrasting effect, arranging them in alternate concentric circles, or divide the top of the cake in quarters with alternate colours. Tiny decorative pastry-cutters can be bought in pretty shapes including diamonds and hearts. Ready-made chocolate leaves are available if you want this effect but are short of time.

Rose leaf gâteau

Hazelnut Cream Bombe

Bombes were originally icecream mixtures served as dessert, moulded in the round moulds that gave them their name. This delectable cake continues the tradition of keeping its contents a secret until the first slice is cut.

100 g (4 oz) hazelnuts, finely chopped
3 eggs
175 g (6 oz) caster sugar
150 g (5 oz) plain flour
grated rind of 2 oranges
To fill and decorate:
300 ml (½ pint) double cream
2 tablespoons orange juice
2 tablespoons Cointreau
1 orange
50 g (2 oz) hazelnuts

Preparation time: 20 minutes
Cooking time: 50 minutes
Oven: 180°C, 350°F, Gas Mark 4

1. Grease a 1.15 litre (2 pint) pudding basin generously with butter.

2. Toast the hazelnuts lightly by spreading them out on a baking sheet and placing them under a preheated grill for 2–3 minutes.

3. Whisk the eggs with the sugar in a bowl until the mixture is pale and thick. Sift the flour over the mixture and fold it in carefully with the hazelnuts and grated orange rind.

4. Turn the mixture into the prepared basin and bake in a preheated oven for 45–50 minutes until well risen, golden brown and springy to the touch. Turn out and cool on a wire rack.

5. Whip the cream with the orange juice and Cointreau until stiff. Cut the cake into three horizontally and sandwich the layers together with some of the cream. Reserve a third of the remaining cream and use the remainder to cover the bombe completely, smoothing the edges with a palette knife.

6. Place the reserved cream in a piping bag with a star nozzle and pipe a ring to crown the top of the cake. Arrange the hazelnuts on the ring of cream.

7. Cut the orange in half. Pare the rind thinly from one half and strew it on top of the cake. Thinly slice the remaining half, cut the slices in quarters, and arrange round the base of the cake.

Mocha Roulade

3 teaspoons coffee powder
1 tablespoon hot water
100 g (4 oz) plain chocolate
4 eggs, separated
100 g (4 oz) caster sugar
To fill and decorate:
300 ml (½ pint) double cream
icing sugar
chocolate triangles (page 68)

Preparation time: 20 minutes, plus cooling overnight
Cooking time: 20 minutes
Oven: 180°C, 350°F, Gas Mark 4

1. Grease and line a 33 × 23 cm (13 × 9 inch) Swiss roll tin with greased greaseproof paper or non-stick silicone paper.

2. Blend the coffee with the hot water in a small heatproof basin. Break the chocolate into small pieces and place it in the basin, set over a pan of hot water. Stir occasionally to melt the chocolate. Leave to cool.

3. Whisk the egg yolks in a mixing bowl with the sugar until thick and pale in colour. Carefully fold in the melted chocolate.

4. In a separate bowl, whisk the egg whites until they form stiff peaks and fold into the mixture with a metal spoon.

5. Pour the mixture into the prepared tin and bake in a preheated oven for 15–20 minutes, until well risen and springy to the touch.

6. As soon as you take the cake out of the oven, cover it – in its tin – with a clean damp tea-towel and leave covered overnight. This ensures that it remains moist enough to roll without cracking.

7. Sprinkle a sheet of grease-proof paper with caster sugar and carefully turn the cake out on to it. Remove the lining paper and trim the edges of the cake if necessary. Whip the cream and spread two thirds of it over the cake, reserving the remainder for piping. Carefully and quickly roll the cake up like a Swiss roll. Place it on a serving dish with the join underneath.

8. Dredge the roulade gener-ously with icing sugar. Place the remaining cream in a piping bag fitted with a medium star nozzle and pipe a line of rosettes along the top of the cake. Arrange chocolate triangles between the rosettes of cream.

Weight Watchers' Note

Because the Mocha Roulade mixture contains no flour, it is relatively light, and is given body by the eggs and chocolate. This gives a delicious but very rich result, and you may prefer not to make the finished cake any richer with the addition of double cream. In this case substitute crème fraîche, either plain or apricot-flavoured, for the cream filling, and decorate the top with a very little icing sugar and slices of fresh fruit, omitting the swirls of cream. Crème fraîche mixed half and half with whipped double cream may also be used to cover the Hazelnut Cream Bombe. In both cases the cakes should be served as soon as possible after being assembled.

From the top: Hazelnut cream bombe
Mocha roulade

Coffee Walnut Crunch Gâteau

175 g (6 oz) digestive biscuits, crushed
50 g (2 oz) walnuts, chopped
100 g (4 oz) unsalted butter, melted
Coffee layer:
150 g (5 oz) butter or margarine
150 g (5 oz) light soft brown sugar, sifted
3 eggs
150 g (5 oz) self-raising flour, sifted
1 ½ tablespoons coffee essence or strong black coffee
To fill and decorate:
1 tablespoon coffee essence or strong black coffee
1 quantity crème pâtissière (page 48)
100 g (4 oz) apricot jam
1 quantity coffee buttercream (page 46)
50 g (2 oz) walnuts, finely chopped
icing sugar
4 walnuts, halved

Preparation time: about 45 minutes, plus chilling
Cooking time: 45–50 minutes
Oven: 190°C, 375°F, Gas Mark 5

1. Grease and line the base of a 20 cm (8 inch) flan ring and set it on a board or plate.

2. Mix together the biscuit crumbs and chopped walnuts and stir in the melted butter. Press over the bottom of the ring and chill until required.

3. To make the coffee layer, cream the butter or margarine and sugar together until light and fluffy. Beat in the eggs, one at a time, following each with 1 tablespoon of the flour. Fold in the remaining flour, followed by the coffee essence.

4. Turn the mixture into a greased and base-lined 20 cm (8 inch) round deep cake tin and level the top. Bake in a preheated oven for 45–50 minutes or until well risen and just firm to the touch. Turn out on to a wire rack, remove the lining paper and leave to cool.

5. For the filling, stir the coffee essence or coffee into the crème pâtissière. Cover with cling film and, if necessary, leave to cool.

6. To assemble the gâteau, remove the flan ring from the biscuit base and spread the apricot jam over it. Cut the cake in half horizontally and set one half over the jam. Cover it with the coffee-flavoured crème pâtissière and place the second layer on top.

7. Put half the coffee buttercream into a piping bag fitted with a star nozzle. Spread the sides of the gâteau with the remaining buttercream and coat with the chopped walnuts. Dredge the top of the gâteau heavily with sifted icing sugar. Pipe a wheel design and a border on top of the cake. Pipe a whirl in each section and top each with a walnut half.

Gingered Gâteau

This cake is best made and filled with crème pâtissière the day before required. Add the cream and brandy cornets just before serving. The cornets may be made several days in advance.

125 g (5 oz) butter or margarine
100 g (4 oz) light soft brown sugar, sifted
175 g (6 oz) plain flour
1 teaspoon bicarbonate of soda
2 teaspoons ground ginger
2 eggs
1 tablespoon black treacle
1 tablespoon golden syrup
1 tablespoon milk
To fill and decorate:
3 tablespoons brandy
1 quantity crème pâtissière (page 48)
150 ml (¼ pint) double or whipping cream
2 tablespoons milk
1 tablespoon icing sugar, sifted
8 brandy cornets (see below)
a few pieces of stem ginger

Preparation time: about 40 minutes
Cooking time: about 25 minutes
Oven: 160°C, 325°F, Gas Mark 3

1. Grease and line a 30 × 23 cm (12 × 9 inch) Swiss roll tin with greased greaseproof paper or non-stick silicone paper.

2. Cream the butter or margarine and sugar together until very light and fluffy.

3. Sift the flour, bicarbonate of soda and ginger together. Beat the eggs into the creamed mixture one at a time, following each with a spoonful of the flour mixture. Fold in the remaining flour, followed by the treacle, syrup and milk.

4. Spread the mixture evenly in the prepared tin, making sure there is plenty in the corners. Place in a preheated oven and bake for about 25 minutes or until set and just firm. Turn out, remove the lining paper, and cool on a wire rack.

5. Beat 2 tablespoons of the brandy into the crème pâtissière. Cover with cling film and, if necessary, leave to cool.

6. Whip the cream and milk together until stiff, then mix in the icing sugar and remaining brandy.

7. Cut the cake into three equal rectangles and sandwich them together with the brandy-flavoured crème pâtissière. Place the cake on a serving plate and spread the top with some of the brandy cream.

8. Place the remaining brandy cream in a piping bag fitted with a star nozzle. Pipe a whirl of cream into each of the brandy cornets and top each with a piece of stem ginger. Arrange the cornets, head to tail, along the top of the gâteau.

Brandy cornets

25 g (1 oz) butter or margarine
25 g (1 oz) caster sugar
25 g (1 oz) golden syrup
25 g (1 oz) plain flour, sifted
good pinch ground ginger

Preparation time: 15 minutes
Cooking time: about 10 minutes per batch, plus cooling
Oven: 160°C, 325°F, Gas Mark

1. Grease 8 small cream horn tins.

2. Melt the butter or margarine in a saucepan with the sugar and syrup. Remove from the heat. Beat the flour and ginger into the melted mixture.

3. Put 4 coffeespoons of the mixture on a baking sheet lined with non-stick silicone paper, spacing them well apart. Bake in a preheated oven for 10 minutes or until an even golden brown.

4. Allow to cool for 1–2 minutes until slightly firm, then carefully ease off the baking sheet one at a time with a palette knife. Immediately wrap round the cream horn tins. Cool on a wire rack until firm, then slide off the tins.

5. Cook and shape the remaining mixture in the same way.

From the top: Coffee walnut crunch gâteau, Gingered gâteau

Praline Gâteau

The Genoese sponge for this cake may be made one day in advance, and the praline up to two weeks in advance and stored in airtight containers.

1 quantity plain or lemon Genoese Sandwich cake mixture (page 22)
Praline:
165 g (5½ oz) sugar
100 g (4 oz) whole blanched almonds
Filling:
4 tablespoons Amaretto liqueur (optional)
300 ml (½ pint) double cream
3 tablespoons milk
To decorate:
2 kiwi fruit, peeled and sliced

Preparation time: about 1 hour, plus cooling
Cooking time: about 40–45 minutes
Oven: 190°C, 375°F, Gas Mark 5

1. Grease and line an 18 cm (7 inch) deep square cake tin with greased greaseproof paper or non-stick silicone paper.

2. Place the cake mixture in the tin and bake in a preheated oven for about 40–45 minutes or until well risen, golden brown and firm to the touch. Turn out on to a wire rack and leave to cool.

3. To make the praline, put the sugar in a heavy-based saucepan and heat gently until it begins to melt. Add the almonds and, stirring occasionally, cook until the caramel is a good golden colour.

4. Turn out immediately on to an oiled baking sheet and cool.

5. Crush the praline until fairly firm, either with a rolling pin, or in a food processor.

6. To assemble the gâteau, split the cake in half horizontally and stand the base on a serving dish. Sprinkle with Amaretto, if used.

7. Whip the cream and milk together until stiff. Mix about one third of the cream with one third of the praline. Use to sandwich the cakes together.

8. Use the remaining cream to cover the top and sides of the cake, covering it completely.

9. Press most of the remaining praline around the sides of the cake using a palette knife.

10. Arrange slices of kiwi fruit from corner to corner of the gâteau, then add a line of praline each side of the fruit and finish by putting two slices of kiwi fruit in the empty corners.

From the top, clockwise: Winston's gâteau, Cranberry orange gâteau (recipe overleaf), Praline gâteau

Winston's Gâteau

Sir Winston Churchill was supposed to have had a particular liking for a gâteau similar to this one.

The shortbreads can be made several days in advance and stored in an airtight container with the paper separating them.

75 g (3 oz) ground rice
175 g (6 oz) plain flour
1 teaspoon mixed spice or ground cinnamon (optional)
175 g (6 oz) butter, cut into pieces
175 g (6 oz) demerara sugar
Filling:
300 ml (½ pint) whipping cream
350–450 g (¾–1 lb) raspberry jam
a few whole fresh raspberries (optional)

Preparation time: about 45 minutes
Cooking time: about 45 minutes
Oven: 180°C, 350°F, Gas Mark 4

1. Sift the ground rice, flour and spice, if used, into a bowl. Add the butter and the sugar. Rub together until the mixture forms a smooth dough. Divide into 3 equal portions.

2. Roll out one portion thinly between 2 sheets of non-stick silicone paper and then cut out a 23 cm (9 inch) fluted circle using a fluted flan ring. Transfer the dough circle, still on its paper base with the flan ring in place, to a baking sheet. Trim off any excess dough from around the flan ring and prick all over with a fork.

3. Use most of the second portion to roll out in the same way and cut into a 20 cm (8 inch) circle with a fluted flan ring. Transfer to a baking sheet and prick as before, with the flan ring in position.

4. Use about three-quarters of the last portion of dough to roll out in the same way and cut into an 18 cm (7 inch) ring.

5. Place each disc of shortbread in a preheated oven and bake for about 25–30 minutes each or until lightly browned and firm to the touch. Remove the flan rings and allow the short-breads to cool, still on the paper, on wire racks.

6. Press all the shortbread trimmings together and roll out, again between 2 sheets of non-stick silicone paper, and cut

into 4–6 rounds using a 7.5 cm (3 inch) fluted cutter. Cut each round across the middle, prick and stand on a baking sheet. Place in a preheated oven and bake for 10–15 minutes. Cool on the paper on a wire rack.

7. To assemble the gâteau, whip the cream until stiff. Peel the paper off the shortbread discs and place the largest one on a flat serving plate. Spread first with a layer of jam and then a layer of cream.

8. Position the middle-size shortbread on top and again spread with jam and cream; and then add the smallest shortbread.

9. Separate the small biscuits to make halves. Put the remaining cream into a piping bag fitted with a star nozzle and pipe a large whirl of cream in the centre of the top using most of the remaining cream. Arrange 8 or 12 half biscuits radiating out from the cream, attaching them with a swirl of cream. Complete the decoration with fresh raspberries, if used.

Cranberry Orange Gâteau

2 eggs
100 g (4 oz) caster sugar
100 g (4 oz) plain flour
grated rind of ½ orange
Filling:
225 g (8 oz) whole cranberries,
*   fresh or frozen and thawed*
150 ml (¼ pint) orange juice
*   (not squash)*
about 75 g (3 oz) caster sugar
300 ml (½ pint) double cream
2–3 tablespoons milk
3–4 tablespoons orange
*   liqueur*
50 g (2 oz) flaked almonds,
*   toasted*
To decorate:
crystallized orange slices

Preparation time: about 1 hour, plus chilling
Cooking time: about 35–40 minutes
Oven: 180°C, 350°F, Gas Mark 4

1. Grease and line a 20 cm (8 inch) round cake tin with greased greaseproof paper or non-stick silicone paper.

2. Whisk the eggs and sugar together in a large electric mixer or by hand in a heatproof bowl over a pan of very gently simmering water until very thick, pale in colour and the whisk leaves a heavy trail.

3. Sift the flour twice. Fold it lightly and evenly through the mixture with the orange rind. Turn into the prepared tin and level the top. Place in a pre-heated oven and bake for 25–30 minutes or until well risen and just firm to the touch. Turn out on to a wire rack and leave until cold.

4. To make the filling, put the cranberries and orange juice into a saucepan, cover and simmer gently for about 10 minutes, until all the cranberries have 'popped' and are tender. If necessary boil uncovered for a few minutes, until thick and pulpy. Sweeten to taste with the sugar and leave to cool.

5. To assemble the gâteau, whip the cream and milk together until stiff. Split the cake in half horizontally and put the base on to a serving dish. Sprinkle with half the orange liqueur then spread with about three quarters of the cranberry mixture and about a quarter of the cream.

6. Top with the other layer of cake and sprinkle with the remaining orange liqueur.

7. Put about a third of the remaining cream into a piping bag fitted with a star vegetable nozzle. Use the remainder to cover the gâteau completely. Swirl the cream on top with a round-bladed knife.

8. Press the toasted almonds all round the sides of the gâteau. Pipe eight whirls of cream around the top edge of the gâteau and then a circle of smaller stars a little in from the whirls, leaving an empty space in the centre.

9. Carefully spoon the remaining cranberry filling into the centre of the cream. Top each large whirl of cream with a slice of crystallized orange and chill the gâteau for 1 hour before serving.

Orange Coffee Gâteau

150 g (6 oz) quantity Victoria
*   Sandwich Cake mixture*
*   (page 18)*
2 tablespoons instant coffee
*   powder*
2 tablespoons sugar
boiling water
2 tablespoons apricot jam
about 50 g (2 oz) finely
*   chopped blanched almonds,*
*   toasted*
about 6 tablespoons whipping
*   or double cream*
1 × 325 g (11 oz) can
*   mandarin oranges in*
*   natural juice, drained*
Filling:
115 g (4½ oz) caster sugar
6 tablespoons water
3 egg yolks
225 g (8 oz) unsalted butter,
*   beaten until soft*

Preparation time: about 45 minutes, plus cooling and standing
Cooking time: about 45 minutes
Oven: 190°C, 375°F, Gas Mark 5

1. Grease and base-line three 20 cm (8 inch) round sandwich tins. Place the cake mixture in the tins and bake in a preheated oven for about 15 minutes each or until well risen, golden brown and firm. Turn on to a wire rack and leave until cold.

2. Put the instant coffee powder and sugar into a measuring jug and make up to 175 ml (6 fl oz) with boiling water. Stir until dissolved and then leave to go cold.

3. To make the filling, gently dissolve the sugar in a heavy-based pan with the water. Boil steadily for 3–4 minutes or until 110°C (225°F) is reached on a sugar thermometer (the thread stage). Pour the syrup in a thin stream on to the egg yolks, whisking constantly until thick and cold. Gradually beat into the butter. Beat in 1 tablespoon of the coffee syrup.

4. To assemble the gâteau, remove the paper from the cakes and put one layer on a serving dish. Sprinkle with about one third of the coffee syrup, then spread with one third of the filling.

5. Add a second layer of cake, sprinkle with coffee syrup, cover with half the remaining filling and place the last layer of cake on top. Sprinkle the remaining coffee syrup over the and spread the remaining filling on top of the cake.

6. Spread the apricot jam thinly around the sides of the cake and use the toasted almonds to coat the sides of the gâteau.

7. Whip the cream and put it into a piping bag fitted with a star nozzle. Arrange an overlapping border of mandarins on top of the cake and pipe a row of rosettes inside the border, then a second circle of mandarins. In the centre of the cake, pipe a close row of cream with an extra rosette on top, and arrange the remaining mandarins around it. Leave the gâteau to stand in a cool place for up to 6 hours before serving.

Variation

For a chocolate, Kirsch and cherry cream gâteau, replace the coffee syrup with the following: dissolve 50 g (2 oz) sugar in 6 tablespoons juice from a 425 g (15 oz) can of black cherries, and add 4 tablespoons of Kirsch when cold. Flavour the filling with 50 (2 oz) of melted chocolate instead of coffee syrup. Use the drained cherries in place of the mandarin oranges to decorate the cake.

Orange coffee gâteau

Malakoff Gâteau

This gâteau makes a sumptuous dessert, and requires no cooking. Natural glacé cherries are best for this recipe: they are much darker and less sweet than the normal glacé cherries and can be bought in most food shops.

1½–2 packets sponge finger
    biscuits
150 g (5 oz) blanched almonds,
    roughly chopped
100 g (4 oz) caster sugar
175 g (6 oz) butter
2 egg yolks
6 tablespoons brandy or dark
    rum
5 tablespoons milk
300 ml (½ pint) whipping
    cream
To decorate:
slivers of blanched almonds,
    toasted
natural glacé cherries

Preparation time: about 30 minutes, plus chilling

1. Grease and line a 23 × 12.5 cm (9 × 5 inch) loaf tin with greased greaseproof paper or non-stick silicone paper. Cover the base with sponge finger biscuits laid lengthways side by side.

2. Put the almonds and 50 g (2 oz) of the sugar in a small heavy-based pan and heat gently until the sugar turns a light caramel colour. Turn on to an oiled baking sheet, leave until cold and then crush finely with a rolling pin or in a food processor.

3. Cream the butter until soft then add the remaining sugar and beat until light and fluffy.

4. Beat in the egg yolks alternating with 3 tablespoons brandy or rum; then stir in the crushed nuts.

5. Combine the milk and remaining brandy or rum and sprinkle 2 tablespoons over the biscuits in the tin, then spread with half the nut mixture.

6. Add a second layer of sponge finger biscuits, sprinkle with another 2 tablespoons of the milk mixture and cover with the remaining nut mixture.

7. Lay a final layer of biscuits on top and sprinkle with the remaining milk mixture. Press down evenly and cover with a sheet of greased greaseproof paper or non-stick silicone paper. Put a sheet of foil on top.

8. If possible put a light weight on the mixture and chill for at least 12 hours, preferably 24 hours.

9. Turn the gâteau out carefully on to a serving dish and gently peel off the paper.

10. Whip the cream and use some of it to cover the whole gâteau. Put the remainder in a piping bag fitted with a star nozzle and pipe diagonal lines on top of the gâteau. Sprinkle toasted almonds between the rows of cream and decorate with glacé cherries. Serve.

Coffee Chestnut Gâteau

1 quantity coffee Genoese
    Sandwich Cake mixture
    (page 22)
1 × 240 g (8½ oz) can chestnut
    spread (sweetened)
1–2 tablespoons Tia Maria or
    Kahlua coffee liqueur
450 ml (¾ pint) whipping
    cream
100 g (4 oz) plain chocolate,
    made into chocolate mini
    curls (page 68)
about 9 chocolate leaves (page
    68)
3–4 marrons glacés or glacé
    cherries

Preparation time: about 1 hour, plus standing
Cooking time: about 40 minutes
Oven: 190°C, 375°F, Gas Mark 5

1. Grease and line a 20 cm (8 inch) deep cake tin with greased greaseproof paper or non-stick silicone paper. Pour in the cake mixture, place in a preheated oven and bake for about 40 minutes, or until well risen, golden brown and firm to the touch. Turn out on to a wire rack and leave until cold.

2. Turn the chestnut spread into a bowl and beat in the liqueur with a wooden spoon until smooth. Divide mixture in half.

3. Whip the cream until stiff. P one third of the cream into a piping bag fitted with a star nozzle; mix 2 tablespoons of cream with one of the chestnut purée mixtures and put into a piping bag fitted with the same sized star nozzle as the cream. Finally add about 6 tablespoon of cream to the remaining chestnut mixture to make a marron cream for the filling.

4. To assemble the gâteau, spl the cake in half horizontally an stand the base on a serving plate. Spread with some of the marron cream and top with the second half of the cake.

5. Spread the remaining marro cream around the sides of the cake and press the chocolate curls against the sides with a palette knife.

6. Using alternate piping bags of cream and chestnut purée, pipe straight lines across the cake to cover the top completely.

7. Arrange the chocolate leaves and pieces of marrons glacé or glacé cherries on the top of the cake. Leave to stand for at least 2 hours for the flavours to marry.

Classic Alternatives

A Malakoff is a rich pudding based on a vanilla-flavoured bavarois (a light mousse-like custard). As well as the biscuits, brandy and almonds, it may include sultanas and currants soaked in a little brandy and very fine strips of orange peel. For decoration, almonds should always be included, but instead of glacé cherries you could use crystallized fruits such as pineapple, orange and lemon cut in small pieces and arranged in clusters of three colours.

The distinctive flavour of chestnuts also combines well with chocolate. Make a 3-egg chocolate-flavoured Whisked Sponge (see page 20), increasing the sugar to 115 g (4½ oz). Bake in a 28 × 18 cm (11 × 7 inch) shallow tin for 30 minutes at 190°C, 375°F, Gas Mark 5. Cut the cake in half lengthways and sprinkle with Grand Marnier. Sandwich with marron cream and decorate.

From the top: Coffee chestnut gâteau, Malakoff gâteau

Tipsy French Ring

225 g (8 oz) plain flour
1 teaspoon salt
1 teaspoon caster sugar
1½ teaspoons easy blend dry
    yeast
3 tablespoons warm water
3 eggs
100 g (4 oz) unsalted butter,
    softened and cut into small
    pieces
Syrup:
175 g (6 oz) sugar
300 ml (½ pint) water
120 ml (4 fl oz) dark rum
To decorate:
2 nectarines, sliced
75 g (3 oz) black grapes, seeded
75 g (3 oz) white grapes, seeded
2 oranges, peeled and
    segmented
2 tablespoons apricot glaze
    (page 38)
25 g (1 oz) flaked almonds

Preparation time: 35 minutes,
plus rising
Cooking time: 20 minutes
Oven: 200°C, 400°F, Gas Mark 6

1. Place the flour, salt, sugar, yeast, water and eggs in a warm bowl. Mix together with a wooden spoon, then beat for 3–4 minutes to form a smooth, elastic batter. (Alternatively, mix in an electric mixer using a dough hook or beater for 1–2 minutes.)

2. Sprinkle the butter pieces over the dough then cover with cling film and leave in a warm place for about an hour, or until the dough has doubled in size.

3. Brush a 23 cm (9 inch) spring-form ring with melted butter and chill until set.

4. Beat the dough with a wooden spoon until all the pieces of butter have been mixed in and the dough is smooth.

5. Carefully spoon the mixture into the ring tin as evenly as possible. Cover the top with cling film and leave in a warm place for about 1 hour, or until the dough has risen almost to the top of the tin.

6. Bake in the centre of a preheated oven for 20 minutes until well risen and golden brown. Remove the ring from the tin and cool on a wire rack.

7. To make the syrup, place the sugar and water in a saucepan and heat gently until the sugar has dissolved. Bring to the boil and boil rapidly for 3 minutes. Allow the syrup to cool, then stir in the rum.

8. Place the ring on a serving plate and pour some of the syrup over. As the ring absorbs the syrup, add some more, and continue in this way until the ring has become saturated with the syrup.

9. Fill the centre with the prepared fruit and arrange any remaining fruit around the base. Brush the ring with apricot glaze and arrange flaked almonds around the top.

10. Pour any leftover syrup into a jug and serve with the ring.

Preparing fruit

To seed the grapes: make a small slit in the top of each grape. Using a small knife, remove the seeds from the centre of the grapes.

To segment an orange: use a small sharp knife and carefully cut the peel including all the white pith away from the orange flesh. Cut in between the membranes carefully to remove each segment from the orange. Discard the membranes and core.

Franzipan Tart

225 g (8 oz) plain flour
100 g (4 oz) butter, softened
    and cut into pieces
25 g (1 oz) caster sugar
1 egg yolk
about 2 tablespoons cold wate
Filling:
4 tablespoons redcurrant jelly
350 g (12 oz) redcurrants
100 g (4 oz) butter, cubed
100 g (4 oz) caster sugar
100 g (4 oz) ground almonds
25 g (1 oz) plain flour
a few drops of almond essence
2 eggs
25 g (1 oz) flaked almonds
1 tablespoon apricot glaze
    (page 38)
To decorate:
whipped cream (optional)

Preparation time: 20 minutes
Cooking time: 50–60 minutes
Oven: 180°C, 350°F, Gas Mark

1. Grease a 25 cm (10 inch) loose-bottomed fluted flan tin.

2. Place the flour in a bowl, ad the butter and rub in until the mixture resembles fine bread-crumbs. Stir in the sugar, egg yolk and enough water to mix to a firm dough.

3. Knead on a lightly floured board until smooth. Roll out to a round large enough to line th flan tin.

4. Press the pastry on to the base and sides of the tin, then trim off the surplus with a knife Reserve the trimmings.

5. Prick the base with a fork an spread with the redcurrant jelly Reserve a few redcurrants for decoration if liked, then distribute the remainder over the jam.

. Place the butter, sugar, ound almonds, flour, almond ssence and eggs in a bowl. Mix gether with a wooden spoon, en beat for 1–2 minutes until nooth.

Spoon the mixture into the stry case and level the top.

Roll out the pastry trimmings d cut into 5 mm (¼ inch) rips. Arrange them in a lattice sign (see right) over the ling and trim the edges.

9. Position the flaked almonds on the exposed filling in between the lattice, then bake in a preheated oven for 50–60 minutes until golden brown and firm to the touch. Leave to cool.

10. When cold, brush the top of the tart with apricot glaze and pipe swirls of cream (if using) around the top.

11. Place one of the reserved redcurrants (if using) on each swirl of cream just before serving.

Making pastry lattice

Knead the pastry trimmings together and roll out thinly to a long thin strip about 25 × 10 cm (10 × 4 inches). Cut the pastry into 5 mm (¼ inch) strips and place half of the strips across the top of

the flan, evenly spaced apart.
    Arrange the remaining strips in the opposite direction and press the pastry strips on to the edge of the tin to make a neat edging. Add a glaze of beaten egg or milk.

From the top: Tipsy French ring, Franzipan tart

CHEESECAKES

Cheesecakes are perfect at picnics, parties, coffee time and dinner time. Aim for contrast but compatibility in combining base, filling and final decoration. A nutty, crunchy base goes well with lemon or chocolate. A sponge base goes best with a mousse type filling.

Cheesecakes make ideal desserts as well as coffee time cakes. Indeed, they are perfectly suited to the modern taste for light-textured sweets with a delicate appearance. With their increasing popularity, a great variety of flavourings and bases have evolved from the traditional baked cheesecake on a pastry base, together with a wide range of decorative effects. The smooth pale surface of a perfect cheesecake is almost like a blank canvas to a painter! You can take a minimalist approach and limit yourself to a small cluster of fruits nicely arranged to one side, or surrender to extravagance with a concoction of whipped cream, nuts and cherries to rival any continental gâteau. The Cherry Cheesecake Torte on page 196 shows how attractive an arrangement of brightly coloured fruits on a creamy surface can be, while the Coffee and Rum Cheesecake on page 194 makes its effect with swirls of cream rippling through the dark cheesecake itself.

A traditional cheesecake is baked. When it is cooked, it should appear well-risen and golden in colour, shrinking away slightly from the sides of the tin. Test by inserting a skewer or wooden toothpick into the centre of the cake, which is always the slowest part to cook, and remove it carefully; if any mixture adheres to the skewer, bake the cake a few minutes longer. Baked cheesecakes tend to crack slightly and collapse as they cool. This does not affect the texture or flavour, but simply adds to their appeal. To decorate, simply dredge lightly with icing sugar and arrange fresh or crystallized fruit on top, as in Torta di Ricotta (page 188) and Baked Fresh Fruit Cheesecake (page 196). These cheesecakes are delicious with morning coffee.

The modern uncooked cheesecake is an American invention which has received the accolade of being imitated and adopted all over the world. Chilled set cheesecakes are perfect endpieces for modern dinner parties, not only because their appearance is so appetizing, but because they can be prepared in advance and kept chilled until required. Many people now favour a cool, fruit-flavoured pudding at the end of a good meal. All fruits enhance cheesecakes, though – like mousses and bavarois – the combination of citrus and creaminess is the longest established. A Lemon Cheesecake such as the one on page 198 will be an invaluable standby in your repertoire, but there are other recipes here for cakes based on apricots, blackberries, cranberries, pineapple and strawberries.

Many uncooked cheesecakes require the use of gelatine. As a rule of thumb, 3 level teaspoons of powdered gelatine will set 500 ml (18 fl. oz) cream. Sprinkle the powder over 75 ml (3 fl. oz) of very hot but not boiling water in a cup and stir to dissolve. If it has not dissolved entirely by the time the water has cooled, stand the cup in a pan of warm water set over a low heat. Stir until the mixture is clear and smooth. Leave to cool at room temperature and trickle slowly into the mixture, beating all the time.

There are a number of bases that can be used for cheesecakes. A biscuitcrumb base is easy to make and very versatile, but experiment with crushed nuts and toasted breadcrumbs, soured cream pastry (page 190) and sweet shortcrust pastry (page 33). For special occasions dark chocolate digestives can also be used successfully, and the sugar quantity of the mixture should be reduced.

Such is the variety of cheesecakes that, like other cakes, there is one for every occasion: for dessert, try Blackberry and Cheese Torte (page 191); for teatime, Citrus Ricotta Cake (page 188), and for a celebration Heavenly Cake (page 192) lives up to its name.

Torta di Ricotta

Serves 10–12
*450 g (1 lb) ricotta cheese,
    drained and sieved
150 g (5 oz) caster sugar
2 drops bitter almond essence
7 eggs, separated
150 g (5 oz) ground almonds
1 tablespoon grated orange zest
50 g (2 oz) candied orange
    peel, chopped
2 tablespoons potato flour, sifted*
To decorate (optional):
*candied orange peel
angelica pieces
icing sugar*

Preparation time: 30 minutes
Cooking time: 50 minutes plus
cooling
Oven: 180°C, 350°F, Gas Mark 4

1. Grease a 25 cm (10 inch)
springform tin and line the base
with non-stick silicone paper.

2. Beat the ricotta cheese with
the sugar until the texture is
creamy; mix in the almond
essence. Add the egg yolks, one
at a time, beating well between
each addition. Mix in the
almonds, orange zest and
candied peel.

3. Whip the egg whites until
they are stiff and gently fold half
into the cheese mixture with a
metal spoon. Sift the potato
flour over the mixture and fold
it in, along with the remaining
egg white.

4. Pour the mixture into the
prepared tin. Rap the tin once
on the work top to disperse any
air pockets, then bake in a
preheated oven for 50 minutes
until nicely browned. Cool in
the tin on a wire rack.

5. When the cake is cool,
carefully remove the sides of
the tin and set the cake on a
serving plate. Decorate if liked
with candied orange peel,
angelica and icing sugar. Serve
with chilled orange sauce (see
below).

Chilled Orange Sauce

*rind of 2 oranges, cut into
    julienne strips
3 tablespoons water
175 g (6 oz) sugar
85 ml (3 fl oz) orange juice
85 ml (3 fl oz) lemon juice*

Preparation time: 30 minutes
plus chilling
Cooking time: 35 minutes

1. Blanch the strips of orange
peel in boiling water for 6
minutes to soften. Drain and set
aside.

2. Put the water and sugar in a
small pan over a low heat and
stir until the sugar has dissolved. Add the orange and
lemon juice, bring to the boil
and add the orange peel.

3. Simmer for 20 minutes. Pour
into a serving jug and chill until
required.

Citrus Ricotta Cake

This pastry can be made up to 4
days in advance. Cover and chill
until required.

Serves 10
*150 g (5 oz) potato flour
150 g (5 oz) plain flour
150 g (5 oz) butter, cubed
1 teaspoon grated lemon zest
2 tablespoons caster sugar
2 egg yolks
1 egg white, lightly beaten
icing sugar, to decorate*
Filling:
*150 ml (¼ pint) milk
piece of vanilla pod 2.5 cm
    (1 inch) long, split
2 tablespoons caster sugar
2 egg yolks
1 tablespoon flour*

*300 g (11 oz) ricotta cheese,
    drained and sieved
3 eggs, separated
50 g (2 oz) icing sugar, sifted
2 tablespoons chopped candied
    orange and lemon peel
2 tablespoons Grand Marnier
1 egg yolk, lightly beaten*

Preparation time: 50 minutes
Cooking time: 40 minutes plus
cooling
Oven: 190°C, 375°F, Gas Mark

1. First make the pastry. Sift the
flours into a bowl and make a
well in the centre. Add the
cubed butter and lightly rub th
mixture with the fingertips to a
fine breadcrumb texture. Stir ir

*From the left: Torta di ricotta with
chilled orange sauce, Citrus ricotta
cake*

e lemon zest and sugar. Add
e egg yolks and work the
ixture into a smooth dough.
oll the dough into a ball, and
ıst it with flour. Wrap in cling
m or foil and chill for 30
inutes.

Grease and flour a 25 cm
0 inch) springform tin.
·serve a third of the pastry.
oll out the rest and line the tin
> that the pastry covers the
ıse and extends about 2.5 cm
inch) up the sides. Brush the
ottom with the lightly beaten
·g white.

3. Roll out the remaining pastry
and cut it into long strips 5 mm
(¼ inch) wide. Set the pastry
strips aside.

4. To make the filling, place the
milk in a small saucepan with
the vanilla pod and bring slowly
just to the boil. Remove from
the heat and leave to infuse
until the milk has cooled.
Remove the vanilla pod.

5. Beat together the sugar and
the egg yolks; sift in the flour
and stir to combine. Pour in
half of the vanilla milk and beat
until well blended.

6. Add the egg mixture to the
remaining milk in the pan.
Bring to the boil very slowly
over a low heat and cook for
4–5 minutes, stirring all the
time. Set this custard aside to
cool.

7. In a mixing bowl, combine
the ricotta cheese, egg yolks,
icing sugar, candied peel and
Grand Marnier, beating well
between each addition. Mix in
the cooled custard.

8. Whip the egg whites until
they are stiff and fold them into

the cheese mixture with a metal
spoon.

9. Pour the mixture into the
pastry shell and gently smooth
over the top with a palette knife.
Lay the reserved strips of pastry
on top in a lattice pattern. Brush
with beaten egg yolk. Bake in a
preheated oven for 40 minutes
until the filling is lightly set and
the pastry is cooked. Cool in the
tin on a wire rack.

10. Carefully remove the sides
of the tin and set the ricotta
cake on a serving plate. Dredge
with icing sugar and serve.

Fresh Cranberry Cheesecake

Serves 8
150 g (5 oz) digestive biscuits, crushed
75 g (3 oz) caster sugar
½ teaspoon ground cinnamon
½ teaspoon ground nutmeg
75 g (3 oz) butter
1½ tablespoons apricot jam
Filling:
350 g (12 oz) fresh canberries, washed, or 330 ml (11 fl oz) cranberry jelly
3 large strips orange peel
150 g (5 oz) granulated sugar
100 g (4 oz) light brown sugar
1 tablespoon powdered gelatine dissolved in 8 tablespoons orange juice
2 tablespoons grated orange zest
200 g (7 oz) cream cheese
200 g (7 oz) curd cheese
100 ml (4 fl oz) double or whipping cream, whipped
To decorate:
julienne strips of orange peel

Preparation time: 40 minutes plus chilling

1. Prepare a biscuitcrumb base in a 22 cm (8½ inch) springform tin as described for Pineapple Refrigerator Cake (page 198) substituting crushed digestive biscuits for the breadcrumbs.

2. If using fresh cranberries, place them in a pan and almost cover with cold water. Add the strips of orange peel. Bring to the boil and simmer for 3–4 minutes until the berries start to pop. Draw off the heat and stir in the granulated sugar. Set aside to cool.

3. To make the filling, mix together the light brown sugar, gelatine and orange juice mixture and zest. Add the cheeses and beat very thoroughly until quite stiff.

4. Whip the cream. Reserve 4 tablespoons for decoration and fold the rest into the filling.

5. Sieve the cooked cranberries without crushing the fruit and discard the juice. Remove the strips of orange peel. Spread half the cooked fruit or half the cranberry jelly over the chilled base in the tin. Cover with the filling mixture. Spread the remaining cooked cranberries or cranberry jelly over. Chill for 5–6 hours.

6. Carefully remove the sides of the tin and set the cheesecake on a serving plate. Decorate with the reserved whipped cream and the julienne strips of orange peel.

Using Gelatine

As a rule of thumb, 10 g (¼ oz) or 3 teaspoons powdered gelatine will set 500 ml (18 fl oz) cream. Gelatine should always be measured in level spoonfuls.
1. Pour 75 ml (3 fl oz) very hot, but not boiling water into a cup. Sprinkle 3 teaspoons of powdered gelatine over and stir to dissolve.
2. If the gelatine has not dissolved entirely by the time the water has cooled, stand the cup in a pan of warm water set over a low heat. Stir until the mixture is quite clear and free of any lumps.
3. Allow to cool to room temperature and trickle slowly into the mixture, beating all the time.

Apricot Cheesecake with Soured Cream Pastry

Serves 8
Soured cream pastry:
150 g (6 oz) plain flour, sifted
100 g (4 oz) butter, cubed
1 tablespoon caster sugar
1 egg yolk
1 tablespoon soured cream
Filling:
2 tablespoons ground almonds
450 g (1 lb) fresh apricots, halved and stoned or 750 g (1½ lb) tinned apricots, well drained, juice reserved
1½ teaspoons ground cinnamon
50 g (2 oz) granulated sugar (if using fresh apricots)
50 g (2 oz) butter
2 eggs yolks
185 g (6½ oz) curd cheese
50 g (2 oz) caster sugar
½ teaspoon grated lemon zest
1 tablespoon double cream
To decorate:
1 teaspoon arrowroot

whipped cream
flaked toasted almonds

Preparation time: 45 minutes plus chilling and cooling
Cooking time: 1 hour 10 minutes
Oven: 180°C, 350°F, Gas Mark 4

1. Grease a 22 cm (8½ inch) springform tin.

2. Sift the flour into a bowl. Add the butter and lightly rub the mixture to a breadcrumb texture. Mix in the sugar. Add the egg yolk and soured cream and blend to a smooth pliable pastry. Roll into a ball, cover with cling film and chill for 1 hour.

3. Roll out the pastry and line the prepared tin, pushing the pastry 2.5 cm (1 inch) up the sides. Scatter the ground almonds on top.

4. Reserve 4 apricot halves for decoration. Pack the rest into the prepared base. Mix together 1 teaspoon of cinnamon with the granulated sugar and sprinkle over the apricots (if using tinned fruit omit the sugar).

5. Beat the butter with the egg yolks until light and creamy. Mix in the curd cheese, caster sugar, lemon zest, double cream and remaining cinnamon.

6. Pour the mixture on to the fruit in the tin and bake in a preheated oven for 1 hour 10 minutes. Cool in the tin on a wire rack.

7. Carefully remove the sides of the tin and set the cheesecake on a serving plate. Slice the reserved apricot halves and arrange them on top. Mix 8 tablespoons of the reserved juice with the arrowroot in a small saucepan and stir over a low heat until thickened. Glaze the apricots with this liquid and leave to cool. Decorate with whipped cream and flaked almonds and serve.

From the top, clockwise: Fresh cranberry cheesecake, Blackberry and cheese torte, Apricot cheesecake with soured cream pastry

Blackberry and Cheese Torte

This pastry must be well chilled before use. If it is difficult to roll out, press it into the tin by hand, patching any small cracks with small pieces of pastry. The texture when cooked is very light.

Serves 8
Pastry:
120 g (4½ oz) plain flour, sifted
pinch of salt
90 g (3½ oz) butter, chilled and cut into cubes
3 tablespoons caster sugar
½ teaspoon grated lemon zest
1 egg yolk
1 egg white, lightly beaten, for brushing

Filling:
400 g (14 oz) blackberries, defrosted if frozen
65 g (2½ oz) caster sugar
65 g (2½ oz) macaroons, coarsely crushed
225 g (8 oz) fromage frais, drained, or curd cheese
2 tablespoons Kirsch
3 tablespoons double cream
2 egg yolks

1 egg white
To decorate:
whipped cream

Preparation time: 30 minutes plus chilling
Cooking time: 45 minutes
Oven: 190°C, 375°F, Gas Mark 5
continued

1. Sift the flour and salt into a bowl and make a well in the centre. Add the cubed butter, then lightly and swiftly rub the mixture to a fine breadcrumb texture. Mix in the sugar and lemon zest.

2. Add the egg yolk and work the mixture with the fingertips to a soft, but not sticky, dough and roll it into a ball.

3. With the heel of your hand, blend the pastry – a small amount at a time – by pushing it away from you on a floured worktop. When it is smooth and pliable gather it into a ball, dredge it with flour and wrap it in cling film. Chill for at least 30 minutes.

4. Roll or press out the pastry and use to line a 20 cm (8 inch) springform tin so that it covers the base and extends about 2.5 cm (1 inch) up the sides. Bake blind (page 31), brushing the base with beaten egg white 5 minutes before the baking is complete.

5. Reserve 50 g (2 oz) black-berries for decoration. Sprinkle 50 g (2 oz) of the sugar over the rest.

6. Scatter half the crushed macaroons over the cooked pastry case and lay the sugared blackberries on top.

7. Beat together the cheese, Kirsch, cream, egg yolks and the remaining sugar. Beat the egg white until stiff and fold it in. Pour the mixture into the tin and scatter the remaining crushed macaroons on top.

8. Bake in a preheated oven for 45 minutes. Cool in the tin on a wire rack.

9. To serve, carefully remove the sides of the tin and put the torte on a serving plate. Decorate with whipped cream and the reserved blackberries.

Cheesecake and Fruit Diplomat

You can use virtually any combination of fruit for this spectacular party dessert: peaches, pears, apricots, gooseberries, black cherries, or red and black currants. Choose fruits which complement each other well in colour and texture.

Serves 14–16
Cheesecake ring:
350 g (12 oz) ricotta or cottage cheese, drained and sieved
75 g (3 oz) caster sugar
3 eggs, separated
1 tablespoon grated orange zest
1 teaspoon grated lemon zest
2 tablespoons lemon juice, strained
150 ml (¼ pint) soured cream
1 tablespoon powdered gelatine, dissolved in 2 tablespoons very hot water
150 ml (¼ pint) double cream
Fruit base:
3 tablespoons apricot jam
1 Fatless Sponge Cake, as page 17 but baked in a 30 cm (12 inch) springform tin
750 g (1½ lb) prepared fresh fruit or drained canned fruit (see below)
To serve:
julienne strips of orange and lemon peel
double quantity Chilled Orange Sauce (page 188)

Preparation time: 1 hour plus chilling
Cooking time: 3 minutes

1. To make the cheesecake ring, beat the cheese, sugar and egg yolks together thoroughly. Beat in the orange and lemon zest, lemon juice and soured cream.

2. Slowly beat in the dissolved gelatine. Put to one side until it is on the point of setting.

3. Whip the egg whites until stiff. Lightly whip the double cream. Fold alternate spoonfuls of egg white and whipped cream into the stiffened mixture.

4. Pour the mixture into a lightly oiled 24 cm (9 inch) ring mould. Chill for 3–4 hours.

5. Meanwhile, gently heat the apricot jam with 3 tablespoons of water and stir to dissolve. Sieve.

6. Place the sponge cake on a large serving plate and brush with the melted apricot jam. Carefully unmould the cheese-cake on top, leaving an even edge all around.

7. Arrange some of the fruits decoratively around the edge of the cheesecake. Place the remaining fruit in the centre of the cheesecake. Chill for 2 hours.

8. Decorate with the julienne strips of peel and serve with the chilled orange sauce.

Heavenly Cake

This light cake should be chilled for 2 days before serving.

Serves 12
Cinnamon pastry:
5 teaspoons ground cinnamon
275 g (10 oz) caster sugar
120 g (4½ oz) butter, softened
4 egg yolks
2 teaspoons grated lemon zest
250 g (9 oz) plain flour
pinch of baking powder
2 tablespoons flaked almonds
Filling:
250 g (9 oz) curd cheese
65 g (2½ oz) caster sugar
2 tablespoons soured cream
2 tablespoons Grand Marnier
150 ml (¼ pint) double cream
225 g (8 oz) redcurrant jelly
To decorate:
whole fresh fruit (redcurrants, raspberries)

Preparation time: about 1 hour 20 minutes plus chilling
Cooking time: 15 minutes
Oven: 180°C, 350°F, Gas Mark 4

1. Mix the cinnamon with half of the sugar and reserve.

2. Beat the butter with the remaining sugar until light and fluffy. Beat in the egg yolks and the lemon zest.

3. Sift the flour with the baking powder and blend into the mixture. Knead until smooth.

4. Divide the pastry in four and press or roll out each piece into a 24 cm (9½ inch) round (cut round the base of a tin as a guide). Sprinkle the cinnamon and sugar mixture over the rounds, and the flaked almonds over one of them.

5. Place on a greased baking sheet and bake in a preheated oven for 15 minutes. Leave to cool on wire racks.

6. Cream the curd cheese with the sugar. Blend in the soured cream and Grand Marnier. Whip the double cream and fold it in.

7. Set the almond-coated round to one side. Spread a layer of redcurrant jelly over each of the remaining pastry rounds, then spread each one with a layer of the cheese and cream filling, dividing it equally between them.

8. Sandwich the layers together and set the almond-coated round on top. Chill for 2 days. To serve, decorate the cake with fresh fruit.

From the top: Cheesecake and fruit diplomat, Heavenly cake

Coffee and Rum Cheesecake

Serves 12
150 g (5 oz) toasted
breadcrumbs
65 g (2½ oz) caster sugar or
vanilla sugar (see page 11)
65 g (2½ oz) grated walnuts
1 heaped teaspoon ground
cinnamon
75 g (3 oz) butter, melted
2 tablespoons apricot jam
Filling:
2 tablespoons instant coffee
powder
3 tablespoons hot water
100 g (4 oz) dark dessert
chocolate, broken in pieces
3 tablespoons dark rum
450 g (1 lb) curd cheese
200 g (7 oz) caster sugar
4 eggs, separated
450 ml (¾ pint) double or
whipping cream
50 g (2 oz) walnuts, chopped
2 tablespoons powdered
gelatine, dissolved in 5
tablespoons very hot water
To decorate:
walnut halves
chocolate curls (see page 68)
icing sugar

Preparation time: 1 hour 15
minutes plus setting and chilling

1. Line the base of a 28 cm
(11 inch) springform tin with
non-stick silicone paper and
grease the sides well.

2. Mix together the breadcrumbs, sugar, grated walnuts
and cinnamon.

3. In a large pan set over a low
heat, melt the butter with the
apricot jam. Remove from the
heat, stir in the crumb mixture
and combine well. Press firmly
into the prepared tin with the
back of a spoon. Leave to chill
while preparing the filling.

4. Dissolve the coffee in the hot
water in a small heatproof bowl.
Add the chocolate pieces. Place
the bowl over a pan of simmering water and stir until the
chocolate has melted. Stir in the
rum. Remove the pan from the
heat and leave to cool.

5. Beat together the cheese, half
the sugar and the egg yolks.
Whip the cream and fold it in.

6. Transfer half the mixture to
another bowl. Add the chocolate and coffee mixture to one
half and combine well. Add the
walnuts to the other half and
stir in.

7. Beat two thirds of the
dissolved gelatine into the
coffee and chocolate mixture
and add the rest to the walnut
mixture. Set both mixtures
aside until they are on the point
of setting.

8. Meanwhile whip the egg
whites until stiff and whisk in
the remaining sugar. Fold half
of the beaten egg white into
each mixture.

9. Pour the walnut mixture on
to the base and smooth over.
Gently spoon the chocolate and
coffee mixture on top. With a
large fork, lightly swirl through
both mixtures. Chill the cake
for at least 6 hours.

10. To serve, carefully remove
the sides of the tin and set the
cheesecake on a serving plate.
Decorate with the walnut
halves, and chocolate curls and
dust with icing sugar.

Cassata Alla Siciliana

This dessert may be prepared
up to 1 day in advance. Cover
and chill until the point of
serving.

Serves 12
3-egg Madeira Cake baked in a
loaf tin and cut into 1 cm
(½ inch) slices
4 tablespoons Maraschino
225 g (8 oz) whole mixed
crystallized fruits
500 g (1 lb) ricotta cheese,
drained and sieved
150 ml (¼ pint) single cream
50 g (2 oz) sugar
1 teaspoon ground cinnamon
100 g (4 oz) dark dessert
chocolate, finely chopped
25 g (1 oz) pistachio nuts,
blanched, peeled and
chopped
½ teaspoon orange-flower
water
Icing:
1 tablespoon lemon juice
250 g (9 oz) icing sugar, sifted
about 5 tablespoons almost
boiling water

Preparation time: 1 hour plus
chilling

1. Line the base and sides of a
1.75 litre (3 pint) charlotte
mould or 18 cm (7 inch) deep
cake tin with non-stick silicone
paper.

2. Use three quarters of the
cake slices to line the base and
sides of the container cutting
and trimming them to a
triangular shape to fit the tin
when placed in a circle. Sprinkle
2 tablespoons of the Maraschino
over the cake.

3. Reserve half the crystallized
fruits for decoration and finely
chop the remainder.

4. Whip the ricotta cheese until
it is creamy then beat in the
cream, sugar, cinnamon,
chocolate, chopped crystallized
fruits and pistachio nuts. Stir in
the orange-flower water. Pour

this mixture into the prepared
mould and smooth over the
top. Trim the remaining cake
slices and arrange them on top
Sprinkle over the remaining
Maraschino. Cover and chill fo
3–4 hours.

5. Carefully unmould the cake
on to a serving plate.

To make the icing, mix the
[le]mon juice with the icing sugar.
[St]ir in tablespoons of hot water
[un]til the mixture is thick
[en]ough to coat the back of a
[sp]oon. Place the bowl over a
[p]an of simmering water and stir
[un]til the icing is lukewarm. Pour
[th]e icing on to the cake, letting
[it] dribble down the sides.
[Sm]ooth over with a hot palette
[kn]ife if necessary.

7. While the icing is still warm,
decorate with the reserved
crystallized fruits. Leave to set
and chill until required.

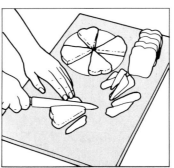

Trim cake slices to fit tin.

*From the left: Coffee and rum
cheesecake, Cassata alla siciliana*

Baked Fresh Fruit Cheesecake

Serves 10
Sweet shortcrust pastry:
165 g (5½ oz) plain flour, sifted
pinch of salt
50 g (2 oz) caster sugar
1 small egg
100 g (4 oz) butter, chilled and
  cut into cubes
20 g (¾ oz) butter, melted
350 g (12 oz) green grapes,
  halved and pipped
Filling:
50 g (2 oz) butter
120 g (4½ oz) caster sugar
3 eggs, separated
1 teaspoon grated lemon zest
2 tablespoons double cream
2 tablespoons Kirsch
450 g (1 lb) curd cheese
20 g (¾ oz) cornflour
Topping:
1 egg yolk
2 tablespoons double cream
2 teaspoons caster sugar
2 tablespoons flaked almonds
To decorate:
icing sugar
whole green grapes

Preparation time: 55 minutes
plus cooling
Cooking time: about 2 hours
Oven: 200°C, 400°F, Gas Mark 6
(for flan case)
then: 190°C, 375°F, Gas Mark 5
(for cheesecake)

1. Grease a 24 cm (9½ inch)
springform tin.

2. Make the pastry as described
for Blackberry and Cheese
Torte (page 191) but omit the
lemon zest. Roll out the pastry
and line the tin so that the
pastry covers the base and
extends 2.5 cm (1 inch) up the
sides. Bake blind (up to step 3,
page 31) for 15–20 minutes in a
preheated oven. Remove the tin
and reduce the oven
temperature.

3. Brush the base of the flan
case with melted butter and
arrange the halved grapes on
top.

4. To make the filling, beat
together the butter and sugar
and mix in the egg yolks. Add
the lemon zest, cream, Kirsch,
curd cheese and cornflour. Mix
well.

5. Whip up the egg whites until
stiff and fold them into the
cheese mixture. Pour the
mixture over the grapes in the
flan case and smooth the top
level.

6. To make the topping, mix
together the egg yolk, double
cream and sugar, and spread
over the filling. Sprinkle the
flaked almonds on top. Bake in
a preheated oven for 1–1¼
hours until golden brown. Cool
in the tin on a wire rack.

7. Carefully remove the sides of
the tin. Arrange the whole
grapes on top, dredge with
icing sugar and serve.

Variation

Any firm fresh fruits may be
used instead of grapes: stoned
black cherries, halved and
stoned Switzen plums or cored
and coarsely sliced apples and
pears.

Cherry Cheesecake Torte

Kirsch is an *eau-de-vie* distilled
from cherries, and its traditional
combination with chocolate
sponge, black cherries and
cream originates in the Black
Forest of Germany. This
variation, with the cream cheese
filling, is an unusual alternative.
It may be prepared up to 1 day
in advance. Cover and chill until
required.

Serves 8
100 g (4 oz) butter
200 g (7 oz) caster sugar
2 eggs, separated
225 g (8 oz) curd cheese
2 teaspoons grated lemon zest
2 tablespoons lemon juice
1 tablespoon powdered gelatine
  dissolved in 4 tablespoons
  very hot water
150 ml (¼ pint) double or
  whipping cream
5 tablespoons Kirsch
1 Fatless Sponge Cake 24 cm
  (9½ inches) in diameter
  (page 17) baked in a deep
  loose-bottomed tin
1 × 850 g (1½ lb) can pitted
  morello or black cherries
50 g (2 oz) flaked almonds,
  toasted
To decorate:
fresh cherries
angelica pieces

Black Forest Special

For an authentic cheesecake
version of a Black Forest
Gâteau, make the Cherry
Cheesecake Torte with a
chocolate sponge base.
Follow the instructions for
the Fatless Sponge, replacing
2 tablespoons of plain flour
with 2 tablespoons of cocoa
and 1 teaspoon of instant
coffee powder. Sift these into
the flour. Decorate the
completed Chocolate Cherry
Cheesecake with chocolate
caraque (see page 68), lightly
dusted with icing sugar.

Preparation time: 50 minutes
plus chilling

1. Cream the butter and sugar
until light and fluffy. Beat in the
egg yolks, one at a time. Beat in
the curd cheese, lemon zest and
lemon juice.

2. Stir the dissolved gelatine into
the mixture. Leave on one side
until on the point of setting.

3. Whip the egg whites until
stiff. Whip the double cream
until stiff. Fold the cream into
the cheese mixture, alternating
with spoonfuls of beaten egg
white. Fold in 2 tablespoons of
Kirsch.

4. Put the cooled sponge cake
back in the cake tin. Drain the
cherries, reserving 3 tablespoons of juice. Mix the
reserved juice with the remaining Kirsch and sprinkle over the
sponge cake to moisten. Scatter
the toasted almond flakes on
top.

5. Divide the cherries in half.
Distribute one half evenly over
the sponge base. Fold the
remainder into the filling
mixture.

6. Spoon the filling on to the
cake in the tin and carefully
smooth over. Chill for 4–5
hours.

7. To serve, carefully remove the
sides of the tin and put the torte
on a serving plate. Decorate
with the fresh cherries and
angelica pieces.

From the top: Cherry cheesecake torte,
Baked fresh fruit cheesecake

Lemon Cheesecake

This refreshing cheesecake is easy to prepare and has an exceptionally light texture. It is the ideal dessert to serve after a rich main course. Prepare it up to 2 days in advance if you wish, and keep chilled until required.

Serves 8
4 eggs, separated
225 g (8 oz) sugar
75 ml (3 fl oz) water
1 tablespoon powdered gelatine dissolved in 5 tablespoons hot water
200 ml (7 fl oz) lemon juice, strained
4 teaspoons grated lemon zest
300 g (11 oz) fromage frais, sieved, or curd cheese
Biscuitcrumb base:
100 g (4 oz) digestive biscuits, crushed
50 g (2 oz) caster sugar
1/2 teaspoon ground cinnamon
1/2 teaspoon ground nutmeg
50 g (2 oz) butter
1 tablespoon apricot jam
To decorate:
whipped cream
lemon slices
green grapes, halved and pipped

Preparation time: 35 minutes plus chilling

Cook's Tip

For a nut and biscuitcrumb base combine 75 g (3 oz) toasted breadcrumbs with 40 g (1 1/2 oz) ground walnuts, 40 g (1 1/2 oz) vanilla sugar and 1/2 teaspoon ground cinnamon. Melt 1/2 teaspoon butter with 1 tablespoon apricot jam in a large pan. Away from the heat, stir in the crumb mixture and combine well. Press into the tin and cool.

1. Prepare a biscuitcrumb base in a 20 cm (8 inch) springform tin as described for Pineapple Refrigerator Cake (below), substituting crushed biscuits for breadcrumbs.

2. Beat the egg yolks until pale and creamy.

3. In a saucepan dissolve the sugar in 75 ml (3 fl oz) water over a low heat. Turn up the heat and boil the syrup to 113°C (235°F)–118°C (245°F) on a sugar thermometer (the soft ball stage or when a small amount dropped into iced water forms a sticky soft ball which loses its shape when removed from the water).

4. Pour the syrup on to the egg yolks in a steady stream, beating all the time. Continue beating until the mixture has cooled. Pour into a large bowl.

5. Stir the dissolved gelatine into the mixture. Stir in the lemon juice and lemon zest, blend well and leave to cool.

6. Fold the cheese into the mixture and set aside until on the point of setting.

7. Whip up the egg whites until stiff then gently fold them into the cheese mixture. Pour the mixture into the prepared tin and gently smooth over the top. Chill for 3–4 hours.

8. To serve, carefully remove the sides of the tin and set the cheesecake on to a serving plate. Decorate with whipped cream, grapes and lemon slices.

From the top: Pineapple refrigerator cake, Lemon cheesecake

Pineapple Refrigerator Cake

This cake may be prepared 2–3 days in advance. Cover and chill until required.

Serves 12
150 g (5 oz) fresh breadcrumbs, toasted
75 g (3 oz) caster sugar
1/2 teaspoon ground cinnamon
1/2 teaspoon ground nutmeg
75 g (3 oz) butter
1 1/2 tablespoons apricot jam
Filling:
2 tablespoons powdered gelatine
175 g (6 oz) sugar
pinch of salt
3 eggs, separated
300 ml (1/2 pint) milk
1 × 225 g (8 oz) can crushed pineapple in natural juice
650 g (1 1/4 lb) curd cheese
2 teaspoons grated lemon zest
3 tablespoons lemon juice
300 ml (1/2 pint) double cream
To decorate:
150 ml (1/4 pint) soured cream
candied pineapple
flaked almonds, toasted
scented geranium leaves (optional)

Preparation time: 50 minutes plus setting and chilling
Cooking time: about 15 minutes

1. Line the base of a 24 cm (9 1/2 inch) springform tin with non-stick silicone paper and grease the sides well.

2. Mix the breadcrumbs with the sugar and spices.

3. Melt the butter and apricot jam in a large pan set over a low heat. Remove the pan from the heat, stir in the crumb mixture and combine well. Press evenly and firmly into the prepared tin using the back of a spoon. Leave to chill while preparing the filling.

4. In a heatproof mixing bowl, mix together the gelatine, sugar and salt.

5. With a fork, lightly beat the egg yolks with the milk and add to the sugar mixture. Mix in the crushed pineapple.

6. Set the mixing bowl over a pan of simmering water and stir for about 15 minutes until the mixture starts to thicken. Draw off the heat and pour into a large mixing bowl. Set aside to cool.

7. Beat together the curd cheese, lemon zest and lemon juice. Gradually add the cooled pineapple mixture and combine well. Set aside until almost on the point of setting.

8. Beat the egg whites until stiff. Whip the double cream until stiff. Fold alternate spoonfuls of whipped cream and egg white into the cheese mixture. Pour on to the chilled base in the tin and carefully smooth over. Chill for 5 hours.

9. To serve, carefully remove the sides of the tin and set the cheesecake on a serving plate. Gently smooth the soured cream over the surface and decorate with the candied pineapple and toasted almond flakes. For a colourful final touch, arrange a few scented geranium leaves on top as well.

Chocolate Orange Cheesecake

Serves 8–10

40 g (1½ oz) plain chocolate
40 g (1½ oz) butter or
* margarine*
175 g (6 oz) digestive biscuits,
* crushed*
Filling:
225 g (8 oz) full fat soft cheese
75 g (3 oz) caster sugar
grated rind of 1 orange
4 tablespoons orange juice
15 g (½ oz) powdered gelatine
1 tablespoon lemon juice
large can evaporated milk,
* chilled overnight*
To decorate:
150 ml (¼ pint) double or
* whipping cream*
1½–2 packets plain chocolate
* finger biscuits*
jellied orange slices

Preparation time: about 30
minutes, plus chilling
Cooking time: about 10
minutes

1. Melt the chocolate and butter
or margarine in a saucepan set
over a gentle heat. Stir in the
crushed biscuits until they are
evenly coated. Press this
mixture over the base of a well-
greased 19–20 cm (7½–8 inch)
loose-based round cake tin.
Chill until set.

2. To make the filling, beat the
cheese and sugar until soft and
smooth. Gradually beat in the
orange rind and juice.

3. Dissolve the gelatine in the
lemon juice in a heatproof bowl
set over a pan of hot water.
Leave to cool, then mix evenly
through the cheese mixture.

4. Whisk the evaporated milk
until very thick and standing in
soft peaks. Fold it quickly
through the cheese mixture.
Pour into the tin over the
biscuit base and chill until set –
preferably overnight.

5. Carefully remove the cheesecake from the tin and place it
on a plate. Whip the cream until
stiff and spread a thin layer all
round the sides of the cheesecake. Arrange the chocolate
finger biscuits round the sides.

6. Place the remaining cream in
a piping bag fitted with a star
nozzle and decorate the top
with whirls of whipped cream.
Complete with jellied orange
slices.

Chocolate orange cheesecake

trawberry Cheesecake Boxes

hese individual cheesecakes
re ideal for an elegant dessert.
he sponge base and filling can
e made the day before, and
he chocolate squares 2–3 days
n advance if stored in a rigid
ontainer in a cool place. On
he day all you need do is
ssemble the cakes and deco-
te the tops.

Makes 9
1 egg
25 g (1 oz) caster sugar
25 g (1 oz) flour, sifted
1 tablespoon warm water
Filling:
150 ml (¼ pint) water
1 × 150 g (5 oz) packet
strawberry jelly
juice of ½ lemon
225 g (8 oz) full fat soft cheese
300 ml (½ pint) whipping
cream
2 tablespoons redcurrant jelly,
warmed
To decorate:
150 g (6 oz) plain chocolate or
cooking chocolate, broken
into pieces
9 fresh strawberries

Preparation time: about 1
hour, plus setting
Cooking time: 10–12 minutes
Oven: 200°C, 400°F, Gas Mark 6

1. Line the base of an 18 cm (7
inch) square cake tin with
greased greaseproof paper or
non-stick silicone paper.

2. Whisk the egg and sugar until
light and foamy and the whisk
leaves a trail when lifted.

3. Gently fold in the flour and
water with a metal spoon, then
pour the mixture into the
prepared tin. Bake in a preheated oven for 10–12 minutes,
until well risen and lightly
golden brown. Turn out the
cake and peel off the paper.
Leave to cool on a wire rack.

4. Break the jelly into sections
and place in a heatproof bowl.
Boil the water and pour it over,
stirring to dissolve the jelly
completely. Add the lemon
juice. Chill until the mixture
becomes syrupy – about 30
minutes.

5. Cream the cheese until it is
smooth, then gradually add the
jelly, beating well between each
addition. Whip the cream and
fold two thirds of it into the
mixture. Pour into an 18 cm (7
inch) square cake tin lined with
greaseproof or non-stick
silicone paper. Chill for about 2
hours, until set.

6. Brush the sponge square
with the redcurrant jelly.
Carefully unmould the cheesecake on to the sponge, matching the edges. Peel off the paper
and trim the edges neatly if
necessary.

7. Draw a 30 cm (12 inch)
square on greaseproof paper.
Melt the chocolate in a heatproof bowl set over a saucepan
of hot water and stir until
smooth. With a palette knife,
spread the chocolate on the
paper to fill the square. Cool
until set.

8. Cut the chocolate into 36
equal squares. Cut the cheesecake into nine 5 cm (2 inch)
squares, trimming the edges if
necessary. Working quickly to
avoid overhandling the chocolate, press a piece of chocolate
on to the four sides of each
cheesecake square.

9. Place the remaining cream in
a greaseproof paper piping bag
fitted with a star nozzle. Pipe a
generous ribbon of cream on
top of each cheesecake.
Decorate each with a
strawberry.

Variations

Vary the flavour of the cheesecake boxes by using a different
flavoured jelly and appropriate
decoration. Orange jelly with a
mandarin segment decoration
or black cherry jelly with a
stoned black cherry on top are
two fruit flavours that combine
well with chocolate. Make all
three kinds for a special dessert
choice.

bove: Strawberry cheesecake boxes

SMALL CAKES & PASTRIES

A quintissential tea time delicacy, small cakes and pastries are back in vogue. Practise your cake design and decorating arts in miniature, and to surprise your friends with their range and variety. Children are sure to enjoy these colourful mouthfuls too.

Diminutive they may be, but the cakes in this chapter have an appeal far outstripping their size. Who can resist an array of tempting little mouthfuls like these?

The small cakes and pastries in the following pages include a number of the basic recipes covered in the preceding chapters: not only cake mixtures, but pastries such as puff, choux and strudel; glacé icing, buttercream and crème pâtissière; meringue, syrups and melted chocolate. These small cakes also demonstrate the skills of the cake-decorator: the importance of design and decoration is even greater when the scale is reduced to individual size. Like a miniature painting, every stroke has to be exact. Before you try these recipes practise the art of making small cakes with Genoese pastries. Make a Genoese Sponge (page 22) and cover the whole cake with buttercream. Decorate with piped buttercream, nuts, cherries and other simple decorations before cutting the cake into fingers. In this chapter the easiest cakes to make and decorate are the Fairy Cakes on page 204. Based on a simple sponge mixture, they are individually cooked and iced with glacé icing. As the number of variations shows, the possibilities are almost endless. Practise small-scale design with these ideas before progressing to more fanciful little cakes.

Although a large and beautiful cake cannot be bettered as the centrepiece to an occasion, most parties require some supporting acts to keep the guests amused before the star turn. This is where a cast of delectable little cakes comes into its own – and may even steal the show, if such delicious examples as Petits Vacherins (page 215) and Marrons Meringues (page 218) make an appearance. Little cakes are a must for children's parties not only because they make the table look colourful and festive, but because children like food of all kinds that's scaled down for them (and no arguments about who's had the biggest slice of cake!). Tortoises (page 206) and Animal Biscuits (page 211) are ideal.

The delicacy of small cakes can bring a touch of luxury to simple family teas, with attractive but easily made cakes like Apple and Ginger Rings and Nutty Angelica Fancies (pages 208–9). They have their practical aspect, too, since you can cater more exactly for a particular number of people. These two recipes are particularly good for picnics – they are easy to transport and just the thing for satisfying fresh-air appetites.

Elegant tea parties are coming back into fashion after a temporary decline, now that people are rediscovering the pleasure of a civilized meal that requires relatively little preparation and fills an otherwise rather vacant spot on Sunday afternoons. As well as the cucumber sandwiches and the China tea, an assortment of pretty little cakes is essential, whether it's tea on the lawn or by the fire. Make sure the selection includes a variety of flavours and textures.

With morning coffee, serve Cranberry Apple Strudels (page 218), a delicious variation on a classic Austrian recipe. There are many continental recipes for small cakes that are luxurious enough to be served as individual desserts, such as Raspberry Vol-au-vents and the renowned Fruit Babas (page 216). When you serve coffee at the end of a special meal, pamper your guests with petits fours such as Italiens or Printaniers (page 212) or bite-sized biscuits like Almond Leaves (page 214). These little cakes make lovely presents, too.

After trying the tempting selection of cakes in this chapter, you are sure to agree that small is beautiful.

Fairy Cakes

Makes 18–20
10 g (4 oz) butter or
  margarine
100 g (4 oz) caster sugar
2 eggs
150 g (5 oz) self-raising flour
To ice and decorate:
225 g (8 oz) glacé icing (see
  page 42)
a few drops of food colouring
small sweets, nuts, glacé
  cherries

Preparation time: 10 minutes
Cooking time: 15–20 minutes
Oven: 180°C, 350°F, Gas Mark 4

1. Cream the butter and sugar together until pale and fluffy. Gradually beat in the eggs. Sift the flour over the mixture and fold it in gently using a wooden spoon.

2. Spoon the mixture into greased patty tins or paper cases placed on a baking tray and bake in a preheated oven for 15–20 minutes or until well risen and golden brown. Turn out of the patty tins and leave to cool on a wire rack.

3. Prepare the glacé icing and tint it delicately with a few drops of any preferred colouring. Coat the tops of the cakes with icing. The cakes may be feather iced with two different colours (see page 43).

4. Decorate with small sweets, nuts, glacé cherries and angelica as preferred.

Variations

Chocolate cup cakes Add 2 tablespoons cocoa powder to the flour. Decorate the cakes with 175 g (6 oz) melted plain chocolate or glacé icing with melted chocolate drizzied on top.

Nutty buns Add 50 g (2 oz) chopped walnuts to the mixture. Decorate with glacé icing and halved walnuts.

Little fruit cakes Add 50 g (2 oz) mixed dried fruit or chopped glacé cherries to the mixture. Mix 100 g (4 oz) sieved icing sugar with 1–2 tablespoons sherry to give a smooth icing. Drizzle the icing over the top of the cakes.

Butterfly cakes Reduce the amount of flour to 100 g (4 oz). This will make 16 cakes. Flavour the mixture with coffee, chocolate, lemon, orange or vanilla. While the cakes are cooling, make up 1 quantity of buttercream (see page 46), coloured and flavoured to blend with the cake. Cut a small piece out of the top of each bun leaving about 1 cm (½ inch) all around the top surface uncut. Cut the round piece in half to form 'wings'.
  Put the buttercream in a piping bag fitted with a star nozzle and pipe small stars all over the cut surface of each cake. Place the wings in position, tilting them up at the edges. Pipe a row of stars between the wings and a border round the top of each cake. Dredge lightly with icing sugar if wished.

Fairy cakes

Iced Fancies

If you have time, make the cake the day before it is to be iced to make cutting it easier.

Makes 22
3 eggs
75 g (3 oz) caster sugar
75 g (3 oz) plain flour
½ teaspoon baking powder
To ice and decorate:
225 g (8 oz) apricot jam,
    warmed and sieved
225 g (8 oz) marzipan
750 g (1½ lb) icing sugar, sifted
boiling water
red, yellow, orange, green and
    blue food colouring
angelica, jelly sweets, dragees
    and mimosa balls

Preparation time: 15 minutes
Cooking time: 25–30 minutes
Oven: 180°C, 350°F, Gas Mark 4

1. Grease and line a 28 × 18 cm (11 × 7 inch) shallow tin with greased greaseproof paper or non-stick silicone paper.

2. Place the eggs and caster sugar in a bowl set over a saucepan of hot water. Whisk until the mixture is thick and pale and leaves a trail when the whisk is lifted. Remove the bowl from the pan and whisk for a further 2 minutes to cool slightly.

3. Sift the flour with the baking powder and carefully fold it in to the egg mixture, using a metal spoon, until evenly mixed. Pour into the prepared tin.

4. Bake the cake in a preheated oven for 25–30 minutes until it is golden brown and firm to the touch. Turn out on to a wire rack, remove the lining paper and leave to cool completely.

5. Brush the top of the cake with some of the jam. Roll out the marzipan and use to cover the top of the cake. Trim the edges of the cake neatly with a sharp knife, reserving the marzipan trimmings for decoration.

6. Cut the cake into rounds, triangles, bars and squares. See the diagram below, right for the most economical way to cut the cake.

7. Brush all the small cakes with the jam. Knead the marzipan trimmings and shape into small rolls and balls. Place on a few of the cakes to give a raised surface when iced. (Sponge trimmings, cut to shape, can be used for the same effect.)

8. Place 450 g (1 lb) of the icing sugar in a bowl set over a saucepan of hot water. Beat in enough boiling water until the icing thickly coats the back of a wooden spoon and is of a smooth pouring consistency.

9. Divide the icing into six portions. Keep one white and colour the others pink, yellow, orange, blue and green. Place one cake of each shape on a wire rack over a tray. Using a tablespoon, coat the cakes with white icing then transfer them to a board. Ice the remaining cakes in this way in the different colours, but remember there are only four square cakes.

10. Mix the remaining icing sugar with boiling water to make icing of a piping consistency. Tint half the icing pink. Fill a piping bag fitted with a thin writing nozzle with white icing and pipe threads of icing across half the cakes. Pipe pink icing threads on the remaining cakes.

11. Decorate the cakes with angelica leaves, jelly sweets, dragees and mimosa balls.

Tortoises

Makes 18
1 tablespoon cocoa
1 tablespoon boiling water
100 g (4 oz) caster sugar
100 g (4 oz) soft margarine
2 eggs
100 g (4 oz) self-raising flour
1 teaspoon baking powder
To ice and decorate:
350 g (12 oz) marzipan
a few drops of green food
    colouring
2 tablespoons apricot jam,
    warmed and sieved
75 g (3 oz) chocolate
silver dragees

Preparation time: 10 minutes
Cooking time: 12–15 minutes
Oven: 190°C, 375°F, Gas Mark 5

1. Blend the cocoa and water to a smooth paste. Allow to cool. Place in a bowl with the remaining cake ingredients. Beat with a wooden spoon for about 2 minutes, until light and fluffy.

2. Divide the mixture between 18 paper cake cases placed in bun tins. Bake in the oven for 12–15 minutes, until firm to the touch, then allow to cool.

3. Knead the marzipan on a board until it is pliable, then gradually knead in food colouring to tint it green.

4. Roll out two thirds of the marzipan and cut into 9 cm (3 inch) rounds, reserving the trimmings. Remove the cakes from the paper cases and invert them on to a board. Brush each cake with jam and cover with a marzipan round.

5. Shape the remaining marzipan into small rolls. Flatten them slightly and attach to the body to form the head and feet. Score the feet with a small sharp knife. Press silver dragees into the head for the eyes. Score the body into hexagonal markings.

6. Melt the chocolate in a bowl set over a pan of hot water. Place the chocolate in a piping bag fitted with a thin writing nozzle and pipe over the tortoise markings. Leave to set.

Variation

To make hedgehogs, colour the marzipan brown with food colouring. Use all the marzipan to cover the cakes. With sharp pointed scissors, make snips over the backs of the hedgehogs to form spines. Pinch out the marzipan to make a snout and press in silver dragees for eyes.

Iced fancies, Tortoises

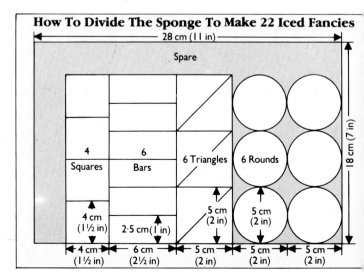

How To Divide The Sponge To Make 22 Iced Fancies

28 cm (11 in)

18 cm (7 in)

Spare

4
Squares

6
Bars

6 Triangles

6 Rounds

4 cm (1½ in)

2·5 cm (1 in)

5 cm (2 in)

5 cm (2 in)

4 cm (1½ in) — 6 cm (2½ in) — 5 cm (2 in) — 5 cm (2 in) — 5 cm (2 in)

Apple and Ginger Rings

Makes 9

2 eggs
100 g (4 oz.) golden syrup
1 cooking apple, weighing
*   about 175 g (6 oz)*
juice of 1 lemon
1 piece preserved ginger,
*   chopped finely*
100 g (4 oz) self-raising flour
¼ teaspoon ground ginger
To ice and decorate:
100 g (4 oz) icing sugar
1–2 tablespoons ginger wine
crystallized ginger
few slices of apple, dipped in
*   lemon juice (optional)*

Preparation time: 10 minutes
Cooking time: 20–25 minutes
Oven: 190°C, 375°F, Gas Mark 5

1. Grease nine 11 cm (4½ inch) ring tins generously.

2. Whisk the eggs with the golden syrup until the mixture is pale and thick.

3. Peel, core and grate the apple. Sprinkle with lemon juice and mix with the preserved ginger. Fold into the eggs.

4. Sieve the flour and ground ginger together and fold into the egg and apple mixture.

5. Divide the mixture evenly between the prepared tins and bake in the oven for 20–25 minutes until well risen and golden brown. Turn out to cool on a wire rack.

6. Sift the icing sugar into a bowl and mix to a smooth consistency with the ginger wine. Drizzle this icing over the cooled cakes and decorate with pieces of crystallized ginger. Just before serving, decorate with apple slices if liked.

...utty Angelica Fancies

...kes 12
...5 g (4 oz) butter or
...margarine
...5 g (4 oz) caster sugar
...ggs, lightly beaten
...5 g (4 oz) self-raising flour,
...sifted
...5 g (4 oz) walnuts, chopped
...g (3 oz) angelica, chopped
...ice and decorate:
...5 g (8 oz) glacé icing (see
...page 42)
...g (1 oz) walnuts, chopped
...g (2 oz) angelica, chopped

Preparation time: 10 minutes
Cooking time: 25–30 minutes
Oven: 180°C, 350°F, Gas Mark 4

1. Lightly grease 12 dariole moulds.

2. Cream the butter with the sugar until light and fluffy. Gradually beat in the eggs and fold in the flour using a metal spoon.

3. Mix together the walnuts and angelica and fold into the cake mixture.

4. Divide the mixture between the prepared moulds and bake in a preheated oven for 25–30 minutes. To make it easier to handle the moulds, place them on a baking sheet. Turn out to cool on a wire rack.

5. Drizzle the glacé icing over the top of each cake, letting it go down the sides of the cakes. Sprinkle with a mixture of chopped walnuts and angelica.

Opposite page: Apple and ginger rings
Below: Nutty angelica fancies

Sponge Dice

These easy-to-make little cakes are fun for a children's tea party or even with the coffee at a bridge party. As an alternative to dots you could cut out diamonds and hearts from the moulding paste.

Makes 16
100 g (4 oz) quantity Chocolate Quick Mix Cake mixture (pages 16–17)
225 g (8 oz) fondant moulding paste (page 44)
red and green food colourings
225 g (8 oz) marzipan (page 37)
6 tablespoons apricot glaze (page 38)
cornflour for dusting

Preparation time: 30 minutes
Cooking time: 35–40 minutes
Oven: 160°C, 325°F, Gas Mark 3

1. Cook the cake mixture in a greased, greaseproof paper-lined 18 cm (7 inch) square tin for 35–40 minutes, until well risen and firm to the touch. Turn out, remove the paper and cool the cake on a wire tray.

2. Cut off a small piece of the fondant moulding paste the size of a walnut and reserve. Colour the remaining moulding paste red with a few drops of red food colouring. Knead a few drops of green food colouring into the marzipan until evenly coloured green.

3. Trim and cut the cake into sixteen 4 cm (1½ inch) squares and brush them evenly with apricot glaze.

4. Roll out the red moulding paste thinly on a surface sprinkled with cornflour and cut out 4 cm (1½ inch) squares, re-rolling the trimmings when necessary. Attach the moulding paste squares to the sides and tops of eight cakes, pressing the joins together.

5. Repeat with the marzipan, cutting out the squares to cover the remaining eight cakes.

6. Use the reserved white moulding paste to roll into tiny dots, and secure one to six dots on each side of the cakes using a little apricot glaze, to make dice.

Animal variety

Children love little cakes shaped like animals. Easy to make using 50 g (2 oz) Quick Mix Cake mixture, are Goldfish Cakes. Bake the mixture in 15 greased boat moulds at 160°C, 325°F, Gas Mark 3 for 15 minutes. Brush the underneath and just the pointed end of the flat tops with apricot glaze and dip in hundreds and thousands to coat well. Colour 175 g (6 oz) marzipan orange. Roll it out thinly and cut out lots of rounds with a 1 cm (½ inch) plain nozzle, 15 'V' shapes for the tails and 15 tiny circles for the eyes. Place the eyes on the pointed end and the tails at the opposite ends. Arrange the small circles like scales, in rows overlapping from head to tail.

Yellow Chicks

Makes 16
2 egg whites
100 g (4 oz) caster sugar
a few drops of yellow food colouring
liquorice food colouring pen
150 ml (¼ pint) double or whipping cream
2 teaspoons grated lemon rind
10 large chocolate buttons

Preparation time: 20 minutes
Cooking time: 2 hours
Oven: 110°C, 225°F, Gas Mark ¼

1. Line two baking sheets with non-stick silicone paper. Place the egg whites in a bowl and whisk until stiff. Gradually whisk in the sugar until the mixture stands up in peaks.

2. Add a few drops of food colouring to the meringue to colour it pale yellow.

3. Place the mixture in a piping bag fitted with a 1 cm (½ inch) plain nozzle. Pipe a small round of the mixture about 2 cm (1 inch) in diameter on to the

From the left: Yellow chicks, Sponge dice, Animal biscuits

king sheet for the body and
ll off to the right to form a
ng. Pipe a smaller round
ove and pull off to the left for
e beak. This makes one half
ick. Pipe another half chick
th the wing to the left and the
ak to the right.

Repeat to pipe another 15
ft-hand chicks and 15 right-
nd chicks. Place in a pre-
ated oven as near to the
ntre as possible and cook for
out 2 hours, or until the
eringue chicks lift easily off
e paper.

5. Using a fine paintbrush and
some yellow colouring, paint
the beak and wing markings on
to each chick. Mark in the eyes
with the food colouring pen.

6. Place the cream and lemon
rind in a bowl and whip until
thick. Spread half of the chicks
with most of the cream leaving a
small amount and sandwich
together with the matching half.

7. Sit each chick on a chocolate
button secured with a little
cream.

Making meringues

Always use 2- to 3-day-old
egg whites if possible when
making meringues as they
dry out more quickly. Also
make sure the sugar is
whisked well into the egg
whites a little at a time,
ensuring a light fluffy
meringue. Dry in a cool oven
until the meringues lift easily
off the paper, and store in a
dry place in an airtight
container.

Animal Biscuits

Makes 25
150 g (5 oz) plain flour
50 g (2 oz) ground rice
75 g (3 oz) caster sugar
150 g (5 oz) soft margarine
1 teaspoon vanilla essence
1 egg, separated
red, yellow and green food
  colourings
currants

Preparation time: about 15
minutes
Cooking time: 10–12 minutes
Oven: 180°C, 350°F, Gas Mark 4
continued

1. Place the flour, ground rice, caster sugar, margarine, vanilla essence and egg white in a mixing bowl. Mix together with a wooden spoon until the mixture begins to bind together, then knead it with the fingers until the mixture forms a soft dough.

2. Roll out thinly on a lightly floured surface. Using different shaped animal cutters, cut out the dough and place the shapes on lightly floured baking sheets.

3. Divide the egg yolk into three portions and colour each portion with a few drops of food colouring so that the egg glazes are red, yellow and green.

4. To decorate the animal shapes, brush on either stripes or dots of different egg glaze colours, or just paint on one plain colour. Make the animals' features with currants.

5. Place the baking sheets in a preheated oven on the centre shelf and just below and bake for 10–12 minutes until pale at the edges.

6. Cool for a few minutes, then remove carefully and place on a wire rack to cool.

Italiens

Because of the cream filling these cakes may be made no further than one day ahead.

Makes 20
1 quantity Genoese Sponge Cake (page 22)
1 quantity crème au beurre mousseline (page 47)
2 tablespoons Kirsch or few drops of almond essence
To finish:
350 g (12 oz) icing sugar, sifted
3 tablespoons water
a few drops of green food colouring
10 blanched almonds

Preparation time: 20 minutes

1. Trim the edges from the sponge and cut it into four strips. Cut each one in half lengthways.

2. Mix the crème au beurre mousseline with the Kirsch or almond essence and spread a layer on each strip of sponge. Put the cake halves back together and place on a wire rack.

3. Put the remaining crème au beurre in a piping bag fitted with a 1 cm (½ inch) plain nozzle. Pipe a band of the cream down the length of each strip. Place in the refrigerator to become firm.

4. Put the icing sugar in a bowl standing over a saucepan of h water, and mix with sufficient water to give a coating consistency. Add a little green food colouring. Stir well until smooth. Pour the icing over each sponge strip, making certain the sides as well as the top are coated with icing. Put plate under the wire rack to catch the surplus icing.

5. Split the almonds in half and place five evenly on top of each band. Dip a knife into hot wat and diagonally cut each strip between each nut. Put into paper cases to serve.

Printaniers

Like the Italiens, these little cakes keep for one day.

Makes 20
1 quantity Genoese Sponge Cake (page 22)
1 quantity crème au beurre mousseline (page 47)
1–2 drops vanilla essence
a few drops of green and pink food colouring
2 teaspoons Kirsch or a few drops of almond essence

Preparation time: 20 minutes

1. Trim the edges from the sponge and cut it into four strips. Cut each one in half lengthways. Spread a thin layer of crème au beurre mousseline on each and put the cake halves back together.

2. Divide the remainder of the buttercream into three. Flavour one third with 1–2 drops vanilla essence, colour one-third pale green and flavour with Kirsch or a little almond essence. Colour the remaining third of the mixture pale pink.

3. With a piping bag(s) fitted with a small star nozzle(s), pipe a band of each colour down the length of each strip, covering the top of the sponge completely. Cut each strip into five. Put in paper cases to serve.

Petits Fours

Italiens and Printaniers look very effective arranged with other petits fours. Little sugared fruits called Friandises make the display very colourful. Make a syrup with 450 g (1 lb) sugar, 50 g (2 oz) powdered glucose and 150 ml (¼ pint) water, cooked to the hard crack stage (see page 49). Using two forks dipped in oil, dip each piece of fruit into the hot syrup to coat. Drain for a moment and leave on an oiled baking sheet to set and cool.

From the left: Printaniers, Italiens

Almond Leaves

These pretty biscuits are simply made with a fluted cutter, marking the veins of a leaf with a knife. They keep up to 4 weeks in an airtight tin.

Makes 30
45 g (1¾ oz) butter
120 g (4½ oz) caster sugar
120 g (4½ oz) ground almonds
1 teaspoon vanilla sugar or few drops of vanilla essence
3 egg yolks
165 g (5½ oz) plain flour, sifted
To finish:
1 egg, beaten
175 g (6 oz) chocolate, broken in pieces

Preparation time: 40 minutes, plus chilling
Cooking time: 15 minutes
Oven: 180°C, 350°F, Gas Mark 4

1. Place the butter in a bowl and beat until soft and creamy. Stir in the sugar, ground almonds and vanilla sugar or essence. Add the egg yolks and mix together to a paste. Gradually work all the flour into the mixture.

2. Cover the pastry with cling film or greaseproof paper and chill for 30 minutes.

3. Roll out the pastry fairly thinly and cut out leaf shapes 5.5 cm (2¼ inch) long, using a 6 cm (2½ inch) fluted cutter. Pinch the fluted edges together to form small points. Mark the veining of a leaf on each biscuit with the back of a small knife.

4. Place on a greased baking sheet and brush with beaten egg. Place in a preheated oven and bake for 15 minutes until golden brown. Cool on a wire rack.

5. Meanwhile, place the chocolate in a bowl set over a saucepan of hot water. When it has melted, dip half of each biscuit into the chocolate. Place on greaseproof paper or cling film until dry.

Rout Biscuits

Rout creams were rich vanilla-flavoured custards popular as desserts in the nineteenth century, and sweet biscuits like these were always served with them. Light as a feather, they keep up to 4 weeks in an airtight tin.

Makes about 36
100 g (4 oz) ground almonds
100 g (4 oz) icing sugar, sifted
1 egg white
rice paper
To decorate:
glacé cherries
crystallized angelica
crystallized pineapple
blanched almond halves
To finish:
2 teaspoons powdered gum arabic
2 tablespoons water

Preparation time: 20 minutes, plus drying
Cooking time: 4–5 minutes
Oven: 230°C, 450°F, Gas Mark 8

1. Mix the ground almonds and icing sugar together in a bowl. Add sufficient egg white to form a soft smooth paste.

2. Cover a baking sheet with rice paper. Put the mixture into a piping bag fitted with a large star nozzle and pipe small shapes on to the prepared sheet.

3. Decorate with small pieces of glacé cherry, angelica, crystallized pineapple or blanched almond halves. Leave for several hours or overnight to dry.

4. Put the gum arabic and water into a bowl set over a bowl of hot water and allow to dissolve

Petits Vacherins

The meringue cases for these sweet little mouthfuls can be kept for up to 3 weeks in an airtight tin. When filled with cream and fruit, eat on the same day.

Makes 20
120 g (4½ oz) icing sugar, sifted
2 egg whites
To finish:
250 ml (8 fl oz) double or whipping cream, whipped
225 g (8 oz) strawberries or other soft fruit

Preparation time: 30 minutes
Cooking time: 1½–2 hours
Oven: 150°C, 300°F, Gas Mark 2

1. Put the icing sugar and egg whites into a large bowl set over a saucepan of hot water. Whisk until the mixture becomes thick and shiny and stands in stiff peaks. Remove from the heat and beat until cool.

2. Place the meringue mixture into a piping bag fitted with a small star nozzle. Pipe small nests no more than 4 cm (1½ inches) in diameter on to baking sheets lined with silicone paper.

3. Place in a preheated oven and bake for 1½–2 hours until dry, firm and easily lifted off the paper. Cool on a wire tray.

4. Place the whipped cream in a piping bag fitted with a small star nozzle and pipe a swirl of cream into the centre of each vacherin. Top with one small strawberry or half a large one.

. Place the biscuits in a reheated oven and bake for −5 minutes to brown the dges. Remove from the oven nd immediately glaze with the um arabic solution. Cool on a wire rack.

Shortbread Specials

Heart-shaped shortbreads can be dipped in chocolate like the Almond Leaves. Cream 175 g (6 oz) butter with 75 g (3 oz) sugar. Beat in 225 g (8 oz) sifted plain flour and chill before kneading and rolling out. Bake the biscuits at 160°C, 325°F, Gas Mark 3 for 15 minutes. Leave to cool before dipping in melted chocolate. A border of shells or stars can be piped with chocolate buttercream.

Clockwise from top left: Almond leaves, Petit vacherins, Rout biscuits

Fruit Babas

These sumptuous cakes make a splendid dessert for a special meal – as long as the preceding course is not too heavy, as these are rather rich. As an alternative, make a single large baba in a 1.5 litre (2½ pint) ring mould, and allow 40 minutes' cooking time. The plain babas can be stored in an airtight tin for 2 days, but should not be filled with the fruit and cream more than 2 hours before serving.

Makes 14–16
lard for greasing
25 g (1 oz) fresh yeast; or 1 tablespoon dried yeast and 1 teaspoon caster sugar
6 tablespoons warm milk
225 g (8 oz) strong plain white flour
½ teaspoon salt
25 g (1 oz) caster sugar
4 eggs, beaten
100 g (4 oz) butter, very soft, but not melted, and cut into pieces
50 g (2 oz) currants (optional)
½ quantity apricot glaze (page 38)
Rum syrup:
4 tablespoons clear honey
4 tablespoons mandarin juice from the can (see filling)
1–2 tablespoons rum or other liqueur
Filling:
1 Ogen or Charentais melon, cut into balls
1 × 325 g (11 oz) can mandarin oranges, drained
1 × 325 g (11 oz) can lychees, drained
about 150 ml (¼ pint) double or whipping cream, whipped (optional)

Preparation time: about 1 hour, plus rising
Cooking time: about 20 minutes
Oven: 200°C, 400°F, Gas Mark 6

1. Grease about 14–16 individual ring tins or moulds with lard.

2. In a bowl blend the fresh yeast (or dried yeast and sugar) with the milk and 50 g (2 oz) of the flour. Stand in a warm place until frothy, allowing about 20 minutes for fresh yeast and 30 minutes for dried.

3. Sift the remaining flour and salt into the yeast batter and add the sugar, eggs, butter and currants. Beat very thoroughly for 3–4 minutes using a wooden spoon.

4. Use the mixture to fill the tins halfway, stand on baking sheets and lay a sheet of oiled polythene lightly over them. Leave to rise in a warm place until the tins are two thirds to three quarters full.

5. Bake in a preheated oven for 15–20 minutes or until well risen and firm to the touch. Cool in the tins for a few minutes, then turn out on to a wire rack.

6. While the babas are still warm, combine the honey, fruit juice and rum or liqueur in a small pan. Gently heat until the honey melts, then spoon over the babas to soak them evenly.

7. Make up the apricot glaze. Use to brush over the outsides of the babas then leave until cold.

8. To serve, place the babas on a serving dish. Fill with a mixture of melon balls, mandarins and lychees (cut in half if large) and top each with a whirl of whipped cream.

Raspberry Vol-au-vents

Other seedless fruits, such as peaches, strawberries, mandarins, melons cut into dice or balls and grapes can be used in place of the raspberries. If wished the fruits can be soaked in a little of the Amaretto di Saronno for a couple of hours.

Makes 8
8 large individual frozen vol-au-vents or 8 ready-baked vol-au-vents or 1 quantity puff pastry (pages 33–4) and beaten egg to glaze
1 quantity crème pâtissière (page 48)
1–2 tablespoons Amaretto di Saronno or the finely grated rind of 1 lemon
175 g (6 oz) raspberries, fresh or frozen and thawed
about 5 tablespoons double or whipping cream, whipped

Preparation time: about 25–30 minutes
Cooking time: about 25 minutes (optional)
Oven: 220°C, 425°F, Gas Mark 7 (optional)

1. If using frozen vol-au-vents, cook them following the instructions on the packet and cool on a wire rack.

   If using puff pastry, roll it out carefully and evenly to about 1 cm (½ inch or less) thickness and cut out 8 × 7.5 cm (3 inch) vol-au-vents. Take a smaller cutter (about 5 cm (2 inches) in diameter) and cut part way through the centre of the pastry rounds, leaving an even margin. Stand on a lightly greased baking sheet and glaze with beaten egg. Leave to stand for 10 minutes then place in a preheated oven and bake for 15 minutes. Turn the trays round in the oven and cook for a further 5–10 minutes or until well risen and golden brown and firm. Carefully remove the soft pastry from the centre and discard. Leave the vol-au-vents to cool on a wire rack.

2. Make up the crème pâtissière and in place of the vanilla essence beat in the Amaretto liqueur to taste or the lemon rind. Cover and leave until cold.

3. Use the crème pâtissière to fill the vol-au-vents, spreading a little over part of the pastry rim.

4. Reserve eight of the best raspberries and arrange the remainder over the tops of the vol-au-vents.

5. Place the whipped cream in a piping bag fitted with a star nozzle and pipe a whirl of cream in the centre of each vol-au-vent on top of the raspberries. Top with the reserved raspberries.

From the top: Fruit babas, Raspberry vol-au-vents

Cranberry Apple Strudels

Strudel pastry is the finest of elastic pastries, and very satisfying to make. This version of the favourite apple strudel is given an extra 'bite' with the cranberries. Serve with cream.

The strudels can be made smaller if preferred by cutting each half of the dough into six instead of four strips. Complete in the same way.

Makes 8
225 g (8 oz) plain flour
½ teaspoon salt
1 egg, beaten
2 tablespoons oil
85 ml (3 fl oz) lukewarm water
icing sugar to dredge
a little extra ground cinnamon
Filling:
900 g (2 lb) cooking apples
225 g (8 oz) cranberries, fresh
*   or frozen and thawed*
½ teaspoon ground cinnamon
about 4 tablespoons water
sugar to taste
50 g (2 oz) butter, melted
100 g (4 oz) ground almonds

Preparation time: about 1 hour, plus resting
Cooking time: 35–40 minutes
Oven: 190°C, 375°F, Gas Mark 5

1. Sift the flour and salt into a bowl and make a well in the centre.

2. Add the egg, oil and water and mix together gradually to make a soft sticky dough. If it feels too sticky, add a sprinkling of flour. Work the dough until it leaves the sides of the bowl clean.

3. Turn on to a lightly floured surface and knead for about 15 minutes or until the dough no longer sticks to the hands or board. Shape into a ball and put on to a cloth; cover with the bowl and leave in a warm place to rest for 1 hour.

4. For the filling, peel, core and slice the apples and put into a saucepan with the cranberries, cinnamon and water. Cover and simmer gently for about 10 minutes or until soft. Beat in the sugar to taste and leave to get cold.

5. Warm a wooden rolling pin and spread a clean cloth on a large flat working surface or table. Dredge lightly with flour.

6. Put the dough on to the cloth and roll out carefully into a square about 3 mm (⅛ inch) thick. Lift the dough and turn it frequently so that it does not stick to the cloth.

7. Using the backs of the hands, put them under the dough and gently lift and stretch it, beginning in the centre and working out to the edge until it is paper thin and measures about 80 cm (32 inches) square. Neaten the edges with a sharp knife and leave to rest for 15 minutes.

8. Brush the dough all over with most of the melted butter and then sprinkle with ground almonds.

9. Cut the dough in half and then each piece into four oblongs of equal size by cutting at right angles to the first cut.

10. Divide the fruit mixture between the pieces of dough, spreading it to within 2.5 cm (1 inch) of two long sides and one short side and 7.5 cm (3 inches) of the other short side. Fold the narrow edges over the filling and beginning at the narrow end, roll up towards the wide border keeping it neat and even. Stand the parcels on greased baking sheets, keeping the join underneath.

11. Brush with melted butter, place in a preheated oven and bake for 25–30 minutes or until golden brown. Remove to a wire tray and when cool, dredge with icing sugar, flavoured with a little ground cinnamon. Leave until cold.

Marron Meringues

The meringues will keep for up to 10 days if stored in an airtight container, but once assembled chill and serve within 2–3 hours.

Makes 8–10
75 g (3 oz) light soft brown
*   sugar*
75 g (3 oz) caster sugar
3 egg whites
2–3 marrons glacés, chopped
*   (optional)*
Filling:
1 × 240 g (8½ oz) can
*   sweetened chestnut spread*
1 tablespoon rum or coffee
*   liqueur*
150 ml (¼ pint) double cream

Preparation time: about 30 minutes
Cooking time: 2–2½ hours
Oven: 110°C, 225°F, Gas Mark ¼

1. Cover two baking sheets with non-stick silicone or greased greaseproof paper.

2. Sift the soft brown sugar and caster sugar together until evenly blended.

3. Put the egg whites into a clean grease-free bowl and whisk until very stiff and standing in peaks. Whisk in the sugar mixture 1 tablespoon at a time until it is thoroughly incorporated and the meringue is stiff again before adding more sugar. The last third of the sugar can be whisked in or folded in as preferred.

4. Put the meringue into a piping bag fitted with a large star vegetable nozzle and pipe into 10 cm (4 inch) twisted bars.

5. Bake in a preheated oven for 2 hours, reversing the trays in the oven after 1 hour. The meringues should then be set and peel easily off the paper; if not, cook for a further 15 minutes and try again. Leave to cool on the paper on a wire rack.

6. When they are cold, peel the meringues off the paper and store in an airtight container until required.

7. To assemble, combine the chestnut spread and rum or liqueur and beat until quite smooth. Whip the cream until stiff and fold through the chestnut mixture.

8. Spread some of the filling over the base of one meringue and cover with another meringue. Stand it on its side on a plate and continue to fill the remainder.

9. Place the remaining filling in a piping bag fitted with a large vegetable nozzle and pipe a line of the filling over the top of each meringue. Add pieces of marrons glacés, if used. Chill until required.

From the top: Cranberry apple strudel
Marron meringues

INDEX